PENGUIN CLASSICS

THE SCHOOL FOR SCANDAL
AND OTHER PLAYS

Richard Brinsley Sheridan was born in 1751, the son of an actor-elocutionist, and educated at Harrow. He escorted the singer Elizabeth Linley to France, fought two duels on her behalf, and married her in 1773. In 1775 he made a spectacular debut as a dramatist with *The Rivals*, *St Patrick's Day* and *The Duenna*, a comic opera. The following year he acquired Garrick's share in the Drury Lane Theatre, which he managed until it was burnt down in 1809. *The School for Scandal* was produced in 1777 and *The Critic* in 1779. From 1780 until 1812 Sheridan was an MP and held several government offices. During 1787 and 1788 he made some celebrated speeches supporting the impeachment of Warren Hastings. He died in 1816.

Eric Rump studied at Pembroke College, Cambridge, for his BA and at the University of Toronto for his Ph.D., and is now an Associate Professor in the English Department of Glendon College, York University, Toronto. He is the author of a number of articles on both Restoration and modern drama, is a contributing author to *Studies in Sheridan* (Cambridge University Press, 1995), and has edited *The Comedies of William Congreve* for the Penguin Classics.

RICHARD BRINSLEY SHERIDAN

The Rivals
The Critic
The School for Scandal

Edited with an Introduction
and Notes by Eric Rump

PENGUIN BOOKS

PENGUIN BOOKS

Published by the Penguin Group
Penguin Books Ltd, 80 Strand, London WC2R 0RL, England
Penguin Putnam Inc., 375 Hudson Street, New York, New York 10014, USA
Penguin Books Australia Ltd, 250 Camberwell Road, Camberwell, Victoria 3124, Australia
Penguin Books Canada Ltd, 10 Alcorn Avenue, Toronto, Ontario, Canada M4V 3B2
Penguin Books India (P) Ltd, 11 Community Centre, Panchsheel Park, New Delhi – 110 017, India
Penguin Books (NZ) Ltd, Cnr Rosedale and Airborne Roads, Albany, Auckland, New Zealand
Penguin Books (South Africa) (Pty) Ltd, 24 Sturdee Avenue, Rosebank 2196, South Africa

Penguin Books Ltd, Registered Offices: 80 Strand, London WC2R 0RL, England

www.penguin.com

This edition first published 1988
16

Introduction, Appendix and Notes copyright © Eric Rump, 1988
All rights reserved

Printed in England by Clays Ltd, St Ives plc
Filmset in 10/12 Linotron Ehrhardt

For Eileen and Gordon

CONTENTS

ACKNOWLEDGEMENTS

I am deeply indebted to the many editors of Sheridan, both to those who have provided far more detailed editions of single plays, such as F. W. Bateson and Elizabeth Duthie in the New Mermaids series, and, of the collected editions, I owe a special debt to Cecil Price, *The Dramatic Works of Richard Brinsley Sheridan* (Oxford, 1973). I would also like to thank for their kindness and co-operation the librarians of Georgetown University, Yale University, the Bodleian Library, Oxford, the British Library, York University, Toronto, and the University of Toronto. I would like to express my gratitude both to my own college, Glendon, and to York University for the financial support that has been provided.

INTRODUCTION

Puff, in Sheridan's play *The Critic*, mentions 'sheer necessity' as being the motive force behind the creation of his own particular 'art', and although 'necessity' may not have been the only reason for Sheridan to try his hand at playwrighting with *The Rivals*, it certainly could have been one of them. In the April of 1773, at the age of 21, he had married, after a complex series of events that involved parental opposition, two duels and an 'elopement' to France, the radiantly beautiful singer Elizabeth Linley, and although there was some money on her side, there was very little on his. It is not altogether surprising, therefore, to find him in one of his letters discussing *The Rivals* chiefly in terms of its ability to make him at least 'six hundred pounds'.[1] However, if these were his initial expectations, then the opening night (17 January 1775) must have been a cruel disappointment indeed.

Much of the critical attack at the first performance was launched at Lee's acting of the part of Sir Lucius O'Trigger, but the part in itself gave concern to some. For the writer from the *Morning Post* it constituted an 'ungenerous attack upon a nation'[2] and for the *Morning Chronicle* the part was 'so far from giving the manners of our brave and worthy neighbours, that it scarce equals the picture of a *respectable* Hottentot'.[3] In consequence, it was the part of Sir Lucius that most occupied Sheridan's attention in the days that intervened between the withdrawal of the play after opening night and its presentation, in a revised form, on Saturday 28 January 1775, and

1. Cecil Price (ed.), *The Letters of Richard Brinsley Sheridan* (Oxford, 1966), Vol. I, p. 85.
2. Cecil Price (ed.), *The Dramatic Works of Richard Brinsley Sheridan* (Oxford, 1973), p. 47.
3. ibid., p. 43.

clearly Sheridan had listened to his critics with some care, for Sir Lucius is remodelled to make him much more the Irish gentleman.

The disapproval of certain expressions voiced by some critics on the grounds of 'ribaldry'[4] or 'low quibbles'[5] led Sheridan not only to make some changes in Sir Lucius's remarks but in Sir Anthony Absolute's as well. He remains irascible in both versions of the play but the vein of earthy humour that can be found in the earlier version disappears almost completely in the revised. No longer does he tell Mrs Malaprop that 'these young soldiers, must never be trusted with a pretty girl, tête à tête – like children, they will be picking at the dish, before mama has pinned the napkin',[6] nor, if 'nunneries' are to be understood as a euphemism for brothels, does he suggest that they get populated through reading because 'the vicious trash . . . not only disturbs the imagination of our girls, but sets their passions afloat'.[7] Likewise, when he discovers that the trinket Jack claims to be taking to Lydia is in fact a sword, he no longer sends him on his way with fatherly instructions to 'let her know you have better trinkets than that'.[8]

As well as making changes such as these, Sheridan also re-designed Bob Acres's challenge to 'Ensign Beverley' and cut the length of the play. Clinch took over the part of Sir Lucius from the unfortunate Lee and, as all the actors were 'better acquainted with their several parts',[9] the revised version received a far warmer reception from the audience, with 'repeated peals of approbation'[10] ringing out at the end. According to an anecdote reported in the *Morning Post*, a gentleman sitting next to David Garrick told him that 'this play will run',[11] a prediction that has clearly proved correct.

Although Sheridan claims, somewhat remarkably, in the preface to

4. Price, ibid., p. 41.
5. Price, ibid., p. 45.
6. Richard L. Purdy (ed.), *The Rivals . . . Edited from the Larpent MS* (Oxford, 1935), p. 83.
7. Purdy, ibid., p. 17.
8. Purdy, ibid., p. 104.
9. Price, *Dramatic Works*, p. 50.
10. ibid.
11. ibid.

The Rivals that he was 'by no means conversant with plays in general, either in reading or at the theatre', a thoroughgoing investigation has been conducted of possible sources in earlier plays and novels.[12] With Lydia, in particular, attention has centred on the possible parallels with the 'heroine', if she can be so called, of George Colman's one-act afterpiece *Polly Honeycombe* (1760). Polly, like Lydia, is a great reader of novels from the circulating library; she has two suitors, one the 'romantic' Mr Scribble and the other the dull, down-to-earth financier Mr Ledger; she too dreams of an elopement with Mr Scribble and, like Lydia, feels that her parents treat her as simply a piece of merchandise. Unlike Polly's two suitors, of course, Lydia's suitors are actually one; nor do we ever hear of Polly putting Mr Scribble through such tests as Lydia apparently has by requiring Jack (or 'Beverley') to court her secretly in the freezing cold of a Bath garden in the depths of winter.

Jack, Lydia's suitor, is called a 'dissembling villain' (IV, ii) by his father, but although he may be a dissembler, a 'villain' he is certainly not. We know this, in part, because we are told by his servant Fag in the opening scene of the play of the reason for Jack's use of disguise:

> Why then the cause of all this is – LOVE – love, Thomas, who (as you may get read to you) has been a masquerader ever since the days of Jupiter.

Although Jack does not share Lydia's romantic fantasies – especially her nominal delight in love-in-poverty – it is clear that it is not only or chiefly for her fortune that he has undertaken the somewhat demanding role of 'Ensign Beverley'. There may be some exaggeration present in his description of Lydia to his father as an 'angel' to whom his 'heart is engaged' (II, i), just as there may be in the opening of one of his letters to her ('my soul's idol, my adored Lydia!') but there is, as well, a sense of genuine emotional commitment behind the language used. It is no surprise, therefore, that the one point in the play where Jack is seriously shaken is when his role-playing has been uncovered,

12. For a summary of this material, see Jack D. Durant, *Richard Brinsley Sheridan* (Boston, 1975), pp. 67–9, and Mark S. Auburn, *Sheridan's Comedies* (Lincoln and London, 1977), p. 33.

so that he feels that his rejection by Lydia (unlike their earlier quarrel) is probably final. It makes emotional sense – as well as tying together two disparate lines of the plot – that the disturbed mood he is in results in his ready acceptance of Sir Lucius's somewhat strange challenge to a duel.

Jack's appeal lies not only in the kind of relationship he has with Lydia but also in his relationship with the audience, which knows from the beginning what he is up to and therefore, because he is trustworthy, shares with him a bemused delight in the situations in which he finds himself. They, like Jack, can take a knowing enjoyment from his promise to Acres that 'Beverley' will certainly receive his challenge, and they can participate in the cordiality with which he joins in Mrs Malaprop's laughter at the very idea that 'Beverley' could ever be clever enough to trick her. Unlike the rest of the characters, he establishes an intimacy with the audience by means of a direct appeal for their sympathy or support. His role as 'Ensign Beverley' may function as a critique of Lydia's naive romantic excesses, but it is also a role he plays with relish – a relish which he invites the audience both to witness and to enjoy:

> Proud of calamity, we will enjoy the wreck of wealth; while the surrounding gloom of adversity shall make the flame of our pure love show doubly bright. – By heavens! I would fling all goods of fortune from me with a prodigal hand to enjoy the scene where I might clasp my Lydia to my bosom, and say, the world affords no smile to me – but here – [*embracing her*]. [*Aside.*] If she holds out now the devil is in it!
>
> [III, iii]

Such inventiveness, combined with a fundamental decency, establishes Jack as very much at the centre of the play. This is true not only of the plot, in which Jack does indeed have a pivotal role, but also in terms – if this is not too heavyhanded – of the play's 'values'. Decency, cleverness, sense combined with sensibility, even 'manliness' perhaps: it is these qualities that seem very close to the play's core.

A lack of such 'manliness' may have been the starting point for the characterization of Faulkland. This, at least, is very much Jack's point of view, for he tells Faulkland to 'love like a man' (II, i) and suggests that his mind is confused by 'a confounded farrago of doubts, fears,

hopes, wishes, and all the flimsy furniture of a country miss's brain'
(II, i). As well, Faulkland's listing of the various meteorological
grounds for apprehension in a lover suggests, by its exaggeration, that
we are being prepared for a comic version of an overheated imagination that could provide a male parallel to Lydia:

> And for her health – does not every hour bring me cause to be
> alarmed? If it rains, some shower may even then have chilled her
> delicate frame! If the wind be keen, some rude blast may have affected
> her! The heat of noon, the dews of the evening, may endanger the life
> of her, for whom only I value mine.
>
> [II, i]

From quite early on in the play, however, grounds are provided for
a more psychologically complex and disturbing portrait than such a
'comic' approach would suggest. Julia, in reply to Lydia's charges
that Faulkland is a creature of 'whim', 'caprice' and 'jealousy', says
that the reason for his actions is a lack of self-confidence or
self-worth; that because he does not see 'why he should be loved to
the degree he wishes', he therefore 'suspects he is not loved enough'
(I, ii). Faulkland, it is true, partly recognizes this himself, but it is not
the sort of recognition that restrains him from probing the genuine-
ness of Julia's love. The tears, then, that he reduces Julia to when they
meet, the cruel trick he plays on her when he pretends he has killed
somebody in a duel and therefore has to flee the country, produce the
cumulative effect of displacing this section from the overall comic
ambit of the play. Sheridan may well, in the Prologue 'spoken on the
tenth night', have declared himself a supporter of 'laughing' as
opposed to 'sentimental' comedy, but one has to wonder how
thoroughgoing that commitment was.[13]

No such questions need be raised about the two 'authority' figures
in the play: Sir Anthony Absolute and Mrs Malaprop. Irascible and
domineering figures like Sir Anthony are, of course, nothing new in
comedy; Sheridan may have had Sir Sampson Legend from Congreve's *Love for Love* vaguely in mind, and a number of similar figures

---

13. Richard Bevis, *The Laughing Tradition* (Athens, Georgia, 1980), is a fine
examination of both 'laughing' and 'sentimental' comedy.

in eighteenth-century comedy have also been examined.[14] His approach to children is one of not overwhelming them with kindness – 'in their younger days, 'twas "Jack, do this" – if he demurred – I knocked him down' (I, ii) – and women he clearly feels are best kept ignorant. His offer to Jack in the second act of a 'noble independence' sounds generous until Jack realizes that this 'independence' is linked to a wife about whom he has been told nothing and who, according to Sir Anthony, could be 'as ugly as I choose' (II, i). All this could result in a somewhat serious and threatening figure but Sheridan, in keeping with the play's generally good-natured approach to people's foibles, prevents this from happening. Although the language that Sir Anthony uses may sound threatening enough, as when he warns Jack not 'to breathe the same air, or use the same light with me' (II, i), one can wonder how much this is simply comic bluster on his part. He certainly has trouble keeping his resolution never to address his son as 'Jack' again, and there is some recognition on his part that in his own youth he was far from being the dutiful son that he now demands Jack should be. More importantly, perhaps, once Jack realizes that the intended wife is one and the same with the Lydia he has been courting as Ensign Beverley, then attention can shift to the skill with which Jack, with due gravity, almost outwits the father by playing the role of the dutiful and obedient son.

Sir Anthony's female counterpart in the play is, of course, Mrs Malaprop. She, like Sir Anthony, expects Lydia to be 'dutiful' and thus to accept whatever husband is proposed, though, unlike Sir Anthony, Mrs Malaprop is involved in the love affairs of the play through her infatuation with Sir Lucius, which leads to her epistolary disguise under the delicately chosen name of 'Delia'. Few audiences, or readers, however, remember Mrs Malaprop for her role as the 'she-dragon' (III, iii), as Jack calls her, or because of her (hoped for) relationship with Sir Lucius; they remember her for her hilariously inappropriate use of language. A character who misuses language is not new with Sheridan – examples can be found as far back as Shakespeare's Dogberry and Mrs Quickly – but, of them all, Sheridan probably owes his most specific debt to Mrs Tryfort, a

14. Mark S. Auburn, *op. cit.*, pp. 44–5.

character in his mother's uncompleted comedy, *A Journey to Bath*. Mrs Tryfort is described by another character, Lady Filmot, as being someone who is fond of 'hard words, which without miscalling, she always takes care to misapply',[15] and at least one of her errors 'contagious countries' – appears in Mrs Malaprop's opening scene. Julia, in a phrase reminiscent of Lady Filmot, describes Mrs Malaprop as someone whose words are 'ingeniously *misapplied*, without being *mispronounced*' (I, ii), but perhaps what distinguishes Mrs Malaprop not only from Mrs Tryfort but from her other predecessors as well is the sheer variety, perverse ingenuity and unshakeable confidence she displays throughout in manifesting that she is 'queen of the dictionary' (II, ii). It is indeed a bravura performance. Some of her slips may be no more ingenious than those devised by earlier writers, but in others – 'pineapple of politeness' (III, iii), 'a nice derangement of epitaphs' (III, iii), 'as headstrong as an allegory on the banks of the Nile' (III, iii) – she (or Sheridan) achieves an unsurpassed creative dottiness. It is perhaps this range and variety – along with the fact that her name has passed into the language – that gives to Mrs Malaprop that curious quality, possessed by a small group of other comic characters, of being part of the work while at the same time possessing an almost autonomous existence outside or apart from it.

The success of the revised version of *The Rivals* may well have increased Sheridan's confidence in his dramatic abilities, for 1775 saw the production not only of that play but of two other pieces as well: *St Patrick's Day*, a two-act farce, and his comic opera, *The Duenna*. Although *The Duenna* is little known these days, it had an unprecedented run of 75 nights in its opening season, was seen by the *Morning Chronicle* as demonstrating a 'fertile imagination, great ability and real genius',[16] and, always important for Sheridan, provided him with some necessary cash. Perhaps it was these extra funds that made it possible for him, along with his father-in-law and a mutual friend, Dr James Ford, to purchase in 1776 David Garrick's

---

15. W. Fraser Rae (ed.), *Sheridan's Plays . . . and His Mother's Unpublished Comedy, 'A Journey to Bath'* (London, 1902), p. 273.
16. Price, *Dramatic Works*, p. 206.

share of Drury Lane Theatre and thereby become not simply a playwright, but a manager as well.

Sheridan did not immediately write a new play for the Drury Lane Company, but his presentation in his first season of two Congreve comedies (with minor alterations),[17] as well as his adaptation of Vanbrugh's *The Relapse* under the new title of *A Trip to Scarborough*, may have had some influence on the more polished language and somewhat darker atmosphere of *The School for Scandal*. This play was first performed in the May of 1777, and was apparently completed in some haste, but Sheridan had clearly been thinking for a while about a play along these lines, for some related jottings and fragments survive, the earliest of which may go back to 1772.[18]

Although Sheridan called his play *The School for Scandal*, to present a satirical portrait of the world of gossip and backbiting is not the only concern of the play; indeed the standards by which that world is judged are found elsewhere, chiefly in the portraits of Charles and his uncle, Sir Oliver Surface. Sir Oliver is important to the play not only as the figure who in his two disguises – as the money-lender, Mr Premium, and as the poor relation, Mr Stanley – is able to find out for himself the true natures of Charles and his brother Joseph, but also because he is the one who, in his commentary, articulates most clearly what at least some of the play's standards or values are.

Sir Oliver has not met his nephews for a number of years, but even before he encounters them again he expresses a distrust of Sir Peter's praise for Joseph's gravity, propriety and 'sentiments', on the grounds that they run counter to youth's natural ebullience: too much youthful 'prudence', as he sees it, can be 'like ivy round a sapling' which 'spoils the growth of the tree' (II, iii). It is not 'prudence' that he is hoping to discover in his two nephews but a moral sense that reveals itself in disdain for anything 'false or mean' (II, iii). There is – and the phrase is probably crucial – to be a 'trial of their hearts' (II, iii).

It is a trial, of course, that Charles soon passes and Joseph rapidly

17. ibid., pp. 834–5.

18. ibid., pp. 287–95; J. R. de J. Jackson, 'The importance of witty dialogue in *The School for Scandal*', *Modern Language Notes*, 76 (1961), 601–7.

fails. In the opening scene of the play Charles has been referred to as a 'libertine', as 'dissipated' and as 'extravagant', but when we do finally meet him in the third act of the play, few, if any, of these faults are in evidence. There is no suggestion that he is a 'libertine' in the sexual sense of the term and though he may be 'extravagant', this appears to result more from generosity to his friends than from reckless or wilful self-indulgence. Sir Oliver may have initial doubts about the depth of Charles's feeling for his own family when he finds out that Charles is quite ready to auction off their portraits, but the kind words he has for the liberality of Sir Oliver, as well as his refusal to sell 'poor Noll's' portrait, quickly reassure Sir Oliver – some may feel too quickly – on that score. His generosity or benevolence is manifested as well by his readiness to give part of the money raised to his impoverished relative, Mr Stanley, and with this final act, although Charles does not realize it at that moment, he has totally won his uncle's approval.

Charles, when discussing the terms of a loan from 'Mr Premium', insists on 'plain dealing' (III, iii), and it is this openness, spontaneity and generosity that, in general, distinguishes Charles from Joseph, his duplicitous brother. It is a contrast that is worked out, with variations, in a number of the play's smaller details. Charles is presumably interested in Maria for herself, Joseph simply because of her fortune; although Charles is accused of being a 'libertine', Joseph is in fact far closer to being one, as shown by his attempted seduction of Lady Teazle; where Charles openly recognizes his uncle's liberality, Joseph falsely depicts him as a victim of avarice; and, even though the purchase by Charles of his father's house is used as an example of his 'extravagance', the emphasis effectively falls less on this 'extravagance' than on Joseph's 'economy' in putting it up for sale in the first place (III, iii). The differences between the two, however, do not slowly emerge as the play progresses but are made clear to the audience from the opening scene. Snake initially suggests what the general perception of the two brothers is – that Joseph is 'the most amiable character' and that Charles is 'dissipated and extravagant' – but Lady Sneerwell quickly sets him right by describing Joseph as 'artful, selfish and malicious – in short, a sentimental knave', and all that Joseph has to say on his first appearance a few lines later confirms the accuracy of her description. Joseph, it is true, occasionally forgets it is a role that he is playing – as when he attempts to be 'moral' before Lady Sneerwell and Snake – but in the main he is perfectly clear about the distinction between the 'silver ore of pure charity' and the 'sentimental French plate' (V, i) that, for much of the play, he successfully substitutes in its place. The audience, in consequence, is in a position both to admire his dexterity in performing his role and to welcome the exposure of this clever rogue at the end.

This dexterity reveals itself both in the moral aphorisms he produces and in the quick-wittedness he displays in handling situations that threaten to reveal the truth. He cleverly explains away the situation when Lady Teazle enters and finds him on his knees before Maria, and much of the comic suspense of the superbly crafted 'screen scene' (IV, iii) arises from the hasty improvisations that Joseph is forced to make. As soon as Lady Teazle is concealed behind the screen on Sir Peter's unexpected entrance, Joseph quickly transforms himself into the thoughtful (if exhausted) student, complete with book and suitably adjusted hair; when Sir Peter almost discovers his concealed wife, she is immediately transformed into a 'little French milliner'; Charles's near revelations of the truth about Joseph and Lady Teazle are successfully hushed up and it is not until the screen collapses that all is finally revealed. A lesser player might have given up at this point but Joseph does not, and even at the play's conclusion he at least tries to pretend that he is not departing out of any sense of disgrace but in an attempt to calm Lady Sneerwell and thereby prevent her from injuring his brother.

The duplicity of Joseph is echoed, in a way, in the 'scandalous college' of which he is a member and over which Lady Sneerwell presides. In the opening conversation between Snake and Lady Sneerwell the topic of scandalmongering is mentioned, but as its practice is discussed more or less in terms of an art form, it is initially presented as almost a witty form of fiction. Indeed, when we first see the other members of the college – Crabtree, Sir Benjamin Backbite and the splendid Mrs Candour – engaging in their scandalmongering, it seems to be an almost fictive world that they are creating. None of the characters mentioned – Lord Buffalo, Sir Harry Bouquet, Tom Saunter – has been introduced earlier nor will be heard of again, and the marvellously detailed anecdote about Miss Letitia Piper and the Nova Scotia sheep, arising as it does out of a perfectly possible misunderstanding, seems harmless enough.

Much the same applies to the second 'scandal' scene (II, ii), except for two differences. The first is that the scandalous attacks are now conducted at a more personal level and revolve around such topics as cosmetics, weight and teeth; the second is that, in the figure of Sir Peter, there is an outside observer and commentator on the scene. It is he who reminds us, both in direct statement and aside, that the people the members of the college are attacking are not fictional creations but actual people whom they know and with whom they dine. Although not overstated, the malice, the lack of generosity, become somewhat more prominent. The college's final appearance is close to the end of the play and though one can revel in the inventiveness displayed in the accounts of the duel and of Sir Peter's wounds – especially the bullet that ricocheted through the window and struck the postman – the complete separation between truth and gossip is at last revealed. Sir Peter's final curses on them – 'fiends! vipers! furies!' – seem almost justified.

Part of the function of the scandal scenes is to form a junction point between the Teazle section and other sections of the play.[19] Lady Teazle, of course, is the young countrywoman who has married the much older Sir Peter, which has enabled her to exchange her somewhat limited country life for the varied social round of London. As such – the younger woman who has married the older man – she is reminiscent of certain characters in Restoration comedy, such as Margery Pinchwife in Wycherley's *The Country Wife*, or even Laetitia Fondlewife in Congreve's first play, *The Old Bachelor*, but the different manner in which both they and their husbands are presented, especially with respect to the possibility or desirability of affairs outside marriage, highlights one way of coming to terms with the change in tone and attitude from the Restoration period to Sheridan's own.[20] Lady Teazle, in the main, simply desires to be

19. For a survey of criticism about the structure of *The School For Scandal* see Jack D. Durant, op. cit., pp. 100–102.

20. There is even a 'softening' of the portrait of Lady Teazle from the early sketches to the finished play: see Mark S. Auburn, op. cit., pp. 116ff.

seen and known as 'fashionable'. It is this which has led her to become part of Lady Sneerwell's circle, and, in her relationship with Joseph, she insists that she will admit him 'as a lover no farther than fashion sanctions' – that is, as he puts it, as 'a mere Platonic *cicisbeo*' (II, ii). It is apparent from the servant's remarks that she has visited Joseph by herself before and, in their encounter in Act IV, Scene iii, she is in an agitated state of mind, but although Joseph's 'logic' is seductive, especially in its conclusion that she should sin in her own defence, it is far from clear that, even if they had not been interrupted by her husband, she would have given in to Joseph's advances. The interruption, however, is particularly fortunate for Lady Teazle because, by hiding behind the screen, she is able to learn about Sir Peter's genuine fondness and affection for her, something the audience, through Sir Peter's monologues and asides, has known all along. It is this new understanding between them, along with the proposed marriage of Charles and Maria, that is chiefly responsible for the play's warmly optimistic conclusion, but it is a conclusion very much tempered by our experience of an alternative world of gossip, vindictiveness and deceit. It is perhaps in this 'balance between sentiment and satire', as John Loftis has expressed it, that the play is 'typical of the Age of Johnson at its best'.[21]

Although *The Critic* is probably the only seventeenth- or eighteenth-century play-about-plays still performed with some regularity, Sheridan, when he wrote it in 1779, had a lively and vigorous tradition of such plays on which to draw. Probably the most important was Buckingham's *The Rehearsal* (1671) – still performed in Sheridan's time – in which a rehearsal of a (mock) heroic play by Bayes (John Dryden) takes place before two baffled spectators, but there were others, such as some of Henry Fielding's plays, or more recent works like Garrick's *A Peep behind the Curtain* (1767) and *The Meeting of the Company* (1774), and Colman's *Occasional Prelude* (1772) and *New Brooms!* (1776).[22] In addition to such plays, Sheridan may also have turned back to one of his earliest dramatic efforts, a

21. John Loftis, *Sheridan and the Drama of Georgian England* (Harvard, 1977), p. 99.
22. See V. C. Clinton-Baddeley, *The Burlesque Tradition in the English Theatre After 1660* (Methuen, 1952), pp. 72–5, and Mark S. Auburn, op. cit., pp. 150–57, for a fuller discussion of these earlier works.

collaboration with a Harrow schoolfriend of his, Nathaniel Halhed. Halhed had composed a burlesque or farcical *burletta* called *Ixion*, which he sent to Sheridan for revision, and, although only a fragment of Sheridan's version exists,[23] it seems that his contribution was to create a rehearsal framework for it and to have its playwright, called Simile, present on stage. In Simile's concern with stage effects and his airy dismissal of any niggling doubts about probability, we may be hearing the earliest voice of Puff:

> MACD.: But pray, Mr Simile, how did Ixion get into heaven?
> SIM.: Why, Sir, what's that to any body? – perhaps by Salmoneus's Brazen Bridge, or the Giant's Mountain, or the Tower of Babel, or on Theobald's bull-dogs, or – who the devil cares how? – he is there, and that's enough.[24]

Although *The Critic* may glance back at earlier plays or even at Sheridan's own (unpublished) work, part of its initial appeal must have been its utilization of so many features or aspects of the actual theatre – Drury Lane – in which the audience was viewing it. For instance, Puff provides, as an illustration of the 'puff direct', this review of a recent play:

> Then for the performance – Mr Dodd was astonishingly great in the character of Sir Harry! That universal and judicious actor Mr Palmer, perhaps never appeared to more advantage than in the Colonel; – but it is not in the power of language to do justice to Mr King! – Indeed he more than merited those repeated bursts of applause which he drew from a most brilliant and judicious audience!
>
> [I, ii]

The Dodd mentioned here was James Dodd, who was onstage playing Dangle; Palmer was John Palmer, who was likewise onstage playing Sneer; and, best of all, King was Thomas King, who was playing Puff, so the 'puff' was very 'direct' indeed. Not only were the actors so identified – along with other members of the organization, such as the scene painter, De Loutherbourg, and the prompter, William Hopkins – but there were also performances in Puff's play

---

23. Price, *Dramatic Works*, pp. 793–7.
24. ibid., p. 795.

which would have reminded the audience of other players. Miss Pope's Tilburina, for instance, managed to parody Mrs Crawford's acting style, and Bannister's portrayal of Don Ferolo Whiskerandos alluded to William Smith's Richard III.[25] In the same vein, Parsons, who played Sir Fretful Plagiary, was able to underline for the audience that this was, in part, a portrayal of the playwright Richard Cumberland – with whom Sheridan had had his difficulties – by imitating Cumberland's mannerisms.[26] Not even Sheridan himself is entirely omitted from this recreation of theatrical life at Drury Lane, though he is not aligned with any one particular character. Like Sir Fretful, he had been accused of plagiarism and was sensitive to criticism, and he had occasionally utilized the newspapers somewhat in the manner of Mr Puff.[27] The manager who 'writes himself' (I, i) is, of course, Sheridan, and Mrs Dangle's complaint about the furniture in her drawing room 'trembling at the probationary starts and unprovoked rants of would-be Richards and Hamlets' (I, i) may be a humorous reflection of what his own drawing room was like from time to time.

Part of the play's initial appeal was no doubt at this local level, but Sheridan had some broader concerns as well. These concerns are first articulated in Richard Fitzpatrick's excellent prologue, which surveys the changes in drama from Dryden's time to Sheridan's, and they surface in the play in a discussion between Dangle, Sneer and Mrs Dangle in the opening act. Dangle and Mrs Sneer are made supporters of 'sentimental' drama, in which the audience can find 'edification' and where 'the conversation [is] always moral at least, if not entertaining'. It would be interesting to know a little more about the two plays for which Sneer is seeking Dangle's support, but both presumably represent the kind of drama that Sneer is encouraging and Sheridan, in the creation of the first act, is rejecting. All we hear about the first play is that it is an example of the 'true sentimental' and therefore has 'nothing ridiculous in it from the beginning to the end', while of the second we at least know the title – *The Reformed*

25. Auburn, op. cit., p. 160.
26. Loftis, op. cit., p. 113.
27. Price, *Dramatic Works*, p. 473.

Housebreaker. This, Sneer explains, is a play which rejects the traditional matter of comedy – the 'follies and foibles of society' – and replaces it with a drama that depicts 'the greater vices and blacker crimes of humanity – gibbeting capital offences in five acts, and pillorying petty larcenies in two'. Dangle is given a comment on the new 'nicety' of the audience, which has led to the re-writing of the plays of such Restoration dramatists as Congreve and Vanbrugh, but although Dangle no doubt has Sheridan's tacit support here, the overall portrayal of this 'head of a band of critics' is not such that the audience is encouraged to put much faith in his perceptiveness.

False and malicious reporting in the newspapers was a subject that Sheridan had touched on in *The School for Scandal* and it is a subject to which he returns in *The Critic*, for Puff is not only the author of *The Spanish Armada*, the rehearsal of which occupies the final two acts of the play, but also the delightfully frank 'journalist' of the opening act. It is from Puff himself that we learn of the various false advertisements of his astonishing catastrophes that he has so successfully directed at the charitable, and it is Puff who likewise provides the splendid disquisition on the whole 'art' of puffing, a commentary no doubt as relevant to the twentieth century as to the eighteenth. Sheridan presumably could have made somebody else, rather than Puff, the author of *The Spanish Armada* – Sir Fretful Plagiary, for instance – but by giving the play to Puff he provided himself with the freedom to move from a specific parody of an individual writer to a depiction of abysmal dramaturgy in general. There may be the occasional reference to a particular play, but in the main what delights is the splendid hodgepodge Puff's play provides. He has, amongst many other things, an underplot which has no relation to the main plot, *three* women in love with the same man, a principal character who says nothing but merely shakes his head, and a mad scene in which the heroine is 'stark mad in white satin' and her confidante 'stark mad in white linen'. The actors have been busily cutting the play before the rehearsal starts, so, in addition to the individual moments, it is the chaotic speed with which it flashes by that informs the whole with a zany, comic energy.

Although *The Spanish Armada* is seen today as just a splendid theatrical burlesque, in its own time it was not without topical reference. Spain had declared war on England in the June of 1779, and the sighting of the combined French and Spanish fleets in the Channel in August led to genuine fears of an invasion.[28] Although such fears were dying down by the time of the first performance of *The Critic* (30 October 1779), it is quite possible that some commentary was intended on the situation and on some of the leading political figures of the day. Lord North is referred to in the opening lines of the play and, if John Loftis is right, is then caricatured as Lord Burleigh;[29] Charles James Fox is to be falsely 'shot' by Puff in the *Morning Post*; and even the emblem of the river Thames may not be without political overtones.[30] Although Puff's play concludes with a magnificent victory celebration, in which he applauds everything, the implicit suggestion could well be that a naval engagement in 1779 might have a very different outcome from what was achieved in 1588.

Politics had long interested Sheridan and it was in that sphere that he was soon to exercise his talents, for with *The Critic* his brief but brilliant career as a dramatist effectively came to an end. He was elected to Parliament in 1780, and with the exception of *Pizarro* (1799), he dedicated the rest of his life to public affairs. Although he was no great innovator, the three comedies by which he is now known are in many ways the best that the Georgian theatre has to offer, and they are comedies which, over the last two hundred years, have added much, as Dr Johnson said about Garrick, to 'the gaiety of nations'.

28. ibid., pp. 465–7.
29. Loftis, op. cit., pp. 120–22.
30. Valerie C. Rudolph, 'Exit *Thames* between his banks: an emblem of order in Sheridan's *The Critic*', *Theatre Survey*, 16 (1975), 93–5.

A NOTE ON THE TEXT

As there are few textual problems with either *The Rivals* or *The Critic*, the text for *The Rivals* is based on the 'third edition corrected' of 1776 and the text of *The Critic* on the first edition of 1781. The textual problems of *The School for Scandal* are very complex and although the text is based on the 1821 edition of *The Works of the Late Right Honourable Richard Brinsley Sheridan*, published by Murray, Ridgway & Wilkie, that text has been emended by readings from earlier manuscripts, as explained in the textual notes to the play (see p. 281).

Spelling has been modernized throughout, but as much of the original punctuation has been preserved as seemed compatible with modern usage.

The Rivals

PREFACE

A preface to a play seems generally to be considered as a kind of closet-prologue, in which – if his piece has been successful – the author solicits that indulgence from the reader which he had before experienced from the audience: but as the scope and immediate object of a play is to please a mixed assembly in the representation (whose judgment in the theatre at least is decisive) its degree of reputation is usually as determined as public, before it can be prepared for the cooler tribunal of the study. Thus any farther solicitude on the part of the writer becomes unnecessary at least, if not an intrusion: and if the piece has been condemned in the performance, I fear an address to the closet, like an appeal to posterity, is constantly regarded as the procrastination of a suit, from a consciousness of the weakness of the cause. From these considerations, the following comedy would certainly have been submitted to the reader, without any further introduction than what it had in the representation, but that its success has probably been founded on a circumstance which the author is informed has not before attended a theatrical trial, and which consequently ought not to pass unnoticed.

I need scarcely add, that the circumstance alluded to, was the withdrawing of the piece, to remove those imperfections in the first representation which were too obvious to escape reprehension, and too numerous to admit of a hasty correction. There are few writers, I believe, who, even in the fullest consciousness of error, do not wish to palliate the faults which they acknowledge; and, however trifling the performance, to second their confession of its deficiencies, by whatever plea seems least disgraceful to their ability. In the present instance, it cannot be said to amount either to candour or modesty in me, to acknowledge an extreme inexperience and want of judgment on matters, in which, without guidance from practice, or spur from success, a young man should scarcely boast of being an adept. If it be said, that under such disadvantages no one should attempt to write a play – I must beg leave to dissent from the position, while the first point of experience that I have gained on the subject is, a knowledge of the candour and judgment with which an impartial public distinguishes between the errors of inexperience and incapacity, and the indulgence which it shows even to a disposition to remedy the defects of either.

It were unnecessary to enter into any farther extenuation of what was thought exceptionable in this play, but that it has been said, that the managers should have prevented some of the defects before its appearance to the public – and in particular the uncommon length of the piece as represented the first night. It were an ill return for the most liberal and gentlemanly conduct on their side, to suffer any censure to rest where none was deserved. Hurry in writing has long been exploded as an excuse for an author; however, in the dramatic line, it may happen, that both an author and a manager may wish to fill a chasm in the entertainment of the public with a hastiness not altogether culpable. The season was advanced when I first put the play into Mr Harris's[1] hand: it was at that time at least double the length of any acting comedy. I profited by his judgment and experience in the curtailing of it – till, I believe, his feeling for the vanity of a young author got the better of his desire for correctness, and he left many excrescences remaining, because he had assisted in pruning so many more. Hence, though I was not uninformed that the acts were still too long, I flattered myself that, after the first trial, I might with safer judgment proceed to remove what should appear to have been most dissatisfactory. Many other errors there were, which might in part have arisen from my being by no means conversant with plays in general, either in reading or at the theatre. Yet I own that, in one respect, I did not regret my ignorance: for as my first wish in attempting a play, was to avoid every appearance of plagiary, I thought I should stand a better chance of effecting this from being in a walk which I had not frequented, and where consequently the progress of invention was less likely to be interrupted by starts of

---

1. *Mr Harris*: Thomas Harris, manager of Covent Garden Theatre.

recollection: for on subjects on which the mind has been much informed, invention is slow of exerting itself. Faded ideas float in the fancy like half-forgotten dreams; and the imagination in its fullest enjoyments becomes suspicious of its offspring, and doubts whether it has created or adopted.

With regard to some particular passages which on the first night's representation seemed generally disliked, I confess, that if I felt any emotion of surprise at the disapprobation, it was not that they were disapproved of, but that I had not before perceived that they deserved it. As some part of the attack on the piece was begun too early to pass for the sentence of judgment, which is ever tardy in condemning, it has been suggested to me, that much of the disapprobation must have arisen from virulence of malice, rather than severity of criticism: but as I was more apprehensive of there being just grounds to excite the latter, than conscious of having deserved the former, I continue not to believe that probable, which I am sure must have been unprovoked. However, if it was so, and I could even mark the quarter from whence it came, it would be ungenerous to retort; for no passion suffers more than malice from disappointment. For my own part, I see no reason why the author of a play should not regard a first night's audience, as a candid and judicious friend attending, in behalf of the public, at his last rehearsal. If he can dispense with flattery, he is sure at least of sincerity, and even though the annotation be rude, he may rely upon the justness of the comment. Considered in this light, that audience, whose *fiat* is essential to the poet's claim, whether his object be fame or profit, has surely a right to expect some deference to its opinion, from principles of politeness at least, if not from gratitude.

As for the little puny critics, who scatter their peevish strictures in private circles, and scribble at every author who has the eminence of being unconnected with them, as they are usually spleen-swollen from a vain idea of increasing their consequence, there will always be found a petulance and illiberality in their remarks, which should place them as far beneath the notice of a gentleman, as their original dullness had sunk them from the level of the most unsuccessful author.

It is not without pleasure that I catch at an opportunity of justifying myself from the charge of intending any national reflection in the character of Sir Lucius O'Trigger. If any gentlemen opposed the piece from that idea, I thank them sincerely for their opposition; and if the condemnation of this comedy (however misconceived the provocation) could have added one spark to the decaying flame of national attachment to the country supposed to be reflected on, I should have been happy in its fate; and might with truth have boasted, that it had done more real service in its failure, than the successful morality of a thousand stage-novels will ever effect.

It is usual, I believe, to thank the performers in a new play, for the exertion of their several abilities. But where (as in this instance) their merit has been so striking and uncontroverted, as to call for the warmest and truest applause from a number of judicious audiences, the poet's after-praise comes like the feeble acclamation of a child to close the shouts of a multitude. The conduct, however, of the principals in a theatre cannot be so apparent to the public. I think it therefore but justice to declare, that from this theatre (the only one I can speak of from experience) those writers who wish to try the dramatic line, will meet with that candour and liberal attention, which are generally allowed to be better calculated to lead genius into excellence, than either the precepts of judgment, or the guidance of experience.

THE AUTHOR

PROLOGUE

BY THE AUTHOR
Spoken by Mr Woodward and Mr Quick[1]

[*Enter* SERJEANT AT LAW, *and* ATTORNEY *following, and giving a paper.*]

SERJEANT
Whats here – a vile cramp hand! I cannot see
Without my spectacles.

ATTORNEY   He means his fee.
Nay, Mr Serjeant, good Sir, try again. [*Gives money.*]

SERJEANT
The scrawl improves – [*More (money is given)*] O come, tis pretty
     plain.
Hey! hows this? Dibble! sure it cannot be!
A poets brief! A poet and a fee!

ATTORNEY
Yea Sir! – though you without reward, I know,
Would gladly plead the muses cause –

SERJEANT   So – So!

ATTORNEY
And if the fee offends – your wrath should fall
On me –

SERJEANT Dear Dibble no offence at all –

ATTORNEY
Some sons of Phoebus in the courts we meet,

SERJEANT
And fifty sons of Phoebus in the Fleet![2]

ATTORNEY
Nor pleads he worse, who with a decent sprig
Of bays adorns his legal waste of wig.

---

1. *Woodward . . . Quick*: Woodward played Captain Absolute and Quick Bob Acres.
2. *Fleet*: the Fleet Prison.

SERJEANT

> Full-bottomed heroes thus, on signs, unfurl
> A leaf of laurel – in a grove of curl!
> Yet tell your client, that, in adverse days,
> This wig is warmer than a bush of bays.

ATTORNEY

> Do you then, Sir, my client's place supply,
> Profuse of robe, and prodigal of tie[3] –
> Do you, with all those blushing powers of face,
> And wonted bashful hesitating grace,
> Rise in the court, and flourish on the case. [*Exit.*]

SERJEANT

> For practice then suppose – this brief will show it –
> Me, Serjeant Woodward, counsel for the poet.
> Used to the ground – I know 'tis hard to deal
> With this dread court from whence there's no appeal;
> No tricking here, to blunt the edge of law,
> Or, damned in equity, escape by flaw:
> But judgment given, your sentence must remain;
> No writ of error lies to Drury Lane![4]
> Yet when so kind you seem, 'tis past dispute
> We gain some favour, if not costs of suit.
> No spleen is here! I see no hoarded fury;
> I think I never faced a milder jury!
> Sad else our plight! – where frowns are transportation,
> A hiss the gallows, and a groan, damnation!
> But such the public candour, without fear
> My client waives all right of challenge here.
> No newsman from our session is dismissed,
> Nor wit nor critic we scratch off the list;
> His faults can never hurt another's ease,
> His crime at worst – a bad attempt to please:
> Thus, all respecting, he appeals to all,
> And by the general voice will stand or fall.

---

3. *tie*: tie-wig.
4. *Drury Lane*: the Drury Lane Theatre.

PROLOGUE

BY THE AUTHOR
Spoken on the tenth night, by Mrs Bulkley[1]

Granted our cause, our suit and trial o'er,
The worthy Serjeant need appear no more:
In pleasing I a different client choose,
He served the poet – I would serve the muse:
Like him, I'll try to merit your applause,
A female counsel in a female's cause.
Look on this form[2] – where humour quaint and sly,
Dimples the cheek, and points the beaming eye;
Where gay invention seems to boast its wiles
In amorous hint, and half-triumphant smiles;
While her light masks or covers satire's strokes,
All hide the conscious blush, her wit provokes.
Look on her well – does she seem formed to teach?
Should you expect to hear this lady – preach?
Is grey experience suited to her youth?
Do solemn sentiments become that mouth?
Bid her be grave, those lips should rebel prove
To every theme that slanders mirth or love.
Yet thus adorned with every graceful art
To charm the fancy and yet reach the heart
Must we displace her? And instead advance
The goddess of the woeful countenance –
The sentimental muse! Her emblems view
The pilgrim's progress and a sprig of rue!
View her – too chaste to look like flesh and blood –
Primly portrayed on emblematic wood!

1. *Mrs Bulkley*: she took the part of Julia.
2. *this form*: the figure of Comedy depicted on one side of the stage.

Thus fixed in usurpation should she stand
She'll snatch the dagger from her sister's hand:
And having made her votaries weep a flood
Good heaven! she'll end her comedies in blood –
Bid Harry Woodward break poor Dunstall's crown!
Imprison Quick – and knock Ned Shuter down;
While sad Barsanti – weeping o'er the scene,
Shall stab herself – or poison Mrs Green.[3]
Such dire encroachments to prevent in time,
Demands the critic's voice – the poet's rhyme.
Can our light scenes add strength to holy laws!
Such puny patronage but hurts the cause:
Fair virtue scorns our feeble aid to ask;
And moral truth disdains the trickster's mask.
For here their favourite stands,[4] whose brow – severe
And sad – claims youth's respect, and pity's tear;
Who – when oppressed by foes her worth creates –
Can point a poignard at the guilt she hates.

3. *Harry Woodward . . . Green*: all actors in the first performances of *The Rivals*.
4. *their favourite*: the figure of Tragedy depicted on the other side of the stage.

DRAMATIS PERSONAE

Men

SIR ANTHONY ABSOLUTE
CAPTAIN ABSOLUTE
FAULKLAND
ACRES
SIR LUCIUS O'TRIGGER
FAG
DAVID
COACHMAN

Women

MRS MALAPROP
LYDIA LANGUISH
JULIA
LUCY

Maid, Boy, Servants, etc.

Scene: Bath
Time of action: within one day

ACT I

Scene i

A street in Bath.

[COACHMAN *crosses the stage. Enter* FAG, *looking after him.*]

FAG: What! – Thomas! – Sure 'tis he? – What! – Thomas! – Thomas!

COACHMAN: Hey! – Odds life! – Mr Fag – give us your hand, my old fellow-servant.

FAG: Excuse my glove, Thomas: I'm devilish glad to see you, my lad: why, my prince of charioteers, you look as hearty! – but who the deuce thought of seeing you in Bath!

COACHMAN: Sure, Master, Madam Julia, Harry, Mrs Kate, and the postillion be all come!

FAG: Indeed!

COACHMAN: Aye! Master thought another fit of the gout was coming to make him a visit: so he'd a mind to gi't the slip, and whip we were all off at an hour's warning.

FAG: Aye, aye! hasty in everything, or it would not be Sir Anthony Absolute!

COACHMAN: But tell us, Mr Fag, how does young Master? Odd! Sir Anthony will stare to see the Captain here!

FAG: I do not serve Captain Absolute now –

COACHMAN: Why sure!

FAG: At present I am employed by Ensign[1] Beverley.

COACHMAN: I doubt, Mr Fag, you ha'n't changed for the better.

FAG: I have not changed, Thomas.

1. *Ensign*: junior officer.

COACHMAN: No! why didn't you say you had left young Master?

FAG: No – well, honest Thomas, I must puzzle you no farther: briefly then – Captain Absolute and Ensign Beverley are one and the same person.

COACHMAN: The devil they are!

FAG: So it is indeed, Thomas; and the *Ensign* half of my master being on guard at present – the *Captain* has nothing to do with me.

COACHMAN: So, so! – what, this is some freak, I warrant! Do, tell us, Mr Fag, the meaning o't – you know I ha' trusted you.

FAG: You'll be secret, Thomas?

COACHMAN: As a coach-horse.

FAG: Why then the cause of all this is – LOVE – love, Thomas, who (as you may get read to you) has been a masquerader ever since the days of Jupiter.

COACHMAN: Aye, aye; I guessed there was a lady in the case: but pray, why does your master pass only for Ensign? – now if he had shammed General indeed –

FAG: Ah! Thomas, there lies the mystery o'the matter. Harkee, Thomas, my master is in love with a lady of a very singular taste: a lady who likes him better as a half-pay Ensign than if she knew he was son and heir to Sir Anthony Absolute, a baronet of three thousand a year!

COACHMAN: That is an odd taste indeed! – but has she got the stuff, Mr Fag; is she rich, hey?

FAG: Rich! – why, I believe she owns half the stocks! Zounds! Thomas, she could pay the national debt as easily as I could my washerwoman! She has a lap-dog that eats out of gold – she feeds her parrot with small pearls – and all her thread-papers[2] are made of bank-notes!

COACHMAN: Bravo! – faith! – Odd! I warrant she has a set of thousands[3] at least: but does she draw kindly with the Captain?

FAG: As fond as pigeons.

COACHMAN: May one hear her name?

FAG: Miss Lydia Languish – but there is an old tough aunt in the way;

2. *thread-papers*: paper folded to hold thread.
3. *a set of thousands*: the phrase probably implies 'a lot of money'.

though by the by – she has never seen my master – for he got acquainted with Miss while on a visit in Gloucestershire.

COACHMAN: Well – I wish they were once harnessed together in matrimony. But pray, Mr Fag, what kind of a place is this Bath? I ha' heard a deal of it – here's a mort[4] o' merry-making – hey?

FAG: Pretty well, Thomas, pretty well – 'tis a good lounge. In the morning we go to the pump-room (though neither my master nor I drink the waters); after breakfast we saunter on the parades or play a game at billiards; at night we dance: but damn the place, I'm tired of it: their regular hours stupefy me – not a fiddle nor a card after eleven! – however Mr Faulkland's gentleman and I keep it up a little in private parties; I'll introduce you there, Thomas – you'll like him much.

COACHMAN: Sure I know Mr Du-Peigne – you know his master is to marry Madam Julia.

FAG: I had forgot. But Thomas you must polish a little – indeed you must: here now – this wig! – what the devil do you do with a *wig*, Thomas? None of the London whips of any degree of *ton* wear *wigs* now.

COACHMAN: More's the pity! more's the pity, I say. Odds life! when I heard how the lawyers and doctors had took to their own hair, I thought how 'twould go next – odd rabbit it! when the fashion had got foot on the Bar, I guessed 'twould mount to the Box![5] – but 'tis all out of character, believe me, Mr Fag: and lookee, I'll never gi' up mine – the lawyers and doctors may do as they will.

FAG: Well, Thomas, we'll not quarrel about that.

COACHMAN: Why, bless you, the gentlemen of they professions ben't all of a mind – for in our village now tho'ff Jack Gauge the exciseman has ta'en to his carrots,[6] there's little Dick the farrier swears he'll never forsake his bob, though all the college[7] should appear with their own heads!

FAG: Indeed! well said Dick! but hold – mark! mark! Thomas.

COACHMAN: Zooks! 'tis the Captain – is that the lady with him?

4. *mort*: a great deal.
5. *Box*: the coachman's box.
6. *carrots*: red hair.
7. *college*: college of doctors.

FAG: No! no! that is Madam Lucy – my master's mistress's maid. They lodge at that house – but I must after him to tell him the news.

COACHMAN: Odd! he's giving her money! – well, Mr Fag –

FAG: Goodbye, Thomas – I have an appointment in Gyde's[8] Porch this evening at eight; meet me there, and we'll make a little party.

[*Exeunt severally.*]

Scene ii

A dressing-room in MRS MALAPROP's *lodgings.*

[LYDIA *sitting on a sofa with a book in her hand.* LUCY, *as just returned from a message.*]

LUCY: Indeed, ma'am, I traversed half the town in search of it: I don't believe there's a circulating library in Bath I ha'n't been at.

LYDIA: And could not you get *The Reward of Constancy*?[9]

LUCY: No, indeed, ma'am.

LYDIA: Nor *The Fatal Connection*?

LUCY: No, indeed, ma'am.

LYDIA: Nor *The Mistakes of the Heart*?

LUCY: Ma'am, as ill-luck would have it, Mr Bull[10] said Miss Sukey Saunter had just fetched it away.

LYDIA: Heigh-ho! – did you inquire for *The Delicate Distress*?

LUCY: Or *The Memoirs of Lady Woodford*? Yes indeed, ma'am. I asked everywhere for it; and I might have brought it from Mr Frederick's,[11] but Lady Slattern Lounger, who had just sent it home, had so soiled and dog's-eared it, it wa'n't fit for a Christian to read.

---

8. *Gyde's*: Gyde's assembly room.
9. See Appendix on p. 280 for more details on Lydia's books.
10. *Mr Bull*: Lewis Bull, a bookseller in Bath.
11. *Mr Frederick*: William Frederick, another Bath bookseller.

LYDIA: Heigh-ho! – yes, I always know when Lady Slattern has been before me. She has a most observing thumb; and I believe cherishes her nails for the convenience of making marginal notes. Well, child, what *have* you brought me?

LUCY: Oh! here ma'am. [*Taking books from under her cloak, and from her pockets*] This is *The Gordian Knot* – and this *Peregrine Pickle*. Here are *The Tears of Sensibility*, and *Humphry Clinker*. This is *The Memoirs of a Lady of Quality, written by herself* – and here the second volume of *The Sentimental Journey*.

LYDIA: Heigh-ho! – what are those books by the glass?[12]

LUCY: The great one is only *The Whole Duty of Man* – where I press a few blondes,[13] ma'am.

LYDIA: Very well – give me the *sal volatile*.[14]

LUCY: Is it in a blue cover, ma'am?

LYDIA: My smelling bottle, you simpleton!

LUCY: Oh, the drops! – here ma'am.

LYDIA: Hold! here's someone coming – quick, see who it is.
      [*Exit* LUCY.]
      Surely I heard my cousin Julia's voice!
      [*Re-enter* LUCY.]

LUCY: Lud! ma'am, here is Miss Melville.

LYDIA: Is it possible!
      [*Enter* JULIA. *Exit* LUCY.]

LYDIA: My dearest Julia, how delighted am I! [*Embrace.*] How unexpected was this happiness!

JULIA: True, Lydia – and our pleasure is the greater; but what has been the matter? You were denied to me at first!

LYDIA: Ah! Julia, I have a thousand things to tell you! But first inform me, what has conjured you to Bath? Is Sir Anthony here?

JULIA: He is – we are arrived within this hour – and I suppose he will be here to wait on Mrs Malaprop as soon as he is dressed.

LYDIA: Then before we are interrupted, let me impart to you some of my distress! I know your gentle nature will sympathize with me,

12. *glass*: mirror.
13. *blondes*: pieces of blonde lace.
14. *sal volatile*: smelling salts.

though your prudence may condemn me! My letters have informed you of my whole connection with Beverley – but I have lost him, Julia! – my aunt has discovered our intercourse by a note she intercepted, and has confined me ever since! – Yet, would you believe it? she has fallen absolutely in love with a tall Irish baronet she met one night since we have been here, at Lady Macshuffle's rout.[15]

JULIA: You jest, Lydia!

LYDIA: No, upon my word. She really carries on a kind of correspondence with him, under a feigned name though, till she chooses to be known to him – but it is a *Delia* or a *Celia*, I assure you.

JULIA: Then, surely, she is now more indulgent to her niece.

LYDIA: Quite the contrary. Since she has discovered her own frailty, she is become more suspicious of mine. Then I must inform you of another plague! That odious Acres is to be in Bath today; so that I protest I shall be teased out of all spirits!

JULIA: Come, come, Lydia, hope the best – Sir Anthony shall use his interest with Mrs Malaprop.

LYDIA: But you have not heard the worst. Unfortunately I had quarrelled with my poor Beverley, just before my aunt made the discovery, and I have not seen him since, to make it up.

JULIA: What was his offence?

LYDIA: Nothing at all! But, I don't know how it was, as often as we had been together, we had never had a quarrel! And, somehow, I was afraid he would never give me an opportunity. So, last Thursday, I wrote a letter to myself, to inform myself that Beverley was at that time paying his addresses to another woman. I signed it *your Friend unknown*, showed it to Beverley, charged him with his falsehood, put myself in a violent passion, and vowed I'd never see him more.

JULIA: And you let him depart so, and have not seen him since?

LYDIA: 'Twas the next day my aunt found the matter out. I intended only to have teased him three days and a half, and now I've lost him for ever.

JULIA: If he is as deserving and sincere as you have represented him

15. *rout*: social gathering.

to me, he will never give you up so. Yet consider, Lydia, you tell me he is but an ensign, and you have thirty thousand pounds!

LYDIA: But you know I lose most of my fortune if I marry without my aunt's consent, till of age; and that is what I have determined to do, ever since I knew the penalty. Nor could I love the man, who would wish to wait a day for the alternative.

JULIA: Nay, this is caprice!

LYDIA: What, does Julia tax me with caprice? I thought her lover Faulkland had inured her to it.

JULIA: I do not love even *his* faults.

LYDIA: But apropos – you have sent to him, I suppose?

JULIA: Not yet, upon my word – nor has he the least idea of my being in Bath. Sir Anthony's resolution was so sudden, I could not inform him of it.

LYDIA: Well, Julia, you are your own mistress (though under the protection of Sir Anthony), yet have you, for this long year, been a slave to the caprice, the whim, the jealousy of this ungrateful Faulkland, who will ever delay assuming the right of a husband, while you suffer him to be equally imperious as a lover.

JULIA: Nay you are wrong entirely. We were contracted before my father's death. That, and some consequent embarrassments, have delayed what I know to be my Faulkland's most ardent wish. He is too generous to trifle on such a point. And for his character, you wrong him there too – no, Lydia, he is too proud, too noble to be jealous; if he is captious, 'tis without dissembling; if fretful, without rudeness. Unused to the fopperies of love, he is negligent of the little duties expected from a lover – but being unhackneyed in the passion, his affection is ardent and sincere; and as it engrosses his whole soul, he expects every thought and emotion of his mistress to move in unison with his. Yet, though his pride calls for this full return – his humility makes him undervalue those qualities in him, which would entitle him to it; and not feeling why he should be loved to the degree he wishes, he still suspects that he is not loved enough. This temper, I must own, has cost me many unhappy hours; but I have learned to think myself his debtor, for those imperfections which arise from the ardour of his attachment.

LYDIA: Well, I cannot blame you for defending him. But tell me candidly, Julia, had he never saved your life, do you think you should have been attached to him as you are? Believe me, the rude blast that overset your boat was a prosperous gale of love to him.

JULIA: Gratitude may have strengthened my attachment to Mr Faulkland, but I loved him before he had preserved me; yet surely that alone were an obligation sufficient –

LYDIA: Obligation! Why a water-spaniel would have done as much! Well, I should never think of giving my heart to a man because he could swim!

JULIA: Come, Lydia, you are too inconsiderate.

LYDIA: Nay, I do but jest – what's here?

[*Enter* LUCY *in a hurry.*]

LUCY: O ma'am, here is Sir Anthony Absolute just come home with your aunt.

LYDIA: They'll not come here – Lucy, do you watch.

[*Exit* LUCY.]

JULIA: Yet I must go – Sir Anthony does not know I am here, and if we meet, he'll detain me, to show me the town. I'll take another opportunity of paying my respects to Mrs Malaprop, when she shall treat me, as long as she chooses, with her select words so ingeniously *misapplied*, without being *mispronounced*.

[*Re-enter* LUCY.]

LUCY: O Lud! ma'am, they are both coming upstairs.

LYDIA: Well, I'll not detain you coz – adieu, my dear Julia, I'm sure you are in haste to send to Faulkland. There – through my room you'll find another staircase.

JULIA: Adieu. [*Embrace.*]

[*Exit* JULIA.]

LYDIA: Here, my dear Lucy, hide these books – quick, quick – fling *Peregrine Pickle* under the toilet[16] – throw *Roderick Random* into the closet – put *The Innocent Adultery* into *The Whole Duty of Man* – thrust *Lord Aimworth* under the sofa – cram Ovid behind the bolster – there – put *The Man of Feeling* into your pocket – so, so, now lay Mrs Chapone in sight, and leave Fordyce's *Sermons* open on the table.

16. *toilet*: dressing-table.

LUCY: O burn it, ma'am, the hairdresser has torn away as far as 'Proper Pride'.

LYDIA: Never mind – open at 'Sobriety' – fling me Lord Chesterfield's *Letters*. Now for 'em.

[*Exit* LUCY.]

[*Enter* MRS MALAPROP *and* SIR ANTHONY ABSOLUTE.]

MRS MALAPROP: There, Sir Anthony, there sits the deliberate simpleton, who wants to disgrace her family, and lavish herself on a fellow not worth a shilling!

LYDIA: Madam, I thought you once –

MRS MALAPROP: You thought, miss! I don't know any business you have to think at all – thought does not become a young woman. But the point we would request of you is, that you will promise to forget this fellow – to illiterate[17] him, I say, quite from your memory.

LYDIA: Ah, Madam! our memories are independent of our wills. It is not so easy to forget.

MRS MALAPROP: But I say it is, miss; there is nothing on earth so easy as to *forget*, if a person chooses to set about it. I'm sure I have as much forgot your poor dear uncle as if he had never existed – and I thought it my duty so to do; and let me tell you, Lydia, these violent memories don't become a young woman.

SIR ANTHONY: Why sure she won't pretend to remember what she's ordered not! Aye, this comes of her reading!

LYDIA: What crime, madam, have I committed to be treated thus?

MRS MALAPROP: Now don't attempt to extirpate[18] yourself from the matter; you know I have proof controvertible[19] of it. But tell me, will you promise to do as you're bid? Will you take a husband of your friend's choosing?

LYDIA: Madam, I must tell you plainly, that had I no preference for anyone else, the choice you have made would be my aversion.

MRS MALAPROP: What business have you, miss, with *preference* and *aversion*? They don't become a young woman; and you ought to know, that as both always wear off, 'tis safest in matrimony to begin

17. *illiterate*: obliterate.
18. *extirpate*: extricate.
19. *controvertible*: incontrovertible.

with a little aversion. I am sure I hated your poor dear uncle before marriage as if he'd been a blackamoor – and yet, miss, you are sensible what a wife I made! – and when it pleased Heaven to release me from him, 'tis unknown what tears I shed! But suppose we were going to give you another choice, will you promise us to give up this Beverley?

LYDIA: Could I belie my thoughts so far, as to give that promise, my actions would certainly as far belie my words.

MRS MALAPROP: Take yourself to your room. You are fit company for nothing but your own ill-humours.

LYDIA: Willingly, ma'am – I cannot change for the worse.

[*Exit* LYDIA.]

MRS MALAPROP: There's a little intricate hussy for you!

SIR ANTHONY: It is not to be wondered at, ma'am – all this is the natural consequence of teaching girls to read. Had I a thousand daughters, by heaven! I'd as soon have them taught the black art as their alphabet!

MRS MALAPROP: Nay, nay, Sir Anthony, you are an absolute misanthropy![20]

SIR ANTHONY: In my way hither, Mrs Malaprop, I observed your niece's maid coming forth from a circulating library! She had a book in each hand – they were half-bound volumes, with marble covers! From that moment I guessed how full of duty I should see her mistress!

MRS MALAPROP: Those are vile places, indeed!

SIR ANTHONY: Madam, a circulating library in a town is as an ever-green tree of diabolical knowledge! It blossoms through the year! And depend on it, Mrs Malaprop, that they who are so fond of handling the leaves, will long for the fruit at last.

MRS MALAPROP: Fie, fie, Sir Anthony, you surely speak laconically![21]

SIR ANTHONY: Why, Mrs Malaprop, in moderation, now, what would you have a woman know?

MRS MALAPROP: Observe me, Sir Anthony. I would by no means

20. *misanthropy*: misanthrope.
21. *laconically*: ironically.

wish a daughter of mine to be a progeny[22] of learning; I don't think so much learning becomes a young woman; for instance – I would never let her meddle with Greek, or Hebrew, or Algebra, or Simony,[23] or Fluxions, or Paradoxes,[24] or such inflammatory branches of learning – neither would it be necessary for her to handle any of your mathematical, astronomical, diabolical instruments. But, Sir Anthony, I would send her, at nine years old, to a boarding-school, in order to learn a little ingenuity and artifice. Then, sir, she should have a supercilious[25] knowledge in accounts; and as she grew up, I would have her instructed in geometry,[26] that she might know something of the contagious[27] countries; but above all, Sir Anthony, she should be mistress of orthodoxy,[28] that she might not misspell, and mispronounce words so shamefully as girls usually do; and likewise that she might reprehend[29] the true meaning of what she is saying. This, Sir Anthony, is what I would have a woman know; and I don't think there is a superstitious[30] article in it.

SIR ANTHONY: Well, well, Mrs Malaprop, I will dispute the point no further with you; though I must confess, that you are a truly moderate and polite arguer, for almost every third word you say is on my side of the question. But, Mrs Malaprop, to the more important point in debate – you say, you have no objection to my proposal.

MRS MALAPROP: None, I assure you. I am under no positive engagement with Mr Acres, and as Lydia is so obstinate against him, perhaps your son may have better success.

SIR ANTHONY: Well, madam, I will write for the boy directly. He knows not a syllable of this yet, though I have for some time had the proposal in my head. He is at present with his regiment.

22. *progeny*: prodigy.
23. *Simony*: cyclometry?
24. *Paradoxes*: parallaxes?
25. *supercilious*: superficial.
26. *geometry*: geography.
27. *contagious*: contiguous.
28. *orthodoxy*: orthography.
29. *reprehend*: apprehend.
30. *superstitious*: superficial.

MRS MALAPROP: We have never seen your son, Sir Anthony; but I hope no objection on his side.

SIR ANTHONY: Objection! – let him object if he dare! No, no, Mrs Malaprop, Jack knows that the least demur puts me in a frenzy directly. My process was always very simple – in their younger days, 'twas 'Jack, do this' – if he demurred – I knocked him down – and if he grumbled at that – I always sent him out of the room.

MRS MALAPROP: Aye, and the properest way, o' my conscience! – nothing is so conciliating[31] to young people as severity. Well, Sir Anthony, I shall give Mr Acres his discharge, and prepare Lydia to receive your son's invocations; and I hope you will represent her to the Captain as an object not altogether illegible.[32]

SIR ANTHONY: Madam, I will handle the subject prudently. Well, I must leave you – and let me beg you, Mrs Malaprop, to enforce this matter roundly to the girl; take my advice – keep a tight hand – if she rejects this proposal – clap her under lock and key: and if you were just to let the servants forget to bring her dinner for three or four days, you can't conceive how she'd come about!

[*Exit* SIR ANTHONY.]

MRS MALAPROP: Well, at any rate I shall be glad to get her from under my intuition.[33] She has somehow discovered my partiality for Sir Lucius O'Trigger – sure, Lucy can't have betrayed me! No, the girl is such a simpleton, I should have made her confess it. [*Calls*] Lucy! – Lucy! Had she been one of your artificial[34] ones, I should never have trusted her.

[*Enter* LUCY.]

LUCY: Did you call, ma'am?

MRS MALAPROP: Yes, girl. Did you see Sir Lucius while you was out?

LUCY: No, indeed, ma'am, not a glimpse of him.

MRS MALAPROP: You are sure, Lucy, that you never mentioned –

LUCY: O Gemini! I'd sooner cut my tongue out.

MRS MALAPROP: Well, don't let your simplicity be imposed on.

31. *conciliating*: constricting?
32. *illegible*: ineligible.
33. *intuition*: tuition.
34. *artificial*: artful.

LUCY: No, ma'am.

MRS MALAPROP: So, come to me presently, and I'll give you another letter to Sir Lucius; but mind Lucy – if ever you betray what you are entrusted with (unless it be other people's secrets to me) you forfeit my malevolence[35] for ever: and your being a simpleton shall be no excuse for your locality.[36]

[*Exit* MRS MALAPROP.]

LUCY: Ha! ha! ha! So, my dear *simplicity*, let me give you a little respite – [*altering her manner*] let girls in my station be as fond as they please of appearing expert, and knowing in their trusts; commend me to a mask of silliness, and a pair of sharp eyes for my own interest under it! Let me see to what account have I turned my *simplicity* lately – [*looks at a paper*]. *For abetting Miss Lydia Languish in a design of running away with an ensign – in money – sundry times – twelve pound twelve – gowns, five – hats, ruffles, caps, etc, etc. – numberless! From the said Ensign, within this last month, six guineas and a half* – about a quarter's pay! Item, *from Mrs Malaprop, for betraying the young people to her* – when I found matters were likely to be discovered – *two guineas, and a black paduasoy.*[37] Item, *from Mr Acres, for carrying divers letters* – which I never delivered – *two guineas, and a pair of buckles.* Item, *from Sir Lucius O'Trigger – three crowns – two gold pocket-pieces*[38] – *and a silver snuff-box!* – Well done, *simplicity*! – yet I was forced to make my Hibernian[39] believe, that he was corresponding, not with the aunt, but with the niece: for, though not over rich, I found he had too much pride and delicacy to sacrifice the feelings of a gentleman to the necessities of his fortune.

[*Exit.*]

35. *malevolence*: benevolence.
36. *locality*: loquacity.
37. *paduasoy*: corded silk fabric or gown of same material.
38. *pocket-piece*: 'a piece of money kept in the pocket as a charm; often one which is damaged or spurious' [*O.E.D.*].
39. *Hibernian*: Irishman.

ACT II

Scene i

[CAPTAIN ABSOLUTE *and* FAG.]

FAG: Sir, while I was there, Sir Anthony came in: I told him, you had sent me to inquire after his health, and to know if he was at leisure to see you.

ABSOLUTE: And what did he say, on hearing I was at Bath?

FAG: Sir, in my life I never saw an elderly gentleman more astonished! He started back two or three paces, rapped out a dozen interjectural oaths, and asked, what the devil had brought you here!

ABSOLUTE: Well, sir, and what did you say?

FAG: Oh, I lied, sir – I forget the precise lie, but you may depend on't; he got no truth from me. Yet, with submission, for fear of blunders in future, I should be glad to fix what *has* brought us to Bath: in order that we may lie a little consistently. Sir Anthony's servants were curious, sir, very curious indeed.

ABSOLUTE: You have said nothing to them –

FAG: Oh, not a word, sir – not a word. Mr Thomas, indeed, the coachman (whom I take to be the discreetest of whips) –

ABSOLUTE: 'Sdeath! – you rascal! you have not trusted him!

FAG: Oh, *no*, sir – no – no – not a syllable, upon my veracity! He was, indeed, a little inquisitive; but I was sly, sir – devilish sly! My master (said I) honest Thomas (you know, sir, one says *honest* to one's inferiors) is come to Bath to *recruit* – yes, sir – I said, *to recruit* – and whether for men, money, or constitution, you know, sir, is nothing to him, nor anyone else.

ABSOLUTE: Well – *recruit* will do – let it be so –

FAG: Oh, sir, recruit will do surprisingly – indeed, to give the thing an air, I told Thomas, that your honour had already enlisted five disbanded chairmen;[1] seven minority waiters,[2] and thirteen billiard markers.

ABSOLUTE: You blockhead, never say more than is necessary.

FAG: I beg pardon, sir – I beg pardon. But with submission, a lie is nothing unless one supports it. Sir, whenever I draw on my invention for a good current lie, I always forge endorsements, as well as the bill.

ABSOLUTE: Well, take care you don't hurt your credit, by offering too much security. Is Mr Faulkland returned?

FAG: He is above, sir, changing his dress.

ABSOLUTE: Can you tell whether he has been informed of Sir Anthony's and Miss Melville's arrival?

FAG: I fancy not, sir; he has seen no one since he came in, but his gentleman, who was with him at Bristol. I think, sir, I hear Mr Faulkland coming down –

ABSOLUTE: Go, tell him I am here.

FAG: Yes, sir – [*going*]. I beg pardon, sir, but should Sir Anthony call, you will do me the favour to remember that we are *recruiting*, if you please.

ABSOLUTE: Well, well.

FAG: And in tenderness to my character, if your honour could bring in the chairmen and waiters, I shall esteem it as an obligation; for though I never scruple a lie to serve my master, yet it hurts one's conscience, to be found out.
[*Exit.*]

ABSOLUTE: Now for my whimsical friend – if he does not know that his mistress is here, I'll tease him a little before I tell him –
[*Enter* FAULKLAND.]
Faulkland, you're welcome to Bath again; you are punctual in your return.

---

1. *chairmen*: sedan chair carriers.
2. *minority waiters*: probably young or part-time waiters.

FAULKLAND: Yes; I had nothing to detain me, when I had finished the business I went on. Well, what news since I left you? How stand matters between you and Lydia?

ABSOLUTE: Faith, much as they were; I have not seen her since our quarrel, however I expect to be recalled every hour.

FAULKLAND: Why don't you persuade her to go off with you at once?

ABSOLUTE: What, and lose two thirds of her fortune? You forget that my friend. No, no, I could have brought her to that long ago.

FAULKLAND: Nay then, you trifle too long – if you are sure of *her*, write to the aunt in your own character, and write to Sir Anthony for his consent.

ABSOLUTE: Softly, softly, for though I am convinced my little Lydia would elope with me as Ensign Beverley, yet am I by no means certain that she would take me with the impediments of our friends' consent, a regular humdrum wedding, and the reversion of a good fortune on my side; no, no, I must prepare her gradually for the discovery, and make myself necessary to her, before I risk it. Well, but Faulkland, you'll dine with us today at the hotel?

FAULKLAND: Indeed I cannot: I am not in spirits to be of such a party.

ABSOLUTE: By heavens! I shall forswear your company. You are the most teasing, captious, incorrigible lover! Do love like a man.

FAULKLAND: I own I am unfit for company.

ABSOLUTE: Am not *I* a lover; aye, and a romantic one too? Yet do I carry everywhere with me such a confounded farrago of doubts, fears, hopes, wishes, and all the flimsy furniture of a country miss's brain!

FAULKLAND: Ah! Jack, your heart and soul are not, like mine, fixed immutably on one only object. You throw for a large stake, but losing – you could stake, and throw again: but I have set my sum of happiness on this cast, and not to succeed, were to be stripped of all.

ABSOLUTE: But for heaven's sake! What grounds for apprehension can your whimsical brain conjure up at present?

FAULKLAND: What grounds for apprehension did you say? Heavens! are there not a thousand! I fear for her spirits – her health – her life. My absence may fret her; her anxiety for my return, her fears for me, may oppress her gentle temper. And for her health – does not every hour bring me cause to be alarmed? If it rains, some shower may even then have chilled her delicate frame! If the wind be keen, some rude blast may have affected her! The heat of noon, the dews of the evening, may endanger the life of her, for whom only I value mine. Oh Jack, when delicate and feeling souls are separated, there is not a feature in the sky, not a movement of the elements, not an aspiration of the breeze, but hints some cause for a lover's apprehension!

ABSOLUTE: Aye, but we may choose whether we will take the hint or not. So then, Faulkland, if you were convinced that Julia were well and in spirits, you would be entirely content?

FAULKLAND: I should be happy beyond measure – I am anxious only for that.

ABSOLUTE: Then to cure your anxiety at once – Miss Melville is in perfect health, and is at this moment in Bath.

FAULKLAND: Nay Jack – don't trifle with me.

ABSOLUTE: She is arrived here with my father within this hour.

FAULKLAND: Can you be serious?

ABSOLUTE: I thought you knew Sir Anthony better than to be surprised at a sudden whim of this kind. Seriously then, it is as I tell you – upon my honour.

FAULKLAND: My dear friend! Hollo, Du-Peigne! my hat – my dear Jack – now nothing on earth can give me a moment's uneasiness.

[*Enter* FAG.]

FAG: Sir, Mr Acres, just arrived, is below.

ABSOLUTE: Stay, Faulkland, this Acres lives within a mile of Sir Anthony, and he shall tell you how your mistress has been ever since you left her. Fag, show the gentleman up.

[*Exit* FAG.]

FAULKLAND: What, is he much acquainted in the family?

ABSOLUTE: Oh, very intimate: I insist on your not going: besides, his character will divert you.

FAULKLAND: Well, I should like to ask him a few questions.

ABSOLUTE: He is likewise a rival of mine – that is of my *other self's*, for he does not think his friend Captain Absolute ever saw the lady in question – and it is ridiculous enough to hear him complain to me of *one Beverley*, a concealed skulking rival, who –

FAULKLAND: Hush! He's here.

[*Enter* ACRES.]

ACRES: Hah! my dear friend, noble captain, and honest Jack, how do'st thou? Just arrived faith, as you see. [*To* FAULKLAND] Sir, your humble servant. Warm work on the roads Jack – odds whips and wheels, I've travelled like a comet, with a tail of dust all the way as long as the Mall.

ABSOLUTE: Ah! Bob, you are indeed an eccentric planet, but we know your attraction hither – give me leave to introduce Mr Faulkland to you; Mr Faulkland, Mr Acres.

ACRES: Sir, I am most heartily glad to see you: sir, I solicit your connections. Hey Jack – what this is Mr Faulkland, who –

ABSOLUTE: Aye, Bob, Miss Melville's Mr Faulkland.

ACRES: Odso! she and your father can be but just arrived before me – I suppose you have seen them. Ah! Mr Faulkland, you are indeed a happy man.

FAULKLAND: I have not seen Miss Melville yet, sir – I hope she enjoyed full health and spirits in Devonshire?

ACRES: Never knew her better in my life, sir – never better. Odds blushes and blooms! she has been as healthy as the German Spa.

FAULKLAND: Indeed! – I did hear that she had been a little indisposed.

ACRES: False, false, sir – only said to vex you: quite the reverse I assure you.

FAULKLAND: There, Jack, you see she has the advantage of me; I had almost fretted myself ill.

ABSOLUTE: Now you are angry with your mistress for not having been sick.

FAULKLAND: No, no, you misunderstand me: yet surely a little trifling indisposition is not an unnatural consequence of absence from those we love. Now confess – isn't there something unkind in this violent, robust, unfeeling health?

ABSOLUTE: Oh, it was very unkind of her to be well in your absence to be sure!

ACRES: Good apartments, Jack.

FAULKLAND: Well sir, but you were saying that Miss Melville has been so *exceedingly* well – what then she has been merry and gay I suppose? Always in spirits – hey?

ACRES: Merry, odds crickets! she has been the belle and spirit of the company wherever she has been – so lively and entertaining! so full of wit and humour!

FAULKLAND: There, Jack, there. Oh, by my soul! there is an innate levity in woman, that nothing can overcome. What! happy, and I away!

ABSOLUTE: Have done: how foolish this is! Just now you were only apprehensive for your mistress's spirits.

FAULKLAND: Why Jack, have I been the joy and spirit of the company?

ABSOLUTE: No indeed, you have not.

FAULKLAND: Have I been lively and entertaining?

ABSOLUTE: Oh, upon my word, I acquit you.

FAULKLAND: Have I been full of wit and humour?

ABSOLUTE: No, faith, to do you justice, you have been confoundedly stupid indeed.

ACRES: What's the matter with the gentleman?

ABSOLUTE: He is only expressing his great satisfaction at hearing that Julia has been so well and happy – that's all – hey, Faulkland?

FAULKLAND: Oh! I am rejoiced to hear it – yes, yes, she has a *happy* disposition!

ACRES: That she has indeed – then she is so accomplished – so sweet a voice – so expert at her harpsichord – such a mistress of flat and sharp, squallante, rumblante, and quiverante![3] There was this time month – odds minims and crotchets! how she did chirrup at Mrs Piano's concert.

FAULKLAND: There again, what say you to this? You see she has been all mirth and song – not a thought of me!

ABSOLUTE: Pho! man, is not music the food of love?[4]

FAULKLAND: Well, well, it may be so. Pray Mr – what's his damned name? – Do you remember what songs Miss Melville sung?

ACRES: Not I, indeed.

3. *squallante . . . quiverante*: Acres coins quasi-Italian terms for 'squalling', 'rumbling' and 'quivering'.

4. *music . . . love*: see *Twelfth Night*, I, i.

ABSOLUTE: Stay now, they were some pretty, melancholy, purling stream airs, I warrant; perhaps you may recollect: did she sing 'When absent from my soul's delight'?

ACRES: No, that wa'n't it.

ABSOLUTE: Or 'Go, gentle gales!'[5] – [Sings] 'Go, gentle gales!'

ACRES: Oh no! nothing like it. Odds! now I recollect one of them – .[Sings] 'My heart's my own, my will is free'.[6]

FAULKLAND: Fool! fool that I am! to fix all my happiness on such a trifler! 'Sdeath! to make herself the pipe and ballad-monger of a circle! To soothe her light heart with catches and glees! What can you say to this, sir?

ABSOLUTE: Why, that I should be glad to hear my mistress had been so merry, sir.

FAULKLAND: Nay, nay, nay – I am not sorry that she has been happy – no, no, I am glad of that – I would not have had her sad or sick – yet surely a sympathetic heart would have shown itself even in the choice of a song – she might have been temperately healthy, and somehow, plaintively gay; but she has been dancing too, I doubt not!

ACRES: What does the gentleman say about dancing?

ABSOLUTE: He says the lady we speak of dances as well as she sings.

ACRES: Aye truly, does she – there was at our last race-ball –

FAULKLAND: Hell and the devil! There! there! – I told you so! I told you so! Oh! she thrives in my absence! – dancing! – but her whole feelings have been in opposition with mine! I have been anxious, silent, pensive, sedentary – my days have been hours of care, my nights of watchfulness. She has been all health! spirit! laugh! song! dance! – Oh! damned, damned levity!

ABSOLUTE: For heaven's sake! Faulkland, don't expose yourself so. Suppose she has danced, what then? – does not the ceremony of society often oblige –

FAULKLAND: Well, well, I'll contain myself – perhaps, as you say – for form sake. What, Mr Acres, you were praising Miss Melville's manner of dancing a minuet – hey?

5. *'When absent . . . gales!'*: both songs are from *Twelve Songs Set to Music by William Jackson of Exeter* (London, n.d.).

6. *'My . . . free'*: from Bickerstaff's *Love in a Village* (1762).

ACRES: Oh, I dare insure her for that – but what I was going to speak of was her *country dancing*: odds swimmings! she has such an air with her!

FAULKLAND: Now disappointment on her! Defend this, Absolute, why don't you defend this? Country dances! jigs, and reels! am I to blame now? A minuet I could have forgiven – I should not have minded that – I say I should not have regarded a minuet – but *country dances*! Zounds! had she made one in a cotillon[7] – I believe I could have forgiven even that – but to be monkey-led for a night! – to run the gauntlet through a string of amorous palming puppies! – to show paces like a managed filly! O Jack, there never can be but *one* man in the world, whom a truly modest and delicate woman ought to pair with in a country dance; and even then, the rest of the couples should be her great uncles and aunts!

ABSOLUTE: Aye, to be sure! – grandfathers and grandmothers!

FAULKLAND: If there be but one vicious mind in the set, 'twill spread like a contagion – the action of their pulse beats to the lascivious movement of the jig – their quivering, warm-breathed sighs impregnate the very air – the atmosphere becomes electrical to love, and each amorous spark darts through every link of the chain! I must leave you – I own I am somewhat flurried – and that confounded looby has perceived it. [*Going.*]

ABSOLUTE: Nay, but stay Faulkland, and thank Mr Acres for his good news.

FAULKLAND: Damn his news!
   [*Exit* FAULKLAND.]

ABSOLUTE: Ha! ha! ha! poor Faulkland five minutes since – 'nothing on earth could give him a moment's uneasiness'!

ACRES: The gentleman wa'n't angry at my praising his mistress, was he?

ABSOLUTE: A little jealous, I believe, Bob.

ACRES: You don't say so? Ha! ha! jealous of me – that's a good joke.

ABSOLUTE: There's nothing strange in that, Bob: let me tell you, that sprightly grace and insinuating manner of yours will do some mischief among the girls here.

7. *cotillon*: French dance.

ACRES: Ah! you joke – ha! ha! mischief – ha! ha! but you know I am not my own property, my dear Lydia has forestalled me. She could never abide me in the country, because I used to dress so badly – but odds frogs[8] and tambours![9] I shan't take matters so here – now ancient Madam has no voice in it – I'll make my old clothes know who's master – I shall straightway cashier the hunting-frock – and render my leather breeches incapable. My hair has been in training some time.

ABSOLUTE: Indeed!

ACRES: Aye – and tho'ff the side-curls are a little restive, my hind-part takes to it very kindly.

ABSOLUTE: Oh, you'll polish, I doubt not.

ACRES: Absolutely I propose so – then if I can find out this Ensign Beverley, odds triggers and flints! I'll make him know the difference o't.

ABSOLUTE: Spoke like a man – but pray, Bob, I observe you have got an odd kind of a new method of swearing –

ACRES: Ha! ha! you've taken notice of it – 'tis genteel, isn't it? I didn't invent it myself though; but a commander in our militia – a great scholar, I assure you – says that there is no meaning in the common oaths, and that nothing but their antiquity makes them respectable; because, he says, the ancients would never stick to an oath or two, but would say by Jove! or by Bacchus! or by Mars! or by Venus! or by Pallas! according to the sentiment – so that to swear with propriety, says my little major, the 'oath should be an echo to the sense';[10] and this we call the *oath referential*, or *sentimental swearing* – ha! ha! ha! 'tis genteel, isn't it?

ABSOLUTE: Very genteel, and very new indeed – and I dare say will supplant all other figures of imprecation.

ACRES: Aye, aye, the best terms will grow obsolete – damns have had their day.

[*Enter* FAG.]

FAG: Sir, there is a gentleman below, desires to see you – shall I show him into the parlour?

8. *frogs*: ornamental fastenings on a military uniform.
9. *tambours*: embroideries produced on a tambour frame.
10. *oath . . . sense*: see Pope, *An Essay on Criticism*, l. 365.

ABSOLUTE: Aye – you may.

ACRES: Well, I must be gone –

ABSOLUTE: Stay; who is it, Fag?

FAG: Your father, sir.

ABSOLUTE: You puppy, why didn't you show him up directly?
    [*Exit* FAG.]

ACRES: You have business with Sir Anthony – I expect a message from Mrs Malaprop at my lodgings – I have sent also to my dear friend Sir Lucius O'Trigger. Adieu, Jack, we must meet at night, when you shall give me a dozen bumpers to little Lydia.

ABSOLUTE: That I will with all my heart.
    [*Exit* ACRES.]

ABSOLUTE: Now for a parental lecture – I hope he has heard nothing of the business that has brought me here. I wish the gout had held him fast in Devonshire, with all my soul!
    [*Enter* SIR ANTHONY.]
    Sir, I am delighted to see you here; and looking so well! – your sudden arrival at Bath made me apprehensive for your health.

SIR ANTHONY: Very apprehensive, I dare say, Jack. What, you are recruiting here, hey?

ABSOLUTE: Yes, sir, I am on duty.

SIR ANTHONY: Well, Jack, I am glad to see you, though I did not expect it, for I was going to write to you on a little matter of business. Jack, I have been considering that I grow old and infirm, and shall probably not trouble you long.

ABSOLUTE: Pardon me, sir, I never saw you look more strong and hearty; and I pray frequently that you may continue so.

SIR ANTHONY: I hope your prayers may be heard with all my heart. Well then, Jack, I have been considering that I am so strong and hearty, I may continue to plague you a long time. Now, Jack, I am sensible that the income of your commission, and what I have hitherto allowed you, is but a small pittance for a lad of your spirit.

ABSOLUTE: Sir, you are very good.

SIR ANTHONY: And it is my wish, while yet I live, to have my boy make some figure in the world. I have resolved, therefore, to fix you at once in a noble independence.

ABSOLUTE: Sir, your kindness overpowers me – such generosity

63

makes the gratitude of reason more lively than the sensations even of filial affection.

SIR ANTHONY: J am glad you are so sensible of my attention – and you shall be master of a large estate in a few weeks.

ABSOLUTE: Let my future life, sir, speak my gratitude: I cannot express the sense I have of your munificence. – Yet, sir, I presume you would not wish me to quit the army?

SIR ANTHONY: Oh, that shall be as your wife chooses.

ABSOLUTE: My wife, sir!

SIR ANTHONY: Aye, aye, settle that between you – settle that between you.

ABSOLUTE: A *wife*, sir, did you say?

SIR ANTHONY: Aye, a wife – why, did not I mention her before?

ABSOLUTE: Not a word of her, sir.

SIR ANTHONY: Odso! – I mustn't forget *her* though. Yes, Jack, the independence I was talking of is by a marriage – the fortune is saddled with a wife – but I suppose that makes no difference.

ABSOLUTE: Sir! Sir! – you amaze me!

SIR ANTHONY: Why, what the devil's the matter with the fool? Just now you were all gratitude and duty.

ABSOLUTE: I was, sir – you talked to me of independence and a fortune, but not a word of a wife.

SIR ANTHONY: Why – what difference does that make? Odds life, sir! if you have the estate, you must take it with the live stock on it, as it stands.

ABSOLUTE: If my happiness is to be the price, I must beg leave to decline the purchase. Pray, sir, who is the lady?

SIR ANTHONY: What's that to you, sir? Come, give me your promise to love, and to marry her directly.

ABSOLUTE: Sure, sir, this is not very reasonable, to summon my affections for a lady I know nothing of!

SIR ANTHONY: I am sure, sir, 'tis more unreasonable in you to *object* to a lady you know nothing of.

ABSOLUTE: Then, sir, I must tell you plainly, that my inclinations are fixed on another – my heart is engaged to an angel.

SIR ANTHONY: Then pray let it send an excuse. It is very sorry – but *business* prevents its waiting on her.

ABSOLUTE: But my vows are pledged to her.

SIR ANTHONY: Let her foreclose, Jack; let her foreclose; they are not worth redeeming: besides, you have the angel's vows in exchange, I suppose; so there can be no loss there.

ABSOLUTE: You must excuse me, sir, if I tell you, once for all, that in this point I cannot obey you.

SIR ANTHONY: Harkee Jack; I have heard you for some time with patience – I have been cool – quite cool; but take care – you know I am compliance itself – when I am not thwarted; no one more easily led – when I have my own way; but don't put me in a frenzy.

ABSOLUTE: Sir, I must repeat it – in this I cannot obey you.

SIR ANTHONY: Now, damn me! if ever I call you Jack again while I live!

ABSOLUTE: Nay, sir, but hear me.

SIR ANTHONY: Sir, I won't hear a word – not a word! not one word! so give me your promise by a nod – and I'll tell you what, Jack – I mean, you dog – if you don't, by –

ABSOLUTE: What, sir, promise to link myself to some mass of ugliness! to –

SIR ANTHONY: Zounds! sirrah! the lady shall be as ugly as I choose: she shall have a hump on each shoulder; she shall be as crooked as the Crescent;[11] her one eye shall roll like the bull's in Cox's[12] museum – she shall have a skin like a mummy, and the beard of a Jew – she shall be all this, sirrah! – yet I'll make you ogle her all day, and sit up all night to write sonnets on her beauty.

ABSOLUTE: This is reason and moderation indeed!

SIR ANTHONY: None of your sneering, puppy! no grinning, jack-anapes!

ABSOLUTE: Indeed, sir, I never was in a worse humour for mirth in my life.

SIR ANTHONY: 'Tis false, sir, I know you are laughing in your sleeve: I know you'll grin when I am gone, sirrah!

ABSOLUTE: Sir, I hope I know my duty better.

11. *Crescent*: the Royal Crescent in Bath.
12. *Cox's*: James Cox, jeweller.

SIR ANTHONY: None of your passion, sir! none of your violence! if you please. It won't do with me, I promise you.

ABSOLUTE: Indeed, sir, I never was cooler in my life.

SIR ANTHONY: 'Tis a confounded lie! I know you are in a passion in your heart; I know you are, you hypocritical young dog! but it won't do.

ABSOLUTE: Nay, sir, upon my word.

SIR ANTHONY: So you will fly out! Can't you be cool, like me? What the devil good can *passion* do! *Passion* is of no service, you impudent, insolent, overbearing reprobate! There you sneer again! – don't provoke me! – but you rely upon the mildness of my temper – you do, you dog! you play upon the meekness of my disposition! Yet take care – the patience of a saint may be overcome at last! – but mark! I give you six hours and a half to consider of this: if you then agree, without any condition, to do everything on earth that I choose, why – confound you! I may in time forgive you – If not, zounds! don't enter the same hemisphere with me! don't dare to breathe the same air, or use the same light with me; but get an atmosphere and a sun of your own! I'll strip you of your commission; I'll lodge a five and threepence in the hands of trustees, and you shall live on the interest. I'll disown you, I'll disinherit you, I'll unget you! And damn me, if ever I call you Jack again!

[*Exit* SIR ANTHONY.]

ABSOLUTE: Mild, gentle, considerate father – I kiss your hands. What a tender method of giving his opinion in these matters Sir Anthony has! I dare not trust him with the truth. I wonder what old, wealthy hag it is that he wants to bestow on me! – yet he himself married for love, and was in his youth a bold intriguer, and a gay companion!

[*Enter* FAG.]

FAG: Assuredly, sir, our father is wrath to a degree; he comes down stairs eight or ten steps at a time – muttering, growling, and thumping the banisters all the way: I, and the cook's dog, stand bowing at the door – rap! he gives me a stroke on the head with his cane; bids me carry that to my master, then kicking the poor turnspit into the area, damns us all, for a puppy triumvirate! –

Upon my credit, sir, were I in your place, and found my father such very bad company, I should certainly drop his acquaintance.

ABSOLUTE: Cease your impertinence, sir, at present. Did you come in for nothing more? Stand out of the way!

[*Pushes him aside, and exit.*]

FAG: So! Sir Anthony trims my master; he is afraid to reply to his father – then vents his spleen on poor Fag! When one is vexed by one person, to revenge oneself on another, who happens to come in the way – is the vilest injustice! Ah! it shows the worst temper – the basest –

[*Enter* ERRAND BOY.]

ERRAND BOY: Mr Fag! Mr Fag! your master calls you.

FAG: Well, you little, dirty puppy, you need not bawl so! – The meanest disposition! the –

ERRAND BOY: Quick, quick, Mr Fag.

FAG: Quick, quick, you impudent jackanapes! Am I to be commanded by you too? You little, impertinent, insolent, kitchen-bred –

[*Exit, kicking and beating him.*]

Scene ii

The North Parade.

[*Enter* LUCY.]

LUCY: So – I shall have another rival to add to my mistress's list – Captain Absolute. – However, I shall not enter his name till my purse has received notice in form. Poor Acres is dismissed! Well, I have done him a last friendly office, in letting him know that Beverley was here before him. Sir Lucius is generally more punctual when he expects to hear from his *dear Dalia*, as he calls her: I wonder he's not here! I have a little scruple of conscience from this deceit; though I should not be paid so well, if my hero knew that *Delia* was near fifty, and her own mistress.

[*Enter* SIR LUCIUS O'TRIGGER.]

SIR LUCIUS: Hah! my little embassadress – upon my conscience I have been looking for you; I have been on the South Parade this half-hour.

LUCY [*speaking simply*]: O gemini! and I have been waiting for your worship here on the North.

SIR LUCIUS: Faith! – maybe that was the reason we did not meet; and it is very comical too, how you could go out and I not see you – for I was only taking a nap at the Parade coffee-house, and I chose the window on purpose that I might not miss you.

LUCY: My stars! Now I'd wager a sixpence I went by while you were asleep.

SIR LUCIUS: Sure enough it must have been so – and I never dreamt it was so late, till I waked. Well, but my little girl, have you got nothing for me?

LUCY: Yes, but I have – I've got a letter for you in my pocket.

SIR LUCIUS: O faith! I guessed you weren't come empty-handed – well – let me see what the dear creature says.

LUCY: There, Sir Lucius. [*Gives him a letter.*]

SIR LUCIUS [*reads*]: *Sir – there is often a sudden incentive impulse in love, that has a greater induction than years of domestic combination: such was the commotion I felt at the first superfluous*[13] *view of Sir Lucius O'Trigger.* Very pretty, upon my word. *Female punctuation*[14] *forbids me to say more; yet let me add, that it will give me joy infallible*[15] *to find Sir Lucius worthy the last criterion of my affections. – Delia.* Upon my conscience! Lucy, your lady is a great mistress of language. Faith, she's quite the queen of the dictionary! – for the devil a word dare refuse coming at her call – though one would think it was quite out of hearing.

LUCY: Aye, sir, a lady of her experience.

SIR LUCIUS: Experience! What, at seventeen?

LUCY: Oh true, sir – but then she reads so – my stars! how she will read off-hand!

SIR LUCIUS: Faith, she must be very deep read to write this way –

---

13. *superfluous*: superficial.
14. *punctuation*: punctilio.
15. *infallible*: ineffable.

though she is a rather arbitrary writer too – for here are a great many poor words pressed into the service of this note, that would get their *habeas corpus* from any court in Christendom.

LUCY: Ah! Sir Lucius, if you were to hear how she talks of you!

SIR LUCIUS: O tell her, I'll make her the best husband in the world, and Lady O'Trigger into the bargain! But we must get the old gentlewoman's consent – and do everything fairly.

LUCY: Nay, Sir Lucius, I thought you wa'n't rich enough to be so nice!

SIR LUCIUS: Upon my word, young woman, you have hit it: I am so poor that I can't afford to do a dirty action. If I did not want money I'd steal your mistress and her fortune with a great deal of pleasure. – However, my pretty girl [*gives her money*], here's a little something to buy you a riband; and meet me in the evening, and I'll give you an answer to this. So, hussy, take a kiss beforehand, to put you in mind.

[*Kisses her.*]

LUCY: O lud! Sir Lucius – I never seed such a gemman! My lady won't like you if you're so impudent.

SIR LUCIUS: Faith she will, Lucy – that same – pho! what's the name of it? – *modesty*! – is a quality in a lover more praised by the women than liked; so, if your mistress asks you whether Sir Lucius ever gave you a kiss, tell her fifty – my dear.

LUCY: What, would you have me tell her a lie?

SIR LUCIUS: Ah then, you baggage! I'll make it a truth presently.

LUCY: For shame now; here is someone coming.

SIR LUCIUS: O faith, I'll quiet your conscience!

[*Sees* FAG. *Exit, humming a tune.*]

[*Enter* FAG.]

FAG: So, so, ma'am. I humbly beg pardon.

LUCY: O lud! – now, Mr Fag, you flurry one so.

FAG: Come, come, Lucy, here's no one by – so a little less simplicity, with a grain or two more sincerity, if you please. – You play false with us, madam. I saw you give the Baronet a letter. My master shall know this – and if he doesn't call him out – I will.

LUCY: Ha! ha! ha! you gentlemen's gentlemen are so hasty. That letter was from Mrs Malaprop, simpleton. She is taken with Sir Lucius's address.

FAG: How! What tastes some people have! Why I suppose I have walked by her window an hundred times. – But what says our young lady? Any message to my master?

LUCY: Sad news! Mr Fag. A worse rival than Acres! Sir Anthony Absolute has proposed his son.

FAG: What, Captain Absolute?

LUCY: Even so – I overheard it all.

FAG: Ha! ha! ha! – very good, faith. Goodbye, Lucy, I must away with this news.

LUCY: Well – you may laugh – but it is true, I assure you. [*Going.*] But, Mr Fag, tell your master not to be cast down by this.

FAG: Oh, he'll be so disconsolate!

LUCY: And charge him not to think of quarrelling with young Absolute.

FAG: Never fear! – never fear!

LUCY: Be sure – bid him keep up his spirits.

FAG: We will – we will.

[*Exeunt severally.*]

ACT III

Scene i

The North Parade.

[*Enter* ABSOLUTE.]

ABSOLUTE: 'Tis just as Fag told me, indeed. Whimsical enough, faith! My father wants to force me to marry the very girl I am plotting to run away with! He must not know of my connection with her yet awhile. – He has too summary a method of proceeding in these matters. – However, I'll read my recantation instantly. My conversion is something sudden, indeed, but I can assure him it is very *sincere*. – So, so – here he comes. He looks plaguy gruff.
[*Steps aside.*]
[*Enter* SIR ANTHONY.]

SIR ANTHONY: No – I'll die sooner than forgive him. *Die*, did I say? I'll live these fifty years to plague him. – At our last meeting, his impudence had almost put me out of temper. An obstinate, passionate, self-willed boy! Who can he take after? This is my return for getting him before all his brothers and sisters! – for putting him, at twelve years old, into a marching regiment, and allowing him fifty pounds a year, besides his pay ever since! But I have done with him – he's anybody's son for me. – I never will see him more – never – never – never – never.

ABSOLUTE: Now for a penitential face.

SIR ANTHONY: Fellow, get out of my way.

ABSOLUTE: Sir, you see a penitent before you.

SIR ANTHONY: I see an impudent scoundrel before me.

ABSOLUTE: A sincere penitent. – I am come, sir, to acknowledge my error, and to submit entirely to your will.

SIR ANTHONY: What's that?

ABSOLUTE: I have been revolving, and reflecting, and considering on your past goodness, and kindness, and condescension to me.

SIR ANTHONY: Well, sir?

ABSOLUTE: I have likewise been weighing and balancing what you were pleased to mention concerning duty, and obedience, and authority.

SIR ANTHONY: Well, puppy?

ABSOLUTE: Why then, sir, the result of my reflections is – a resolution to sacrifice every inclination of my own to your satisfaction.

SIR ANTHONY: Why now, you talk sense – absolute sense – I never heard anything more sensible in my life. – Confound you; you shall be Jack again.

ABSOLUTE: I am happy in the appellation.

SIR ANTHONY: Why, then, Jack, my dear Jack, I will now inform you who the lady really is. – Nothing but your passion and violence, you silly fellow, prevented my telling you at first. Prepare, Jack, for wonder and rapture – prepare. What think you of Miss Lydia Languish?

ABSOLUTE: Languish! What, the Languishes of Worcestershire?

SIR ANTHONY: Worcestershire! No. Did you never meet Mrs Malaprop and her niece, Miss Languish, who came into our country just before you were last ordered to your regiment?

ABSOLUTE: Malaprop! Languish! I don't remember ever to have heard the names before. Yet, stay – I think I do recollect something. – Languish! Languish! She squints, don't she? A little, red-haired girl?

SIR ANTHONY: Squints? A red-haired girl! Zounds, no.

ABSOLUTE: Then I must have forgot; it can't be the same person.

SIR ANTHONY: Jack! Jack! what think you of blooming, love-breathing seventeen?

ABSOLUTE: As to that, sir, I am quite indifferent. If I can please you in the matter, 'tis all I desire.

SIR ANTHONY: Nay, but Jack, such eyes! such eyes! so innocently wild! so bashfully irresolute! Not a glance but speaks and kindles some thought of love! Then, Jack, her cheeks! her cheeks, Jack! so deeply blushing at the insinuations of her tell-tale eyes! Then, Jack, her lips! O Jack, lips smiling at their own discretion; and if not smiling, more sweetly pouting; more lovely in sullenness!

ABSOLUTE [*aside*]: That's she indeed. Well done, old gentleman!

SIR ANTHONY: Then, Jack, her neck. O Jack! Jack!

ABSOLUTE: And which is to be mine, sir, the niece or the aunt?

SIR ANTHONY: Why, you unfeeling, insensible puppy, I despise you. When I was of your age, such a description would have made me fly like a rocket![1] The *aunt*, indeed! Odds life! when I ran away with your mother, I would not have touched anything old or ugly to gain an empire.

ABSOLUTE: Not to please your father, sir?

SIR ANTHONY: To please my father! Zounds! not to please – O my father! – odso! – yes – yes! if my father indeed had desired – that's quite another matter. Though he wa'n't the indulgent father that I am, Jack.

ABSOLUTE: I dare say not, sir.

SIR ANTHONY: But, Jack, you are not sorry to find your mistress is so beautiful.

ABSOLUTE: Sir, I repeat it; if I please you in this affair, 'tis all I desire. Not that I think a woman the worse for being handsome; but, sir, if you please to recollect, you before hinted something about a hump or two, one eye, and a few more graces of that kind – now, without being very nice, I own I should rather choose a wife of mine to have the usual number of limbs, and a limited quantity of back: and though *one* eye may be very agreeable, yet as the prejudice has always run in favour of *two*, I would not wish to affect a singularity in that article.

SIR ANTHONY: What a phlegmatic sot it is! Why, sirrah, you're an anchorite! – a vile insensible stock.[2] You a soldier! – you're a walking block, fit only to dust the company's regimentals on – odds life! I've a great mind to marry the girl myself.

ABSOLUTE: I am entirely at your disposal, sir; if you should think of

1. *rocket*: firework.
2. *stock*: block of wood.

addressing Miss Languish yourself, I suppose you would have me marry the aunt; or if you should change your mind, and take the old lady – 'tis the same to me – I'll marry the niece.

SIR ANTHONY: Upon my word, Jack, thou'rt either a very great hypocrite, or – but come, I know your indifference on such a subject must be all a lie – I'm sure it must – come, now – damn your demure face! – come, confess, Jack – you have been lying – ha'n't you? You have been playing the hypocrite, hey! – I'll never forgive you, if you ha'n't been lying and playing the hypocrite.

ABSOLUTE: I'm sorry, sir, that the respect and duty which I bear to you should be so mistaken.

SIR ANTHONY: Hang your respect and duty! But, come along with me, I'll write a note to Mrs Malaprop, and you shall visit the lady directly. Her eyes shall be the Promethean torch to you – come along, I'll never forgive you, if you don't come back, stark mad with rapture and impatience – if you don't, egad, I'll marry the girl myself!

[*Exeunt.*]

Scene ii

JULIA's *dressing-room.*

[FAULKLAND *solus.*]

FAULKLAND: They told me Julia would return directly; I wonder she is not yet come! How mean does this captious, unsatisfied temper of mine appear to my cooler judgment! Yet I know not that I indulge it in any other point: but on this one subject, and to this one subject, whom I think I love beyond my life, I am ever ungenerously fretful, and madly capricious! I am conscious of it – yet I cannot correct myself! What tender, honest joy sparkled in her eyes when we met! How delicate was the warmth of her expressions! I was ashamed to appear less happy – though I had come resolved to wear a face of coolness and upbraiding. Sir Anthony's presence prevented my proposed expostulations: yet I must be satisfied that she has not been so *very* happy in my absence. – She is coming! – yes! – I know the nimbleness of her tread, when she thinks her impatient Faulkland counts the moments of her stay.

[*Enter* JULIA.]

JULIA: I had not hoped to see you again so soon.

FAULKLAND: Could I, Julia, be contented with my first welcome – restrained as we were by the presence of a third person?

JULIA: O Faulkland, when your kindness can make me thus happy, let me not think that I discovered something of coldness in your first salutation.

FAULKLAND: 'Twas but your fancy, Julia. I *was* rejoiced to see you – to see you in such health – sure I had no cause for coldness?

JULIA: Nay then, I see you have taken something ill. You must not conceal from me what it is.

FAULKLAND: Well then – shall I own to you that my joy at hearing of your health and arrival here, by your neighbour Acres, was somewhat damped, by his dwelling much on the high spirits you had enjoyed in Devonshire – on your mirth – your singing – dancing, and I know not what! For such is my temper, Julia, that I should regard every mirthful moment in your absence as a treason to constancy: the mutual tear that steals down the cheek of parting lovers is a compact, that no smile shall live there till they meet again.

JULIA: Must I never cease to tax my Faulkland with this teasing minute caprice? Can the idle reports of a silly boor weigh in your breast against my tried affection?

FAULKLAND: They have no weight with me, Julia: no, no – I am happy if you have been so – yet only say, that you did not sing with *mirth* – say that you *thought* of Faulkland in the dance.

JULIA: I never can be happy in your absence. If I wear a countenance of content, it is to show that my mind holds no doubt of my Faulkland's truth. If I seemed sad, it were to make malice triumph; and say, that I had fixed my heart on one, who left me to lament his roving, and my own credulity. Believe me, Faulkland, I mean not to upbraid you, when I say, that I have often dressed sorrow in smiles, lest my friends should guess whose unkindness had caused my tears.

FAULKLAND: You were ever all goodness to me. Oh, I am a brute, when I but admit a doubt of your true constancy!

JULIA: If ever, without such cause from you as I will not suppose possible, you find my affections veering but a point, may I become a proverbial scoff for levity, and base ingratitude.

FAULKLAND: Ah! Julia, that *last* word is grating to me. I would I had no title to your *gratitude*! Search your heart, Julia; perhaps what you have mistaken for love is but the warm effusion of a too thankful heart!

JULIA: For what quality must I love you?

FAULKLAND: For no quality! To regard me for any quality of mind or understanding, were only to *esteem* me. And for person – I have often wished myself deformed, to be convinced that I owed no obligation *there* for any part of your affection.

JULIA: Where nature has bestowed a show of nice attention in the features of a man, he should laugh at it, as misplaced. I have seen men, who in *this* vain article perhaps might rank above you; but my heart has never asked my eyes if it were so or not.

FAULKLAND: Now this is not well from *you*, Julia – I despise person in a man. Yet if you loved me as I wish, though I were an Ethiop, you'd think none so fair.

JULIA: I see you are determined to be unkind. The contract which my poor father bound us in gives you more than a lover's privilege.

FAULKLAND: Again, Julia, you raise ideas that feed and justify my doubts. I would not have been more free – no – I am proud of my restraint – yet – yet – perhaps your high respect alone for this solemn compact has fettered your inclinations, which else had made a worthier choice. How shall I be sure, had you remained unbound in thought and promise, that I should still have been the object of your persevering love?

JULIA: Then try me now. Let us be free as strangers as to what is past: *my* heart will not feel more liberty!

FAULKLAND: There now! so hasty, Julia! so anxious to be free! If your love for me were fixed and ardent, you would not loose your hold, even though I wished it!

JULIA: Oh, you torture me to the heart! I cannot bear it.

FAULKLAND: I do not mean to distress you. If I loved you less, I should never give you an uneasy moment. But hear me. All my fretful doubts arise from this – women are not used to weigh, and separate the motives of their affections: the cold dictates of prudence, gratitude, or filial duty, may sometimes be mistaken for the pleadings of the heart. – I would not boast – yet let me say, that I have neither age, person, or character, to found dislike on; my fortune such as few ladies could be charged with *indiscretion* in the match. – O Julia! when *love* receives such countenance from *prudence*, nice minds will be suspicious of its birth.

JULIA: I know not whither your insinuations would tend: but as they seem pressing to insult me – I will spare you the regret of having done so. – I have given you no cause for this!

[*Exit in tears.*]

FAULKLAND: In tears! stay Julia, stay but for a moment. – The door is fastened! – Julia! – my soul – but for one moment – I hear her sobbing! 'Sdeath! what a brute am I to use her thus! Yet stay – aye – she is coming now: how little resolution there is in woman! – how a few soft words can turn them! No, faith! – she is *not* coming either. Why, Julia – my love – say but that you forgive me – come but to tell me that – now, this is being *too* resentful: stay! she *is* coming too – I thought she would – no *steadiness* in anything! Her going away must have been a mere trick then – she shan't see that I was hurt by it. I'll affect indifference – [*hums a tune: then listens*] – no – zounds! she's *not* coming! – nor don't intend it, I suppose. This is not *steadiness*, but *obstinacy*! Yet I deserve it. What, after so long an absence, to quarrel with her tenderness! – 'twas barbarous and unmanly! I should be ashamed to see her now. I'll wait till her just resentment is abated – and when I distress her so again, may I lose her for ever! and be linked instead to some antique virago, whose gnawing passions, and long-hoarded spleen, shall make me curse my folly half the day, and all the night!

[*Exit.*]

Scene iii

MRS MALAPROP's *lodgings.*

[MRS MALAPROP,[3] *and* CAPTAIN ABSOLUTE.]

MRS MALAPROP: Your being Sir Anthony's son, Captain, would itself be a sufficient accommodation;[4] but from the ingenuity[5] of your appearance, I am convinced you deserve the character here given of you.

ABSOLUTE: Permit me to say, madam, that as I never yet have had the pleasure of seeing Miss Languish, my principal inducement in this affair at present, is the honour of being allied to Mrs Malaprop; of whose intellectual accomplishments, elegant manners, and unaffected learning, no tongue is silent.

MRS MALAPROP: Sir, you do me infinite honour! I beg, Captain, you'll be seated. [(*They*) *sit.*] Ah! few gentlemen, nowadays, know how to value the ineffectual[6] qualities in a woman! Few think how a little knowledge becomes a gentlewoman! Men have no sense now but for the worthless flower of beauty!

ABSOLUTE: It is but too true indeed, ma'am – yet I fear our ladies should share the blame – they think our admiration of beauty so great, that knowledge in them would be superfluous. Thus, like garden-trees, they seldom show fruit, till time has robbed them of the more specious blossom. Few, like Mrs Malaprop and the orange-tree, are rich in both at once!

MRS MALAPROP: Sir – you overpower me with good breeding. He is the very pineapple[7] of politeness! You are not ignorant, Captain, that this giddy girl has somehow contrived to fix her affections on a beggarly, strolling, eavesdropping Ensign, whom none of us have seen, and nobody knows anything of.

3. I have omitted '*with a letter in her hand*' from this stage direction, as Mrs Malaprop later finds it in her pocket (*Ed.*).

4. *accommodation*: recommendation.

5. *ingenuity*: ingenuousness.

6. *ineffectual*: intellectual.

7. *pineapple*: pinnacle.

ABSOLUTE: Oh, I have heard the silly affair before. I'm not at all prejudiced against her on *that* account.

MRS MALAPROP: You are very good, and very considerate, Captain. I am sure I have done everything in my power since I exploded[8] the affair! Long ago I laid my positive conjunctions[9] on her, never to think on the fellow again – I have since laid Sir Anthony's preposition[10] before her – but I'm sorry to say she seems resolved to decline every particle[11] that I enjoin her.

ABSOLUTE: It must be very distressing indeed, ma'am.

MRS MALAPROP: Oh! it gives me the hydrostatics[12] to such a degree! I thought she had persisted[13] from corresponding with him; but behold this very day, I have interceded[14] another letter from the fellow! I believe I have it in my pocket.

ABSOLUTE [*aside*]: O the devil! my last note.

MRS MALAPROP: Aye, here it is.

ABSOLUTE [*aside*]: Aye, my note indeed! O the little traitress Lucy.

MRS MALAPROP: There, perhaps you may know the writing.
[*Gives him the letter.*]

ABSOLUTE: I think I have seen the hand before – yes, I certainly must have seen this hand before –

MRS MALAPROP: Nay, but read it, Captain.

ABSOLUTE [*reads*]: *My soul's idol, my adored Lydia!* Very tender indeed!

MRS MALAPROP: Tender! aye, and profane too, o' my conscience!

ABSOLUTE: *I am excessively alarmed at the intelligence you send me, the more so as my new rival* –

MRS MALAPROP: That's you, sir.

ABSOLUTE: – *has universally the character of being an accomplished gentleman, and a man of honour.* Well, that's handsome enough.

MRS MALAPROP: Oh, the fellow had some design in writing so –

8. *exploded*: exposed.
9. *conjunctions*: injunctions.
10. *preposition*: proposition.
11. *particle*: article.
12. *hydrostatics*: hysterics.
13. *persisted*: desisted.
14. *interceded*: intercepted.

ABSOLUTE: That he had, I'll answer for him, ma'am.

MRS MALAPROP: But go on, sir – you'll see presently.

ABSOLUTE: *As for the old weather-beaten she-dragon who guards you –* who can he mean by that?

MRS MALAPROP: Me, sir – *me* – he means *me* there – what do you think now? But go on a little further.

ABSOLUTE: Impudent scoundrel! – *it shall go hard but I will elude her vigilance, as I am told that the same ridiculous vanity, which makes her dress up her coarse features, and deck her dull chat with hard words which she don't understand –*

MRS MALAPROP: There, sir! an attack upon my language! what do you think of that? An aspersion upon my parts of speech! Was ever such a brute! Sure if I reprehend[15] anything in this world, it is the use of my oracular[16] tongue, and a nice derangement[17] of epitaphs![18]

ABSOLUTE: He deserves to be hanged and quartered! Let me see – *same ridiculous vanity –*

MRS MALAPROP: You need not read it again, sir.

ABSOLUTE: I beg pardon, ma'am – *does also lay her open to the grossest deceptions from flattery and pretended admiration –* an impudent coxcomb! – *so that I have a scheme to see you shortly with the old harridan's consent, and even to make her a go-between in our interviews.* – Was ever such assurance?

MRS MALAPROP: Did you ever hear anything like it? He'll elude my vigilance, will he? Yes, yes! ha! ha! He's very likely to enter these doors! – we'll try who can plot best.

ABSOLUTE: So we will ma'am – so we will. Ha! ha! ha! a conceited puppy, ha! ha! ha! Well, but Mrs Malaprop, as the girl seems so infatuated by this fellow, suppose you were to wink at her corresponding with him for a little time – let her even plot an elopement with him – then do you connive at her escape – while *I,* just in the nick, will have the fellow laid by the heels, and fairly contrive to carry her off in his stead.

15. *reprehend*: apprehend.
16. *oracular*: vernacular.
17. *derangement*: arrangement.
18. *epitaphs*: epithets.

MRS MALAPROP: I am delighted with the scheme, never was anything better perpetrated!

ABSOLUTE: But, pray, could not I see the lady for a few minutes now? I should like to try her temper a little.

MRS MALAPROP: Why, I don't know – I doubt she is not prepared for a visit of this kind. There is a decorum in these matters.

ABSOLUTE: O Lord! she won't mind *me* – only tell her Beverley –

MRS MALAPROP: Sir!

ABSOLUTE [*aside*]: Gently, good tongue.

MRS MALAPROP: What did you say of Beverley?

ABSOLUTE: Oh, I was going to propose that you should tell her, by way of jest, that it was Beverley who was below – she'd come down fast enough then – ha! ha! ha!

MRS MALAPROP: 'Twould be a trick she well deserves – besides you know the fellow tells her he'll get my consent to see her – ha! ha! Let him if he can, I say again. [*Calling*] Lydia, come down here! He'll make me a *go-between in their interviews*! – ha! ha! ha! Come down, I say, Lydia! I don't wonder at your laughing, ha! ha! ha! his impudence is truly ridiculous.

ABSOLUTE: 'Tis very ridiculous, upon my soul, ma'am, ha! ha! ha!

MRS MALAPROP: The little hussy won't hear. Well, I'll go and tell her at once who it is – she shall know that Captain Absolute is come to wait on her. And I'll make her behave as becomes a young woman.

ABSOLUTE: As you please, ma'am.

MRS MALAPROP: For the present, Captain, your servant – ah! you've not done laughing yet, I see – *elude my vigilance*! Yes, yes, ha! ha! ha!
[*Exit.*]

ABSOLUTE: Ha! ha! ha! one would think now that I might throw off all disguise at once, and seize my prize with security – but such is Lydia's caprice, that to undeceive her were probably to lose her. I'll see whether she knows me.
[*Walks aside, and seems engaged in looking at the pictures.*]
[*Enter* LYDIA.]

LYDIA: What a scene am I now to go through! Surely nothing can be more dreadful than to be obliged to listen to the loathsome addresses of a stranger to one's heart. I have heard of girls persecuted as I am, who have appealed in behalf of their favoured lover to the generosity of his rival: suppose I were to try it – there stands the hated rival – an officer too! – but oh, how unlike my Beverley! – I wonder he don't begin – truly he seems a very negligent wooer! Quite at his ease, upon my word! I'll speak first – Mr Absolute.

ABSOLUTE: Madam.

    [*Turns round.*]

LYDIA: O heavens! Beverley!

ABSOLUTE: Hush! – hush, my life! – softly! be not surprised!

LYDIA: I am so astonished! and so terrified! and so overjoyed! For heaven's sake! how came you here?

ABSOLUTE: Briefly – I have deceived your aunt – I was informed that my new rival was to visit here this evening, and contriving to have him kept away, have passed myself on her for Captain Absolute.

LYDIA: Oh, charming! And she really takes you for young Absolute?

ABSOLUTE: Oh, she's convinced of it.

LYDIA: Ha! ha! ha! I can't forbear laughing to think how her sagacity is overreached!

ABSOLUTE: But we trifle with our precious moments – such another opportunity may not occur – then let me now conjure my kind, my condescending angel, to fix the time when I may rescue her from undeserved persecution, and with a licensed warmth plead for my reward.

LYDIA: Will you then, Beverley, consent to forfeit that portion of my paltry wealth – that burden on the wings of love?

ABSOLUTE: Oh, come to me – rich only thus – in loveliness – bring no portion to me but thy love – 'twill be generous in you, Lydia – for well you know, it is the only dower your poor Beverley can repay.

LYDIA: How persuasive are his words! How charming will poverty be with him!

ABSOLUTE: Ah! my soul, what a life will we then live? Love shall be our idol and support! We will worship him with a monastic strictness; abjuring all worldly toys, to centre every thought and action there. Proud of calamity, we will enjoy the wreck of wealth; while the surrounding gloom of adversity shall make the flame of our pure love show doubly bright. – By heavens! I would fling all goods of fortune from me with a prodigal hand to enjoy the scene where I might clasp my Lydia to my bosom, and say, the world affords no smile to me – but here – [*embracing her*]. [*Aside*] If she holds out now the devil is in it!

LYDIA: Now could I fly with him to the Antipodes! but my persecution is not yet come to a crisis.

[*Enter* MRS MALAPROP, *listening.*]

MRS MALAPROP: I'm impatient to know how the little hussy deports herself.

ABSOLUTE: So pensive, Lydia! – is then your warmth abated?

MRS MALAPROP: Warmth abated! – so! – she has been in a passion, I suppose.

LYDIA: No – nor ever can while I have life.

MRS MALAPROP: An ill-tempered little devil! She'll be in a passion all her life, will she?

LYDIA: Think not the idle threats of my ridiculous aunt can ever have any weight with me.

MRS MALAPROP: Very dutiful, upon my word!

LYDIA: Let her choice be Captain Absolute, but Beverley is mine.

MRS MALAPROP: I am astonished at her assurance! – to his face! – this to his face!

ABSOLUTE [*kneeling*]: Thus then let me enforce my suit.

MRS MALAPROP: Aye – poor young man! – down on his knees entreating for pity! – I can contain no longer. – [*Reveals herself*] Why thou vixen! – I have overheard you.

ABSOLUTE [*aside*]: Oh, confound her vigilance!

MRS MALAPROP: Captain Absolute – I know not how to apologize for her shocking rudeness.

ABSOLUTE [*aside*]: So – all's safe, I find. [*Aloud*] I have hopes, madam, that time will bring the young lady –

MRS MALAPROP: Oh there's nothing to be hoped for from her! She's as headstrong as an allegory[19] on the banks of Nile.

LYDIA: Nay, madam, what do you charge me with now?

MRS MALAPROP: Why, thou unblushing rebel – didn't you tell this gentleman to his face that you loved another better? Didn't you say you never would be his?

19. *allegory*: alligator.

LYDIA: No, madam – I did not.

MRS MALAPROP: Good heavens! what assurance! Lydia, Lydia, you ought to know that lying don't become a young woman! Didn't you boast that Beverley – that stroller Beverley, possessed your heart? Tell me that, I say.

LYDIA: 'Tis true, ma'am, and none but Beverley –

MRS MALAPROP: Hold; hold Assurance! you shall not be so rude.

ABSOLUTE: Nay, pray Mrs Malaprop, don't stop the young lady's speech: she's very welcome to talk thus – it does not hurt *me* in the least, I assure you.

MRS MALAPROP: You are *too* good, Captain – *too* amiably patient – but come with me, Miss – let us see you again soon, Captain – remember what we have fixed.

ABSOLUTE: I shall, ma'am.

MRS MALAPROP: Come, take a graceful leave of the gentleman.

LYDIA: May every blessing wait on my *Beverley*, my loved *Bev* –

MRS MALAPROP: Hussy! I'll choke the word in your throat! Come along – come along.

[*Exeunt severally*, (ABSOLUTE) *kissing his hand to* LYDIA, MRS MALAPROP *stopping her from speaking.*]

Scene iv

ACRES's *lodgings.*

[ACRES *and* DAVID. ACRES *as just dressed.*]

ACRES: Indeed, David – do you think I become it so?

DAVID: You are quite another creature, believe me Master, by the Mass! An' we've any luck we shall see the Devon monkeyrony[20] in all the print-shops in Bath!

ACRES: Dress *does* make a difference, David.

DAVID: 'Tis all in all, I think – difference! Why, an' you were to go now to Clod Hall, I am certain the old lady wouldn't know you:

20. *monkeyrony*: fop.

Master Butler wouldn't believe his own eyes, and Mrs Pickle would cry, 'Lard presarve me!'. Our dairymaid would come giggling to the door, and I warrant Dolly Tester, your honour's favourite, would blush like my waistcoat. Oons! I'll hold a gallon, there an't a dog in the house but would bark, and I question whether Phillis would wag a hair of her tail!

ACRES: Aye, David, there's nothing like polishing.

DAVID: So I says of your honour's boots; but the boy never heeds me!

ACRES: But, David, has Mr De-la-Grace been here? I must rub up my balancing, and chasing, and boring.[21]

DAVID: I'll call again, sir.

ACRES: Do – and see if there are any letters for me at the post-office.

DAVID: I will. – By the Mass, I can't help looking at your head! If I hadn't been by at the cooking, I wish I may die if I should have known the dish again myself!

[*Exit.*]

[ACRES *comes forward, practising a dancing step.*]

ACRES: Sink, slide – coupee[22] – confound the first inventors of cotillons! say I – they are as bad as algebra to us country gentlemen – I can walk a minuet easy enough when I'm forced! – and I have been accounted a good stick in a country dance. Odds jigs and tabors! I never valued your cross over to couple – figure in – right and left – and I'd foot it with e'er a captain in the county! – but these outlandish heathen allemandes[23] and cotillons are quite beyond me! – I shall never prosper at 'em, that's sure – mine are true-born English legs – they don't understand their cursed French lingo! – their *pas*[24] this, and *pas* that, and *pas* t'other! – damn me, my feet don't like to be called paws! No, 'tis certain I have most antigallican toes!

[*Enter* SERVANT.]

SERVANT: Here is Sir Lucius O'Trigger to wait on you, sir.

ACRES: Show him in.

21. *balancing ... boring*: dance movements; 'chasing' from French *chassé* and 'boring' from French *bourrée*.

22. *Sink ... coupee*: dance movements.

23. *allemandes*: German dances.

24. *pas*: step (French).

[*Enter* SIR LUCIUS.]

SIR LUCIUS: Mr Acres, I am delighted to embrace you.

ACRES: My dear Sir Lucius, I kiss your hands.

SIR LUCIUS: Pray, my friend, what has brought you so suddenly to Bath?

ACRES: Faith! I have followed Cupid's jack-a-lantern, and find myself in a quagmire at last. In short, I have been very ill-used, Sir Lucius. I don't choose to mention names, but look on me as a very ill-used gentleman.

SIR LUCIUS: Pray, what is the case? I ask no names.

ACRES: Mark me, Sir Lucius, I fall as deep as need be in love with a young lady – her friends take my part – I follow her to Bath – send word of my arrival; and receive answer, that the lady is to be otherwise disposed of. This, Sir Lucius, I call being ill-used.

SIR LUCIUS: Very ill, upon my conscience. Pray, can you divine the cause of it?

ACRES: Why, there's the matter: she has another lover, one *Beverley*, who, I am told, is now in Bath. Odds slanders and lies! he must be at the bottom of it.

SIR LUCIUS: A rival in the case, is there? And you think he has supplanted you unfairly?

ACRES: Unfairly! – to be sure he has. He never could have done it fairly.

SIR LUCIUS: Then sure you know what is to be done!

ACRES: Not I, upon my soul!

SIR LUCIUS: We wear no swords here, but you understand me.

ACRES: What! fight him!

SIR LUCIUS: Aye, to be sure: what can I mean else?

ACRES: But he has given me no provocation.

SIR LUCIUS: Now, I think he has given you the greatest provocation in the world. – Can a man commit a more heinous offence against another than to fall in love with the same woman? Oh, by my soul, it is the most unpardonable breach of friendship!

ACRES: Breach of friendship! Aye, aye; but I have no acquaintance with this man. I never saw him in my life.

SIR LUCIUS: That's no argument at all – he has the less right then to take such a liberty.

ACRES: Gad that's true – I grow full of anger, Sir Lucius! – I fire apace! Odds hilts and blades! I find a man may have a deal of valour in him, and not know it! But couldn't I contrive to have a little right of my side?

SIR LUCIUS: What the devil signifies *right*, when your *honour* is concerned? Do you think Achilles, or my little Alexander the Great ever inquired where the right lay? No, by my soul, they drew their broadswords, and left the lazy sons of peace to settle the justice of it.

ACRES: Your words are a grenadier's march to my heart! I believe courage must be catching! I certainly do feel a kind of valour rising as it were – a kind of courage, as I may say – odds flints, pans, and triggers! I'll challenge him directly.

SIR LUCIUS: Ah, my little friend! if we had Blunderbuss Hall here – I could show you a range of ancestry, in the O'Trigger line, that would furnish the new room;[25] every one of whom had killed his man! – For though the mansion-house and dirty acres have slipped through my fingers, I thank heaven our honour, and the family pictures, are as fresh as ever.

ACRES: O Sir Lucius! I have had ancestors too! Every man of 'em colonel or captain in the militia! Odds balls and barrels! say no more – I'm braced for it. The thunder of your words has soured the milk of human kindness in my breast! Zounds! as the man in the play says, 'I could do such deeds!'[26]

SIR LUCIUS: Come, come, there must be no passion at all in the case – these things should always be done civilly.

ACRES: I must be in a passion, Sir Lucius – I must be in a rage – dear Sir Lucius, let me be in a rage, if you love me. – Come, here's pen and paper. [*Sits down to write.*] I would the ink were red! Indite, I say, indite! How shall I begin? Odds bullets and blades! I'll write a good bold hand, however.

SIR LUCIUS: Pray compose yourself.

ACRES: Come – now shall I begin with an oath? Do, Sir Lucius, let me begin with a damme.

---

25. *new room*: Assembly rooms in Bath, opened 1771.
26. *I . . . deeds*: cf. *Lear*, II, iv: 'I will do such things –'.

SIR LUCIUS: Pho! pho! do the thing decently and like a Christian. Begin now – *Sir* –

ACRES: That's too civil by half.

SIR LUCIUS: *To prevent the confusion that might arise* –

ACRES: Well –

SIR LUCIUS: *From our both addressing the same lady* –

ACRES: Aye – there's the reason – [*writing*] *same lady* – well –

SIR LUCIUS: *I shall expect the honour of your company* –

ACRES: Zounds! I'm not asking him to dinner.

SIR LUCIUS: Pray be easy.

ACRES: Well then, *honour of your company*.

SIR LUCIUS: *To settle our pretensions* –

ACRES: Well.

SIR LUCIUS: Let me see, aye, Kingsmead Fields will do – *in Kingsmead Fields*.

ACRES: So that's done. Well, I'll fold it up presently; my own crest – a hand and dagger shall be the seal.

SIR LUCIUS: You see now this little explanation will put a stop at once to all confusion or misunderstanding that might arise between you.

ACRES: Aye, we fight to prevent any misunderstanding.

SIR LUCIUS: Now, I'll leave you to fix your own time. Take my advice, and you'll decide it this evening if you can; then let the worst come of it, 'twill be off your mind tomorrow.

ACRES: Very true.

SIR LUCIUS: So I shall see nothing more of you, unless it be by letter, till the evening. I would do myself the honour to carry your message; but, to tell you a secret, I believe I shall have just such another affair on my own hands. There is a gay captain here, who put a jest on me lately, at the expense of my country, and I only want to fall in with the gentleman, to call him out.

ACRES: By my valour, I should like to see you fight first! Odds life! I should like to see you kill him, if it was only to get a little lesson.

SIR LUCIUS: I shall be very proud of instructing you. – Well for the present – but remember now, when you meet your antagonist, do everything in a mild and agreeable manner. Let your courage be as keen, but at the same time as polished as your sword.

[*Exeunt severally.*]

ACT IV

Scene i

ACRES's *lodgings.*

[ACRES *and* DAVID.]

DAVID: Then, by the Mass, sir! I would do no such thing – ne'er a Sir Lucius O'Trigger in the kingdom should make me fight, when I wa'n't so minded. Oons! what will the old lady say, when she hears o't!

ACRES: Ah! David, if you had heard Sir Lucius! – odds sparks and flames! he would have roused your valour.

DAVID: Not he, indeed. I hates such bloodthirsty cormorants. Lookee Master, if you'd wanted a bout at boxing, quarterstaff,[1] or short-staff,[2] I should never be the man to bid you cry off: but for your cursed sharps[3] and snaps,[4] I never knew any good come of 'em.

ACRES: But my honour, David, my honour! I must be very careful of my honour.

DAVID: Aye, by the Mass! and I would be very careful of it; and I think in return my *honour* couldn't do less than to be very careful of *me.*

ACRES: Odds blades! David, no gentleman will ever risk the loss of his honour!

DAVID: I say then, it would be but civil in *honour* never to risk the loss of the *gentleman.* – Lookee, Master, this *honour* seems to me to be a

1. *quarterstaff*: an iron-tipped pole.
2. *short-staff*: short cudgel.
3. *sharps*: swords.
4. *snaps*: pistols.

marvellous false friend; aye, truly, a very courtier-like servant. – Put the case, I was a gentleman (which, thank God, no one can say of me); well – my honour makes me quarrel with another gentleman of my acquaintance. So – we fight (pleasant enough that). Boh! – I kill him (the more's my luck). Now, pray, who gets the profit of it? Why, my *honour*. But put the case that he kills me! – by the Mass! I go to the worms, and my honour whips over to my enemy.

ACRES: No, David – in that case – odds crowns and laurels! your honour follows you to the grave.

DAVID: Now, that's just the place where I could make a shift to do without it.

ACRES: Zounds, David, you're a coward! It doesn't become my valour to listen to you. What, shall I disgrace my ancestors? Think of that, David – think what it would be to disgrace my ancestors!

DAVID: Under favour, the surest way of not disgracing them, is to keep as long as you can out of their company. Lookee now, Master, to go to them in such haste – with an ounce of lead in your brains – I should think might as well be let alone. Our ancestors are very good kind of folks; but they are the last people I should choose to have a visiting acquaintance with.

ACRES: But David, now, you don't think there is such very, very, *very* great danger, hey? Odds life! people often fight without any mischief done!

DAVID: By the Mass, I think 'tis ten to one against you! Oons! here to meet some lion-headed fellow, I warrant, with his damned double-barrelled swords, and cut and thrust pistols! Lord bless us! it makes me tremble to think o't! – Those be such desperate bloody-minded weapons! Well, I never could abide 'em – from a child I never could fancy 'em! I suppose there a'n't so merciless a beast in the world as your loaded pistol!

ACRES: Zounds! I *won't* be afraid – odds fire and fury! you shan't make me afraid. Here is the challenge, and I have sent for my dear friend Jack Absolute to carry it for me.

DAVID: Aye, i'the name of mischief, let *him* be the messenger. For my part, I wouldn't lend a hand to it for the best horse in your stable. By the Mass! it don't look like another letter! It is, as I may say, a designing and malicious-looking letter! – and I warrant smells of gunpowder like a soldier's pouch! Oons! I wouldn't swear it mayn't go off!

ACRES: Out, you poltroon! – you ha'n't the valour of a grasshopper.

DAVID: Well, I say no more – 'twill be sad news, to be sure, at Clod Hall! – but I ha' done. How Phillis will howl when she hears of it! – aye, poor bitch, she little thinks what shooting her master's going after! And I warrant old Crop, who has carried your honour, field and road, these ten years, will curse the hour he was born. [*Whimpering.*]

ACRES: It won't do, David – I am determined to fight – so get along, you coward, while I'm in the mind.

　　[*Enter* SERVANT.]

SERVANT: Captain Absolute, sir.

ACRES: Oh! Show him up.

　　[*Exit* SERVANT.]

DAVID: Well, heaven send we be all alive this time tomorrow.

ACRES: What's that! Don't provoke me, David!

DAVID [*whimpering*]: Goodbye, Master.

ACRES: Get along, you cowardly, dastardly, croaking raven.

　　[*Exit* DAVID.]

　　[*Enter* ABSOLUTE.]

ABSOLUTE: What's the matter, Bob?

ACRES: A vile, sheep-hearted blockhead! If I hadn't the valour of St George and the dragon to boot –

ABSOLUTE: But what did you want with me, Bob?

ACRES: Oh! – there – [*Gives him the challenge.*]

ABSOLUTE [*aside*]: *To Ensign Beverley.* So – what's going on now? – Well, what's this?

ACRES: A challenge!

ABSOLUTE: Indeed! Why, you won't fight him; will you, Bob?

ACRES: Egad but I will, Jack. Sir Lucius has wrought me to it. He has left me full of rage – and I'll fight this evening, that so much good passion mayn't be wasted.

ABSOLUTE: But what have I to do with this?

ACRES: Why, as I think you know something of this fellow, I want you to find him out for me, and give him this mortal defiance.

ABSOLUTE: Well, give it to me, and trust me he gets it.

ACRES: Thank you, my dear friend, my dear Jack; but it is giving you a great deal of trouble.

ABSOLUTE: Not in the least – I beg you won't mention it. – No trouble in the world, I assure you.

ACRES: You are very kind. What it is to have a friend! You couldn't be my second – could you, Jack?

ABSOLUTE: Why no, Bob – not in *this* affair – it would not be quite so proper.

ACRES: Well then, I must get my friend Sir Lucius. I shall have your good wishes, however, Jack.

ABSOLUTE: Whenever he meets you, believe me.

[*Enter* SERVANT.]

SERVANT: Sir Anthony Absolute is below, inquiring for the Captain.

ABSOLUTE: I'll come instantly. – Well, my little hero, success attend you.

[*Going.*]

ACRES: Stay – stay, Jack. If Beverley should ask you what kind of a man your friend Acres is, do tell him I am a devil of a fellow – will you, Jack?

ABSOLUTE: To be sure I shall. I'll say you are a determined dog – hey, Bob!

ACRES: Aye, do, do – and if that frightens him, egad perhaps he mayn't come. So tell him I generally kill a man a week; will you, Jack?

ABSOLUTE: I will, I will; I'll say you are called in the country 'Fighting Bob'!

ACRES: Right, right – 'tis all to prevent mischief; for I don't want to take his life if I clear my honour.

ABSOLUTE: No! – that's very kind of you.

ACRES: Why, you don't wish me to kill him – do you, Jack?

ABSOLUTE: No, upon my soul, I do not. But a devil of a fellow, hey?

[*Going.*]

ACRES: True, true – but stay – stay, Jack – you may add that you never saw me in such a rage before – a most devouring rage!

ABSOLUTE: I will, I will.

ACRES: Remember, Jack – a determined dog!

ABSOLUTE: Aye, aye, 'Fighting Bob'!
  [*Exeunt severally.*]

Scene ii

MRS MALAPROP's *lodgings.*

[MRS MALAPROP *and* LYDIA.]

MRS MALAPROP: Why, thou perverse one! – tell me what you can object to him? Isn't he a handsome man? Tell me that. A genteel man? A pretty figure of a man?

LYDIA [*aside*]: She little thinks whom she is praising! – So is Beverley, ma'am.

MRS MALAPROP: No caparisons,[5] Miss, if you please! Caparisons don't become a young woman. No Captain Absolute is indeed a fine gentleman!

LYDIA [*aside*]: Aye, the Captain Absolute *you* have seen.

MRS MALAPROP: Then he's *so* well bred – *so* full of alacrity, and adulation! – and has *so much* to say for himself: in such good language too! His physiognomy[6] so grammatical! Then his presence is so noble! I protest, when I saw him, I thought of what Hamlet says in the play: 'Hesperian curls! – the front of Job himself! – an eye, like March, to threaten at command! – a station, like Harry Mercury, new' – something about kissing – on a hill[7] – however, the similitude struck me directly.

LYDIA [*aside*]: How enraged she'll be presently when she discovers her mistake!
  [*Enter* SERVANT.]

SERVANT: Sir Anthony and Captain Absolute are below ma'am.

MRS MALAPROP: Show them up here.
  [*Exit* SERVANT.]

5. *caparisons*: comparisons.
6. *physiognomy*: phraseology.
7. '*Hesperian . . . hill*: see *Hamlet*, III, iv.

Now, Lydia, I insist on your behaving as becomes a young woman. Show your good breeding at least, though you have forgot your duty.

LYDIA: Madam, I have told you my resolution; I shall not only give him no encouragement, but I won't even speak to, or look at him.

[*Flings herself into a chair, with her face from the door.*]

[*Enter* SIR ANTHONY *and* ABSOLUTE.]

SIR ANTHONY: Here we are, Mrs Malaprop; come to mitigate the frowns of unrelenting beauty – and difficulty enough I had to bring this fellow. I don't know what's the matter; but if I hadn't held him by force, he'd have given me the slip.

MRS MALAPROP: You have infinite trouble, Sir Anthony, in the affair. I am ashamed for the cause! [*Aside to her*] Lydia, Lydia, rise I beseech you! – pay your respects!

SIR ANTHONY: I hope, madam, that Miss Languish has reflected on the worth of this gentleman, and the regard due to her aunt's choice, and *my* alliance. [*Aside to him*] Now, Jack, speak to her!

ABSOLUTE [*aside*]: What the devil shall I do! – You see, sir, she won't even look at me, whilst you are here. I knew she wouldn't! I told you so. Let me entreat you, sir, to leave us together!

[ABSOLUTE *seems to expostulate with his father.*]

LYDIA [*aside*]: I wonder I ha'n't heard my aunt exclaim yet! sure she can't have looked at him! – perhaps their regimentals are alike, and she is something blind.

SIR ANTHONY: I say, sir, I won't stir a foot yet.

MRS MALAPROP: I am sorry to say, Sir Anthony, that my affluence[8] over my niece is very small. [*Aside to her*] Turn round Lydia, I blush for you!

SIR ANTHONY: May I not flatter myself that Miss Languish will assign what cause of dislike she can have to my son. [*Aside to him*] Why don't you begin, Jack? Speak, you puppy – speak!

MRS MALAPROP: It is impossible, Sir Anthony, she can have any. She will not say she has. [*Aside to her*] Answer, hussy! why don't you answer?

SIR ANTHONY: Then, madam, I trust that a childish and hasty

8. *affluence*: influence.

predilection will be no bar to Jack's happiness. [*Aside to him*]
Zounds! sirrah! why don't you speak?

LYDIA [*aside*]: I think my lover seems as little inclined to conversation
as myself. How strangely blind my aunt must be!

ABSOLUTE: Hem! hem! – madam – hem! [ABSOLUTE *attempts to
speak, then returns to* SIR ANTHONY] Faith! Sir, I am so confounded! – and so – so – confused! I told you I should be so, sir – I
knew it – the – the – tremor of my passion, entirely takes away my
presence of mind.

SIR ANTHONY: But it don't take away your voice, fool, does it? Go up,
and speak to her directly!

[ABSOLUTE *makes signs to* MRS MALAPROP *to leave them together.*]

MRS MALAPROP: Sir Anthony, shall we leave them together? [*Aside to
her*] Ah! you stubborn little vixen!

SIR ANTHONY: Not yet, ma'am, not yet! [*Aside to him*] What the devil
are you at? Unlock your jaws, sirrah, or –

[ABSOLUTE *draws near* LYDIA.]

ABSOLUTE: Now heaven send she may be too sullen to look round!
[*Aside*] I must disguise my voice. [*Speaks in a low hoarse tone.*] Will
not Miss Languish lend an ear to the mild accents of true love? Will
not –

SIR ANTHONY: What the devil ails the fellow? Why don't you speak
out? – not stand croaking like a frog in a quinsy!

ABSOLUTE: The – the – excess of my awe, and my – my – my
modesty, quite choke me!

SIR ANTHONY: Ah! your *modesty* again! I'll tell you what, Jack; if you
don't speak out directly, and glibly too, I shall be in such a rage!
Mrs Malaprop, I wish the lady would favour us with something
more than a side-front!

[MRS MALAPROP *seems to chide* LYDIA.]

ABSOLUTE [*aside*]: So! – all will out I see! [*Goes up to* LYDIA, *speaks
softly.*] Be not surprised, my Lydia, suppress all surprise at present.

LYDIA [*aside*]: Heavens! 'tis Beverley's voice! Sure he can't have
imposed on Sir Anthony too! [*Looks round by degrees, then starts
up.*] Is this possible! – my Beverley! – how can this be? – my
Beverley?

ABSOLUTE [*aside*]: Ah! 'tis all over.

SIR ANTHONY: Beverley! – the devil – Beverley! – What can the girl mean? This is my son, Jack Absolute!

MRS MALAPROP: For shame, hussy! for shame! – your head runs so on that fellow, that you have him always in your eyes! Beg Captain Absolute's pardon directly.

LYDIA: I see no Captain Absolute, but my loved Beverley!

SIR ANTHONY: Zounds! the girl's mad! – her brain's turned by reading!

MRS MALAPROP: O' my conscience, I believe so! What do you mean by Beverley, hussy? You saw Captain Absolute before today; there he is – your husband that shall be.

LYDIA: With all my soul, ma'am – when I refuse my Beverley –

SIR ANTHONY: Oh! she's as mad as Bedlam![9] – or has this fellow been playing us a rogue's trick! Come here, sirrah! Who the devil are you?

ABSOLUTE: Faith, sir, I am not quite clear myself; but I'll endeavour to recollect.

SIR ANTHONY: Are you my son, or not? Answer for your mother, you dog, if you won't for me.

MRS MALAPROP: Aye, sir, who are you? O mercy! I begin to suspect –

ABSOLUTE [aside]: Ye powers of impudence befriend me! – Sir Anthony, most assuredly I am your wife's son; and that I sincerely believe myself to be *yours* also, I hope my duty has always shown. Mrs Malaprop, I am your most respectful admirer – and shall be proud to add affectionate nephew. I need not tell my Lydia, that she sees her faithful *Beverley*, who, knowing the singular generosity of her temper, assumed that name, and a station, which has proved a test of the most disinterested love, which he now hopes to enjoy in a more elevated character.

LYDIA [*sullenly*]: So! – there will be no elopement after all!

SIR ANTHONY: Upon my soul, Jack, thou art a very impudent fellow! To do you justice, I think I never saw a piece of more consummate assurance!

ABSOLUTE: Oh, you flatter me, sir – you compliment – 'tis my *modesty* you know, sir – my *modesty* that has stood in my way.

9. *Bedlam*: Hospital of St Mary of Bethlehem, a lunatic asylum.

SIR ANTHONY: Well, I am glad you are not the dull, insensible varlet you pretended to be, however! I'm glad you have made a fool of your father, you dog – I am. – So this was your *penitence*, your *duty*, and *obedience*! I thought it was damned sudden! You *never heard their names before*, not you! – What, the Languishes of Worcestershire, hey? – *if you could please me in the affair, 'twas all you desired!* Ah! you dissembling villain! What! [*pointing to* LYDIA] *she squints, don't she? – a little red-haired girl!* – hey? Why, you hypocritical young rascal – I wonder you a'n't ashamed to hold up your head!

ABSOLUTE: 'Tis with much difficulty, sir – I *am* confused – very much confused, as you must perceive.

MRS MALAPROP: O Lud! Sir Anthony! – a new light breaks in upon me! – hey! how! what! Captain, did *you* write the letters then? What! am I to thank *you* for the elegant compilation of 'an old weather-beaten she-dragon' – hey? O mercy! – was it *you* that reflected on my parts of speech?

ABSOLUTE [*aside to* SIR ANTHONY]: Dear Sir! my modesty will be overpowered at last, if you don't assist me. I shall certainly not be able to stand it!

SIR ANTHONY: Come, come, Mrs Malaprop, we must forget and forgive; odds life! matters have taken so clever a turn all of a sudden, that I could find it in my heart, to be so good-humoured! and so gallant! – hey! Mrs Malaprop!

MRS MALAPROP: Well, Sir Anthony, since *you* desire it, we will not anticipate the past; so mind young people – our retrospection will now be all to the future.

SIR ANTHONY: Come, we must leave them together, Mrs Malaprop; they long to fly into each other's arms, I warrant! Jack, isn't the cheek as I said, hey? And the eye, you rogue! and the lip – hey? Come, Mrs Malaprop, we'll not disturb their tenderness – theirs is the time of life for happiness! [*Sings.*] 'Youth's the season made for joy'[10] hey! – odds life! I'm in such spirits – I don't know what I couldn't do! [*Gives his hand to* MRS MALAPROP.] Permit me, ma'am – [*Sings.*] Tol-de-rol – gad I should like a little fooling myself – tol-de-rol! de-rol!

10. *'Youth's . . . joy'*: from John Gay, *The Beggar's Opera* (1728).

[*Exit singing, and handing* MRS MALAPROP.]

[LYDIA *sits sullenly in her chair.*]

ABSOLUTE [*aside*]: So much thought bodes me no good. – So grave, Lydia!

LYDIA: Sir!

ABSOLUTE [*aside*]: So! – egad! I thought as much! – that damned monosyllable has froze me! – What, Lydia, now that we are as happy in our friends' consent, as in our mutual vows –

LYDIA [*peevishly*]: *Friends' consent*, indeed!

ABSOLUTE: Come, come, we must lay aside some of our romance – a little *wealth* and *comfort* may be endured after all. And for your fortune, the lawyers shall make such settlements as –

LYDIA: *Lawyers!* I hate lawyers!

ABSOLUTE: Nay then, we will not wait for their lingering forms, but instantly procure the licence, and –

LYDIA: The *licence*! I hate licence!

ABSOLUTE: O my love! Be not so unkind! – thus let me entreat – [*Kneeling.*]

LYDIA: Pshaw! – what signifies kneeling, when you know I *must* have you?

ABSOLUTE [*rising*]: Nay, madam, there shall be no constraint upon your inclinations, I promise you. If I have lost your heart – I resign the rest. [*Aside*] Gad, I must try what a little *spirit* will do.

LYDIA [*rising*]: Then, sir, let me tell you, the interest you had there was acquired by a mean, unmanly imposition, and deserves the punishment of fraud. What, you have been treating *me* like a *child*! – humouring my romance! and laughing, I suppose, at your success!

ABSOLUTE: You wrong me, Lydia, you wrong me – only hear –

LYDIA [*walking about in heat*]: So, while *I* fondly imagined we were deceiving my relations, and flattered myself that I should outwit and incense them all – behold! my hopes are to be crushed at once, by my aunt's consent and approbation! – and *I* am myself the only dupe at last! – But here, sir, here is the picture – *Beverley's* picture! [*taking a miniature from her bosom*] which I have worn, night and day, in spite of threats and entreaties! There, sir [*flings it to him*], and be assured I throw the original from my heart as easily!

ABSOLUTE: Nay, nay, ma'am, we will not differ as to that. Here [*taking out a picture*], here is Miss Lydia Languish. What a difference! – aye, *there* is the heavenly assenting smile, that first gave soul and spirit to my hopes! – those are the lips which sealed a vow, as yet scarce dry in Cupid's calendar! – and there the half resentful blush, that *would* have checked the ardour of my thanks. – Well, all that's past! – all over indeed! There, madam – in beauty, that copy is not equal to you, but in my mind its merit over the original, in being still the same, is such – that – I cannot find in my heart to part with it.

[*Puts it up again.*]

LYDIA [*softening*]: 'Tis your own doing, sir – I – I – I suppose you are perfectly satisfied.

ABSOLUTE: Oh, most certainly – sure now this is much better than being in love! – ha! ha! ha! – there's some spirit in *this*! What signifies breaking some scores of solemn promises – all that's of no consequence you know. To be sure people will say, that Miss didn't know her own mind – but never mind that: or perhaps they may be ill-natured enough to hint, that the gentleman grew tired of the lady and forsook her – but don't let that fret you.

LYDIA: There's no bearing his insolence.

[*Bursts into tears.*]

[*Enter* MRS MALAPROP *and* SIR ANTHONY.]

MRS MALAPROP [*entering*]: Come, we must interrupt your billing and cooing a while.

LYDIA [*sobbing*]: This is worse than your treachery and deceit, you base ingrate!

SIR ANTHONY: What the devil's the matter now! Zounds! Mrs Malaprop, this is the oddest *billing* and *cooing* I ever heard! – but what the deuce is the meaning of it? I'm quite astonished!

ABSOLUTE: Ask the lady, sir.

MRS MALAPROP: O mercy! – I'm quite analysed[11] for my part! Why, Lydia, what is the reason of this?

LYDIA: Ask the gentleman, ma'am.

---

11. *analysed*: paralysed.

SIR ANTHONY: Zounds! I shall be in a frenzy! Why Jack, you are not come out to be anyone else, are you?

MRS MALAPROP: Aye, sir, there's no more trick, is there? You are not like Cerberus,[12] *three* gentlemen at once, are you?

ABSOLUTE: You'll not let me speak – I say the lady can account for this much better than I can.

LYDIA: Ma'am, you once commanded me never to think of Beverley again – there is the man – I now obey you: for, from this moment, I renounce him for ever.

[*Exit* LYDIA.]

MRS MALAPROP: O mercy! and miracles! what a turn here is – why sure, Captain, you haven't behaved disrespectfully to my niece.

SIR ANTHONY: Ha! ha! ha! – ha! ha! ha! – now I see it – ha! ha! ha! – now I see it – you have been too lively, Jack.

ABSOLUTE: Nay, sir, upon my word –

SIR ANTHONY: Come, no lying, Jack – I'm sure '*twas* so.

MRS MALAPROP: O Lud! Sir Anthony! – O fie, Captain!

ABSOLUTE: Upon my soul, ma'am –

SIR ANTHONY: Come, no excuses, Jack; why, your father, you rogue, was so before you: the blood of the Absolutes was always impatient. Ha! ha! ha! poor little Lydia! – why, you've frightened her, you dog, you have.

ABSOLUTE: By all that's good, sir –

SIR ANTHONY: Zounds! say no more, I tell you. Mrs Malaprop shall make your peace. You must make his peace, Mrs Malaprop; you must tell her 'tis Jack's way – tell her 'tis all our ways – it runs in the blood of our family! Come, away, Jack – ha! ha! ha! Mrs Malaprop – a young villain!

[*Pushes him out.*]

MRS MALAPROP: Oh! Sir Anthony! O fie, Captain!

[*Exeunt severally.*]

12. *Cerberus*: the three-headed dog which guarded the entrance to the underworld.

Scene iii

The North Parade.

[*Enter* SIR LUCIUS O'TRIGGER.]

SIR LUCIUS: I wonder where this Captain Absolute hides himself. Upon my conscience! these officers are always in one's way in love affairs: I remember I might have married Lady Dorothy Carmine, if it had not been for a little rogue of a Major, who ran away with her before she could get a sight of me! – And I wonder too what it is the ladies can see in them to be so fond of them – unless it be a touch of the old serpent in 'em, that makes the little creatures be caught, like vipers with a bit of red cloth. – Hah! – isn't this the Captain coming? Faith it is! There is a probability of succeeding about that fellow, that is mighty provoking! Who the devil is he talking to?

[*Steps aside.*]

[*Enter* CAPTAIN ABSOLUTE.]

ABSOLUTE: To what fine purpose I have been plotting! A noble reward for all my schemes, upon my soul! – a little gipsy! I did not think her romance could have made her so damned absurd either – 'sdeath, I never was in a worse humour in my life! I could cut my own throat, or any other person's, with the greatest pleasure in the world!

SIR LUCIUS: Oh, faith! I'm in the luck of it – I never could have found him in a sweeter temper for my purpose – to be sure I'm just come in the nick! Now to enter into conversation with him, and so quarrel genteelly. [SIR LUCIUS *goes up to* ABSOLUTE.] With regard to that matter, Captain, I must beg leave to differ in opinion with you.

ABSOLUTE: Upon my word then, you must be a very subtle disputant: because, sir, I happened just then to be giving no opinion at all.

SIR LUCIUS: That's no reason. For give me leave to tell you, a man may *think* an untruth as well as *speak* one.

ABSOLUTE: Very true, sir, but if the man never utters his thoughts, I should think they might stand a chance of escaping controversy.

SIR LUCIUS: Then, sir, you differ in opinion with me, which amounts to the same thing.

ABSOLUTE: Harkee, Sir Lucius – if I had not before known you to be a gentleman, upon my soul, I should not have discovered it at this interview: for what you can drive at, unless you mean to quarrel with me, I cannot conceive!

SIR LUCIUS [*bowing*]: I humbly thank you, sir, for the quickness of your apprehension – you have named the very thing I would be at.

ABSOLUTE: Very well, sir – I shall certainly not baulk your inclinations – but I should be glad you would please to explain your motives.

SIR LUCIUS: Pray, sir, be easy – the quarrel is a very pretty quarrel as it stands – we should only spoil it, by trying to explain it. However, your memory is very short – or you could not have forgot an affront you passed on me within this week. So, no more, but name your time and place.

ABSOLUTE: Well, sir, since you are so bent on it, the sooner the better; let it be this evening – here, by the Spring Gardens. We shall scarcely be interrupted.

SIR LUCIUS: Faith! that same interruption in affairs of this nature shows very great ill-breeding. I don't know what's the reason, but in England, if a thing of this kind gets wind, people make such a pother, that a gentleman can never fight in peace and quietness. However, if it's the same to you, Captain, I should take it as a particular kindness, if you'd let us meet in Kingsmead Fields, as a little business will call me there about six o'clock, and I may dispatch both matters at once.

ABSOLUTE: 'Tis the same to me exactly. A little after six, then, we will discuss this matter more seriously.

SIR LUCIUS: If you please, sir, there will be very pretty small-sword[13] light, though it won't do for a long shot. – So that matter's settled! and my mind's at ease.

[*Exit* SIR LUCIUS.]

[*Enter* FAULKLAND, *meeting* ABSOLUTE.]

ABSOLUTE: Well met – I was going to look for you. O Faulkland! all the demons of spite and disappointment have conspired against me! I'm so vexed, that if I had not the prospect of a resource in

13. *small-sword*: light sword used in fencing.

being knocked o'the head by and by, I should scarce have spirits to tell you the cause.

FAULKLAND: What can you mean? Has Lydia changed her mind? I should have thought her duty and inclination would now have pointed to the same object.

ABSOLUTE: Aye, just as the eyes do of a person who squints: when her love eye was fixed on me – t'other, her eye of duty, was finely obliqued: but when duty bid her point that the same way – off t'other turned on a swivel, and secured its retreat with a frown!

FAULKLAND: But what's the resource you –

ABSOLUTE: Oh, to wind up the whole, a good-natured Irishman here has [*mimicking* SIR LUCIUS] begged leave to have the pleasure of cutting my throat – and I mean to indulge him – that's all.

FAULKLAND: Prithee, be serious.

ABSOLUTE: 'Tis fact, upon my soul. Sir Lucius O'Trigger – you know him by sight – for some affront, which I am sure I never intended, has obliged me to meet him this evening at six o'clock: 'tis on that account I wished to see you – you must go with me.

FAULKLAND: Nay, there must be some mistake, sure. Sir Lucius shall explain himself – and I dare say matters may be accommodated: but this evening, did you say? I wish it had been any other time.

ABSOLUTE: Why? – there will be light enough: there will (as Sir Lucius says) 'be very pretty small-sword light, though it won't do for a long shot'. Confound his long shots!

FAULKLAND: But I am myself a good deal ruffled, by a difference I have had with Julia – my vile tormenting temper had made me treat her so cruelly, that I shall not be myself till we are reconciled.

ABSOLUTE: By heavens, Faulkland, you don't deserve her.

[*Enter* SERVANT, *gives* FAULKLAND *a letter.* (*Exit* SERVANT.)]

FAULKLAND: O Jack! this is from Julia – I dread to open it – I fear it may be to take a last leave – perhaps to bid me return her letters – and restore – oh! how I suffer for my folly!

ABSOLUTE: Here – let me see. [*Takes the letter and opens it.*] Aye, a final sentence indeed! – 'tis all over with you, faith!

FAULKLAND: Nay, Jack – don't keep me in suspense.

ABSOLUTE: Hear then. *As I am convinced that my dear Faulkland's own reflections have already upbraided him for his last unkindness to me, I will not add a word on the subject. I wish to speak with you as soon as possible. Yours ever and truly, Julia.* – There's stubbornness and resentment for you! [*Gives him the letter.*] Why, man, you don't seem one whit the happier at this.

FAULKLAND: Oh, yes, I am – but – but –

ABSOLUTE: Confound your *buts*. You never hear anything that would make another man bless himself, but you immediately damn it with a *but*.

FAULKLAND: Now, Jack, as you are my friend, own honestly – don't you think there is something forward – something indelicate in this haste to forgive? Women should never sue for reconciliation: that should always come from us. They should retain their coldness till *wooed* to kindness – and their *pardon*, like their *love*, should 'not unsought be won'.[14]

ABSOLUTE: I have not patience to listen to you: thou'rt incorrigible! – so say no more on the subject. I must go to settle a few matters – let me see you before six – remember – at my lodgings. A poor industrious devil like me, who have toiled, and drudged, and plotted to gain my ends, and am at last disappointed by other people's folly – may in pity be allowed to swear and grumble a little; but a captious sceptic in love – a slave to fretfulness and whim – who has no difficulties but of his own creating – is a subject more fit for ridicule than compassion!

[*Exit* ABSOLUTE.]

FAULKLAND: I feel his reproaches! Yet I would not change this too exquisite nicety, for the gross content with which *he* tramples on the thorns of love. His engaging me in this duel has started an idea in my head, which I will instantly pursue. I'll use it as the touchstone of Julia's sincerity and disinterestedness – if her love prove pure and sterling ore – my name will rest on it with honour! And once I've stamped it there, I lay aside my doubts for ever: but if the dross of selfishness, the allay[15] of pride predominate – 'twill be best to leave her as a toy for some less cautious fool to sigh for.

[*Exit* FAULKLAND.]

14. 'not . . . won': see *Paradise Lost*, VIII, 503.
15. *allay*: alloy.

ACT V

Scene i

JULIA's *dressing-room.*

[JULIA, *sola.*]

JULIA: How this message has alarmed me! what dreadful accident can he mean? why such charge to be alone? O Faulkland! how many unhappy moments! how many tears have you cost me!

[*Enter* FAULKLAND.]

JULIA: What means this? – Why this caution, Faulkland?

FAULKLAND: Alas! Julia, I am come to take a long farewell.

JULIA: Heavens! what do you mean?

FAULKLAND: You see before you a wretch, whose life is forfeited. Nay, start not! The infirmity of my temper has drawn all this misery on me. I left you fretful and passionate – an untoward accident drew me into a quarrel – the event is, that I must fly this kingdom instantly. O Julia, had I been so fortunate as to have called you mine entirely, before this mischance had fallen on me, I should not so deeply dread my banishment!

JULIA: My soul is oppressed with sorrow at the nature of your misfortune: had these adverse circumstances arisen from a less fatal cause, I should have felt strong comfort in the thought that I could now chase from your bosom every doubt of the warm sincerity of my love. My heart has long known no other guardian – I now entrust my person to your honour – we will fly together. When safe from pursuit, my father's will may be fulfilled – and I receive a legal claim to be the partner of your sorrows, and tenderest comforter. Then on the bosom of your wedded Julia, you may lull your keen regret to slumbering; while virtuous love, with a cherub's hand, shall smooth the brow of upbraiding thought, and pluck the thorn from compunction.

FAULKLAND: O Julia! I am bankrupt in gratitude! but the time is so pressing, it calls on you for so hasty a resolution. Would you not wish some hours to weigh the advantages you forego, and what little compensation poor Faulkland can make you beside his solitary love?

JULIA: I ask not a moment. No, Faulkland, I have loved you for yourself: and if I now, more than ever, prize the solemn engagement which so long has pledged us to each other, it is because it leaves no room for hard aspersions on my fame, and puts the seal of duty to an act of love. But let us not linger – perhaps this delay –

FAULKLAND: 'Twill be better I should not venture out again till dark. Yet am I grieved to think what numberless distresses will press heavy on your gentle disposition!

JULIA: Perhaps your fortune may be forfeited by this unhappy act. I know not whether 'tis so – but sure that alone can never make us unhappy. The little I have will be sufficient to support us; and exile never should be splendid.

FAULKLAND: Aye, but in such an abject state of life, my wounded pride perhaps may increase the natural fretfulness of my temper, till I become a rude, morose companion, beyond your patience to endure. Perhaps the recollection of a deed my conscience cannot justify, may haunt me in such gloomy and unsocial fits, that I shall hate the tenderness that would relieve me, break from your arms, and quarrel with your fondness!

JULIA: If your thoughts should assume so unhappy a bent, you will the more want some mild and affectionate spirit to watch over and console you: one who, by bearing *your* infirmities with gentleness and resignation, may teach you *so* to bear the evils of your fortune.

FAULKLAND: Julia, I have proved you to the quick! and with this useless device I throw away all my doubts. How shall I plead to be forgiven this last unworthy effect of my restless, unsatisfied disposition?

JULIA: Has no such disaster happened as you related?

FAULKLAND: I am ashamed to own that it was all pretended; yet, in pity, Julia, do not kill me with resenting a fault which never can be repeated: but sealing, this once, my pardon, let me tomorrow, in the face of heaven, receive my future guide and monitress, and expiate my past folly, by years of tender adoration.

JULIA: Hold, Faulkland! That you are free from a crime, which I before feared to name, heaven knows how sincerely I rejoice! These are tears of thankfulness for that! But that your cruel doubts should have urged you to an imposition that has wrung my heart, gives me now a pang, more keen than I can express!

FAULKLAND: By heavens! Julia –

JULIA: Yet hear me. – My father loved you, Faulkland! and you preserved the life that tender parent gave me; in his presence I pledged my hand – joyfully pledged it – where before I had given my heart. When, soon after, I lost that parent, it seemed to me that providence had, in Faulkland, shown me whither to transfer, without a pause, my grateful duty, as well as my affection. Hence I have been content to bear from you what pride and delicacy would have forbid me from another. I will not upbraid you, by repeating how you have trifled with my sincerity –

FAULKLAND: I confess it all! yet hear –

JULIA: After such a year of trial – I might have flattered myself that I should not have been insulted with a new probation of my sincerity, as cruel as unnecessary! I now see it is not in your nature to be content, or confident in love. With this conviction – I never will be yours. While I had hopes that my persevering attention, and unreproaching kindness might in time reform your temper, I should have been happy to have gained a dearer influence over you; but I will not furnish you with a licensed power to keep alive an incorrigible fault, at the expense of one who never would contend with you.

FAULKLAND: Nay, but Julia, by my soul and honour, if after this –

JULIA: But one word more. As my faith has once been given to you, I never will barter it with another. I shall pray for your happiness with the truest sincerity; and the dearest blessing I can ask of heaven to send you, will be to charm you from that unhappy temper, which alone has prevented the performance of our solemn engagement. All I request of *you* is, that you will yourself reflect upon this infirmity, and when you number up the many true delights it has deprived you of – let it not be your *least* regret, that it lost you the love of one – who would have followed you in beggary through the world!

[*Exit.*]

FAULKLAND: She's gone! – for ever! There was an awful resolution in her manner, that riveted me to my place. – O fool! – dolt! – barbarian! Curst as I am, with more imperfections than my fellow-wretches, kind fortune sent a heaven-gifted cherub to my aid, and, like a ruffian, I have driven her from my side! I must now haste to my appointment. Well, my mind is tuned for such a scene. I shall wish only to become a principal in it, and reverse the tale my cursed folly put me upon forging here. O love! – tormentor! – fiend! – whose influence, like the moon's, acting on men of dull souls, makes idiots of them, but meeting subtler spirits, betrays their course, and urges sensibility to madness!

[*Exit.*]

[*Enter* MAID *and* LYDIA.]

MAID: My mistress, ma'am, I know, was here just now – perhaps she is only in the next room.

[*Exit* MAID.]

LYDIA: Heigh ho! – though he has used me so, this fellow runs strangely in my head. I believe one lecture from my grave cousin will make me recall him.

[*Enter* JULIA.]

LYDIA: O Julia, I am come to you with such an appetite for consolation. Lud! child, what's the matter with you? You have been crying! I'll be hanged, if that Faulkland has not been tormenting you!

JULIA: You mistake the cause of my uneasiness – something *has* flurried me a little – nothing that you can guess at. – [*Aside*] I would not accuse Faulkland to a sister!

LYDIA: Ah! whatever vexations you may have, I can assure you mine surpass them. You know who Beverley proves to be?

JULIA: I will now own to you, Lydia, that Mr Faulkland had before informed me of the whole affair. Had young Absolute been the person you took him for, I should not have accepted your confidence on the subject, without a serious endeavour to counteract your caprice.

LYDIA: So, then, I see I have been deceived by everyone! – but I don't care – I'll never have him.

JULIA: Nay, Lydia –

LYDIA: Why, is it not provoking; when I thought we were coming to the prettiest distress imaginable, to find myself made a mere Smithfield bargain[1] of at last. – There had I projected one of the most sentimental elopements! – so becoming a disguise! – so amiable a ladder of ropes! – conscious[2] moon – four horses – Scotch parson[3] – with such surprise to Mrs Malaprop – and such paragraphs in the newspapers! – Oh, I shall die with disappointment.

JULIA: I don't wonder at it!

LYDIA: Now – sad reverse! – what have I to expect, but, after a deal of flimsy preparation with a bishop's licence, and my aunt's blessing, to go simpering up to the altar; or perhaps be cried three times in a country church, and have an unmannerly fat clerk ask the consent of every butcher in the parish to join John Absolute and Lydia Languish, spinster! Oh, that I should live to hear myself called spinster!

JULIA: Melancholy, indeed!

LYDIA: How mortifying, to remember the dear delicious shifts I used to be put to, to gain half a minute's conversation with this fellow! How often have I stole forth, in the coldest night in January, and found him in the garden, stuck like a dripping statue! There would he kneel to me in the snow, and sneeze and cough so pathetically! he shivering with cold, and I with apprehension! and while the freezing blast numbed our joints, how warmly would he press me to pity his flame, and glow with mutual ardour! – Ah, Julia! that was something like being in love.

JULIA: If I were in spirits, Lydia, I should chide you only by laughing

1. *Smithfield bargain*: 'a marriage of interest, in which money is the chief consideration' (*O.E.D.*).

2. *conscious*: sympathetic; sharing in human feelings and actions.

3. *Scotch parson*: in Scotland, parental consent was not required for the marriage of minors.

heartily at you: but it suits more the situation of my mind, at present, earnestly to entreat you, not to let a man, who loves you with sincerity, suffer that unhappiness from your caprice, which I know too well caprice can inflict.

LYDIA: O Lud! what has brought my aunt here!

[*Enter* MRS MALAPROP, FAG, *and* DAVID.]

MRS MALAPROP: So! so! Here's fine work! Here's fine suicide, paracide,[4] and simulation[5] going on in the fields! and Sir Anthony not to be found to prevent the antistrophe![6]

JULIA: For heaven's sake, madam, what's the meaning of this?

MRS MALAPROP: That gentleman can tell you – 'twas he enveloped[7] the affair to me.

LYDIA [*to* FAG:]: Do, sir, will you inform us.

FAG: Ma'am, I should hold myself very deficient in every requisite that forms the man of breeding, if I delayed a moment to give all the information in my power to a lady so deeply interested in the affair as you are.

LYDIA: But quick! quick, sir!

FAG: True, ma'am, as you say, one should be quick in divulging matters of this nature; for should we be tedious, perhaps while we are flourishing on the subject, two or three lives may be lost!

LYDIA: O patience! Do, ma'am, for heaven's sake! tell us what is the matter?

MRS MALAPROP: Why, murder's the matter! slaughter's the matter! killing's the matter! – but he can tell you the perpendiculars.[8]

LYDIA: Then, prithee, sir, be brief.

FAG: Why then, ma'am – as to murder – I cannot take upon me to say – and as to slaughter, or manslaughter, that will be as the jury finds it.

LYDIA: But who, sir – who are engaged in this?

FAG: Faith, ma'am, one is a young gentleman whom I should be very

---

4. *paracide*: parricide.
5. *simulation*: dissimulation.
6. *antistrophe*: catastrophe.
7. *enveloped*: developed.
8. *perpendiculars*: particulars.

sorry anything was to happen to – a very pretty behaved gentleman! We have lived much together, and always on terms.

LYDIA: But who is this? who! who! who!

FAG: My master, ma'am – my master – I speak of my master.

LYDIA: Heavens! What, Captain Absolute!

MRS MALAPROP: Oh, to be sure, you are frightened now!

JULIA: But who are with him, sir?

FAG: As to the rest, ma'am, this gentleman can inform you better than I.

JULIA [*to* DAVID]: Do speak, friend.

DAVID: Lookee, my lady – by the Mass! there's mischief going on. – Folks don't use to meet for amusement with firearms, firelocks,[9] fire-engines, fire-screens, fire-office,[10] and the devil knows what other crackers besides! – This, my lady, I say, has an angry favour.[11]

JULIA: But who is there beside Captain Absolute, friend?

DAVID: My poor master – under favour, for mentioning him first. You know me, my lady – I am David – and my master of course is, or *was*, Squire Acres. Then comes Squire Faulkland.

JULIA: Do, ma'am, let us instantly endeavour to prevent mischief.

MRS MALAPROP: O fie – it would be very inelegant in us: we should only participate[12] things.

DAVID: Ah! do, Mrs Aunt, save a few lives – they are desperately given, believe me. Above all, there is that bloodthirsty Philistine, Sir Lucius O'Trigger.

MRS MALAPROP: Sir Lucius O'Trigger! O mercy! have they drawn poor little dear Sir Lucius into the scrape? Why, how you stand, girl! you have no more feeling than one of the Derbyshire putrefactions![13]

LYDIA: What are we to do, madam?

MRS MALAPROP: Why, fly with the utmost felicity[14] to be sure, to

9. *firelocks*: muskets.
10. *fire-office*: insurance office dealing with fires.
11. *favour*: appearance.
12. *participate*: precipitate.
13. *putrefactions*: petrifactions.
14. *felicity*: velocity.

prevent mischief: here, friend – you can show us the place?

FAG: If you please, ma'am, I will conduct you. David, do you look for Sir Anthony.

[*Exit* DAVID.]

MRS MALAPROP: Come, girls! this gentleman will exhort[15] us. Come, sir, you're our envoy[16] – lead the way, and we'll precede.[17]

FAG: Not a step before the ladies for the world!

MRS MALAPROP: You're sure you know the spot.

FAG: I think I can find it, ma'am; and one good thing is, we shall hear the report of the pistols as we draw near, so we can't well miss them; never fear, ma'am, never fear.

[*Exeunt, he talking.*]

Scene ii

South Parade.

[*Enter* ABSOLUTE, *putting his sword under his greatcoat.*]

ABSOLUTE: A sword seen in the streets of Bath would raise as great an alarm as a mad dog. How provoking this is in Faulkland! – never punctual! I shall be obliged to go without him at last. Oh, the devil! here's Sir Anthony! – how shall I escape him?

[*Muffles up his face, and takes a circle to go off.*]

[*Enter* SIR ANTHONY.]

SIR ANTHONY: How one may be deceived at a little distance! Only that I see he don't know me, I could have sworn that was Jack! Hey! Gad's life, it is. Why, Jack, what are you afraid of? Hey! sure I'm right. Why, Jack – Jack Absolute!

[*Goes up to him.*]

ABSOLUTE: Really, sir, you have the advantage of me: I don't remember ever to have had the honour – my name is Saunderson, at your service.

15. *exhort*: escort.
16. *envoy*: convoy.
17. *precede*: proceed.

SIR ANTHONY: Sir, I beg your pardon – I took you – hey! – why, zounds! it is – stay – [*Looks up to his face.*] So, so – your humble servant, Mr Saunderson! Why, you scoundrel, what tricks are you after now?

ABSOLUTE: Oh! a joke, sir, a joke! I came here on purpose to look for you, sir.

SIR ANTHONY: You did! Well, I am glad you were so lucky: but what are you muffled up so for? What's this for? – hey?

ABSOLUTE: 'Tis cool, sir; isn't it? – rather chilly somehow: but I shall be late – I have a particular engagement.

SIR ANTHONY: Stay – why, I thought you were looking for me? Pray, Jack, where is't you are going?

ABSOLUTE: Going, sir!

SIR ANTHONY: Aye – where are you going?

ABSOLUTE: Where am I going?

SIR ANTHONY: You unmannerly puppy!

ABSOLUTE: I was going, sir, to – to – to – to Lydia – sir to Lydia – to make matters up if I could; and I was looking for you, sir, to – to –

SIR ANTHONY: To go with you, I suppose – well, come along.

ABSOLUTE: Oh! zounds! no, sir, not for the world! I wished to meet with you, sir, to – to – to – you find it cool, I'm sure, sir – you'd better not stay out.

SIR ANTHONY: Cool! not at all – well, Jack – and what will you say to Lydia?

ABSOLUTE: Oh, sir, beg her pardon, humour her – promise and vow: but I detain you, sir – consider the cold air on your gout.

SIR ANTHONY: Oh, not at all! – not at all! – I'm in no hurry. Ah! Jack, you youngsters when once you are wounded here. [*Putting his hand to* ABSOLUTE*'s breast*] Hey! what the deuce have you got here?

ABSOLUTE: Nothing, sir – nothing.

SIR ANTHONY: What's this? – here's something damned hard!

ABSOLUTE: Oh, trinkets, sir! trinkets – a bauble for Lydia!

SIR ANTHONY: Nay, let me see your taste. [*Pulls his coat open, the sword falls.*] Trinkets! – a bauble for Lydia! Zounds! sirrah, you are not going to cut her throat, are you?

ABSOLUTE: Ha! ha! ha! – I thought it would divert you, sir, though I didn't mean to tell you till afterwards.

SIR ANTHONY: You didn't? Yes, this is a very diverting trinket, truly.

ABSOLUTE: Sir, I'll explain to you. You know, sir, Lydia is romantic – devilish romantic, and very absurd of course: now, sir, I intend, if she refuses to forgive me – to unsheath this sword – and swear – I'll fall upon its point, and expire at her feet!

SIR ANTHONY: Fall upon a fiddlestick's end! Why, I suppose it is the very thing that would please her. Get along, you fool.

ABSOLUTE: Well, sir, you shall hear of my success – you shall hear. 'Oh, Lydia! forgive me, or this pointed steel' – says I.

SIR ANTHONY: 'Oh, booby! stab away, and welcome' – says she. Get along! and damn your trinkets!

[*Exit* ABSOLUTE.]

[*Enter* DAVID, *running.*]

DAVID: Stop him! stop him! murder! thief! fire! Stop fire! stop fire! Oh! Sir Anthony – call! call! bid 'em stop! Murder! Fire!

SIR ANTHONY: Fire! murder! where?

DAVID: Oons! he's out of sight! and I'm out of breath, for my part! Oh, Sir Anthony, why didn't you stop him? why didn't you stop him?

SIR ANTHONY: Zounds! the fellow's mad! – Stop whom? Stop Jack?

DAVID: Aye, the Captain, sir! – there's murder and slaughter –

SIR ANTHONY: Murder!

DAVID: Aye, please you, Sir Anthony, there's all kinds of murder, all sorts of slaughter to be seen in the fields: there's fighting going on, sir – bloody sword-and-gun fighting!

SIR ANTHONY: Who are going to fight, dunce?

DAVID: Everybody that I know of, Sir Anthony: everybody is going to fight, my poor master, Sir Lucius O'Trigger, your son, the Captain –

SIR ANTHONY: Oh, the dog! I see his tricks – do you know the place?

DAVID: Kingsmead Fields.

SIR ANTHONY: You know the way?

DAVID: Not an inch; but I'll call the mayor – aldermen – constables – churchwardens – and beadles – we can't be too many to part them.

SIR ANTHONY: Come along – give me your shoulder! We'll get assistance as we go – the lying villain! Well, I shall be in such a frenzy – so – this was the history of his damned trinkets! I'll bauble him!

[*Exeunt.*]

Scene iii

Kingsmead Fields.

[SIR LUCIUS *and* ACRES, *with pistols.*]

ACRES: By my valour! then, Sir Lucius, forty yards is a good distance – odds levels and aims! I say it is a good distance.

SIR LUCIUS: Is it for muskets or small field-pieces?[18] Upon my conscience, Mr Acres, you must leave those things to me. Stay now – I'll show you. [*Measures paces along the stage.*] There now, that is a very pretty distance – a pretty gentleman's distance.

ACRES: Zounds! we might as well fight in a sentry-box! I tell you, Sir Lucius, the farther he is off, the cooler I shall take my aim.

SIR LUCIUS: Faith! then I suppose you would aim at him best of all if he was out of sight!

ACRES: No, Sir Lucius – but I should think forty or eight and thirty yards –

SIR LUCIUS: Pho! pho! nonsense! Three or four feet between the mouths of your pistols is as good as a mile.

ACRES: Odds bullets, no! – by my valour! there is no merit in killing him so near: do, my dear Sir Lucius, let me bring him down at a long shot: a long shot, Sir Lucius, if you love me!

SIR LUCIUS: Well – the gentleman's friend and I must settle that. But tell me now, Mr Acres, in case of an accident, is there any little will or commission I could execute for you?

ACRES: I am much obliged to you, Sir Lucius – but I don't under-stand –

SIR LUCIUS: Why, you may think there's no being shot at without a little risk – and if an unlucky bullet should carry a quietus[19] with

18. *field-pieces*: light cannon.
19. *quietus*: deadly wound.

it – I say it will be no time then to be bothering you about family matters.

ACRES: A quietus!

SIR LUCIUS: For instance now – if that should be the case – would you choose to be pickled and sent home? or would it be the same to you to lie here in the Abbey? I'm told there is very snug lying in the Abbey.

ACRES: Pickled! Snug lying in the Abbey! Odds tremors! Sir Lucius, don't talk so!

SIR LUCIUS: I suppose, Mr Acres, you never were engaged in an affair of this kind before?

ACRES: No, Sir Lucius, never before.

SIR LUCIUS: Ah! that's a pity! – there's nothing like being used to a thing. Pray now, how would you receive the gentleman's shot?

ACRES: Odds files! I've practised that – there, Sir Lucius – there [*puts himself in an attitude*] – a side-front, hey? Odd! I'll make myself small enough – I'll stand edge-ways.

SIR LUCIUS: Now – you're quite out – for if you stand so when I take my aim – [*Levelling at him.*]

ACRES: Zounds! Sir Lucius – are you sure it is not cocked?

SIR LUCIUS: Never fear.

ACRES: But – but – you don't know – it may go off of its own head!

SIR LUCIUS: Pho! be easy. Well, now if I hit you in the body, my bullet has a double chance – for if it misses a vital part on your right side – 'twill be very hard if it don't succeed on the left!

ACRES: A vital part!

SIR LUCIUS: But, there – fix yourself so – [*placing him*] let him see the broad side of your full front – there – now a ball or two may pass clean through your body, and never do any harm at all.

ACRES: Clean through me! – a ball or two clean through me!

SIR LUCIUS: Aye – may they – and it is much the genteelest attitude into the bargain.

ACRES: Lookee! Sir Lucius – I'd just as lieve[20] be shot in an awkward posture as a genteel one – so, by my valour! I will stand edge-ways.

20. *lieve*: willingly.

SIR LUCIUS [*looking at his watch*]: Sure they don't mean to disappoint us. Hah! No, faith – I think I see them coming.

ACRES: Hey! – what! – coming! –

SIR LUCIUS: Aye – who are those yonder getting over the stile?

ACRES: There are two of them, indeed! Well – let them come – hey, Sir Lucius! – we – we – we –we – won't run –

SIR LUCIUS: Run!

ACRES: No – I say – we *won't* run, by my valour!

SIR LUCIUS: What the devil's the matter with you?

ACRES: Nothing – nothing – my dear friend – my dear Sir Lucius – but – I – I – I don't feel quite so bold, somehow – as I did.

SIR LUCIUS: O fie! – consider your honour.

ACRES: Aye – true – my honour – do, Sir Lucius, edge in a word or two every now and then about my honour.

SIR LUCIUS [*looking*]: Well, here they're coming.

ACRES: Sir Lucius – if I wa'n't with you, I should almost think I was afraid – if my valour should leave me! – Valour will come and go.

SIR LUCIUS: Then pray keep it fast, while you have it.

ACRES: Sir Lucius – I doubt it is going – yes – my valour is certainly going! – it is sneaking off! – I feel it oozing out as it were at the palms of my hands!

SIR LUCIUS: Your honour – your honour – here they are.

ACRES: O mercy! – now – that I were safe at Clod Hall! or could be shot before I was aware!

[*Enter* FAULKLAND *and* ABSOLUTE.]

SIR LUCIUS: Gentlemen, your most obedient – hah! – what Captain Absolute! So, I suppose, sir, you are come here, just like myself – to do a kind of office, first for your friend – then to proceed to business on your own account.

ACRES: What, Jack! – my dear Jack! – my dear friend!

ABSOLUTE: Harkee, Bob, Beverley's at hand.

SIR LUCIUS: Well, Mr Acres – I don't blame your saluting the gentleman civilly. So, Mr Beverley [*to* FAULKLAND], if you'll choose your weapons, the Captain and I will measure the ground.

FAULKLAND: *My* weapons, sir.

ACRES: Odds life! Sir Lucius, I'm not going to fight Mr Faulkland; these are my particular friends.

SIR LUCIUS: What, sir, did not you come here to fight Mr Acres?

FAULKLAND: Not I, upon my word, sir.

SIR LUCIUS: Well, now, that's mighty provoking! But I hope, Mr Faulkland, as there are three of us come on purpose for the game, you won't be so cantankerous as to spoil the party by sitting out.

ABSOLUTE: O pray, Faulkland, fight to oblige Sir Lucius.

FAULKLAND: Nay, if Mr Acres is so bent on the matter.

ACRES: No, no, Mr Faulkland – I'll bear my disappointment like a Christian. Lookee, Sir Lucius, there's no occasion at all for me to fight; and if it is the same to you, I'd as lieve let it alone.

SIR LUCIUS: Observe me, Mr Acres – I must not be trifled with. You have certainly challenged somebody – and you came here to fight him. Now, if that gentleman is willing to represent him – I can't see, for my soul, why it isn't just the same thing.

ACRES: Why no – Sir Lucius – I tell you, 'tis one Beverley I've challenged – a fellow, you see, that dare not show his face! If *he* were here, I'd make him give up his pretensions directly!

ABSOLUTE: Hold, Bob – let me set you right – there is no such man as *Beverley* in the case. The person who assumed that name is before you; and as his pretensions are the same in both characters, he is ready to support them in whatever way you please.

SIR LUCIUS: Well, this is lucky – now you have an opportunity –

ACRES: What, quarrel with my dear friend Jack Absolute – not if he were fifty Beverleys! Zounds! Sir Lucius, you would not have me be so unnatural.

SIR LUCIUS: Upon my conscience, Mr Acres, your valour has *oozed* away with a vengeance!

ACRES: Not in the least! Odds backs and abettors! I'll be your second with all my heart – and if you should get a *quietus*, you may command me entirely. I'll get you a *snug lying* in the *Abbey here*; or *pickle* you, and send you over to Blunderbuss Hall, or anything of the kind with the greatest pleasure.

SIR LUCIUS: Pho! pho! you are little better than a coward.

ACRES: Mind, gentlemen, he calls me a *coward*; coward was the word, by my valour!

SIR LUCIUS: Well, sir?

ACRES: Lookee, Sir Lucius, 'tisn't that I mind the word coward –

coward may be said in joke. But if you had called me a *poltroon*, odds daggers and balls!

SIR LUCIUS: Well, sir?

ACRES: I should have thought you a very ill-bred man.

SIR LUCIUS: Pho! you are beneath my notice.

ABSOLUTE: Nay, Sir Lucius, you can't have a better second than my friend, Acres. He is a most *determined dog* – called in the country, 'Fighting Bob'. He generally *kills a man a week*; don't you, Bob?

ACRES: Aye – at home!

SIR LUCIUS: Well then, Captain, 'tis we must begin – so come out, my little counsellor [*draws his sword*], and ask the gentleman, whether he will resign the lady, without forcing you to proceed against him?

ABSOLUTE: Come on then, sir [*draws*]; since you won't let it be an amicable suit, here's my reply.

[*Enter* SIR ANTHONY, DAVID, *and the* WOMEN.]

DAVID: Knock 'em down, sweet Sir Anthony, knock down my master in particular – and bind his hands over to their good behaviour!

SIR ANTHONY: Put up, Jack, put up, or I shall be in a frenzy – how came you in a duel, sir?

ABSOLUTE: Faith, sir, that gentleman can tell you better than I; 'twas he called on me, and you know, sir, I serve his Majesty.

SIR ANTHONY: Here's a pretty fellow; I catch him going to cut a man's throat, and he tells me, he serves his Majesty! – Zounds! sirrah, then how durst you draw the King's sword against one of his subjects?

ABSOLUTE: Sir, I tell you! That gentleman called me out, without explaining his reasons.

SIR ANTHONY: Gad! Sir, how came you to call my son out, without explaining your reasons?

SIR LUCIUS: Your son, sir, insulted me in a manner which my honour could not brook.

SIR ANTHONY: Zounds! Jack, how durst you insult the gentleman in a manner which his honour could not brook?

MRS MALAPROP: Come, come, let's have no honour before ladies. Captain Absolute, come here – how could you intimidate us so? Here's Lydia has been terrified to death for you.

ABSOLUTE: For fear I should be killed, or escape, ma'am?

MRS MALAPROP: Nay, no delusions[21] to the past – Lydia is convinced; speak child.

SIR LUCIUS: With your leave, ma'am, I must put in a word here – I believe I could interpret the young lady's silence. Now mark –

LYDIA: What is it you mean, sir?

SIR LUCIUS: Come, come, Delia, we must be serious now – this is no time for trifling.

LYDIA: 'Tis true, sir; and your reproof bids me offer this gentleman my hand, and solicit the return of his affections.

ABSOLUTE: Oh! my little angel, say you so? – Sir Lucius, I perceive there must be some mistake here – with regard to the affront which you affirm I have given you – I can only say, that it could not have been intentional. And as you must be convinced, that I should not fear to support a real injury – you shall now see that I am not ashamed to atone for an inadvertency – I ask your pardon. But for this lady, while honoured with her approbation, I will support my claim against any man whatever.

SIR ANTHONY: Well said, Jack, and I'll stand by you, my boy.

ACRES: Mind, I give up all my claim – I make no pretensions to anything in the world – and if I can't get a wife, without fighting for her, by my valour! I'll live a bachelor.

SIR LUCIUS: Captain, give me your hand – an affront handsomely acknowledged becomes an obligation – and as for the lady – if she chooses to deny her own handwriting here – [*Takes out letters.*]

MRS MALAPROP: Oh, he will dissolve[22] my mystery! Sir Lucius, perhaps there's some mistake – perhaps, I can illuminate –

SIR LUCIUS: Pray, old gentlewoman, don't interfere, where you have no business. Miss Languish, are you my Delia, or not?

LYDIA: Indeed, Sir Lucius, I am not.

[LYDIA *and* ABSOLUTE *walk aside.*]

MRS MALAPROP: Sir Lucius O'Trigger – ungrateful as you are – I own the soft impeachment – pardon my blushes, I am Delia.

SIR LUCIUS: You Delia – pho! pho! be easy.

MRS MALAPROP: Why, thou barbarous Vandyke[23] – those letters are

21. *delusions*: allusions.
22. *dissolve*: resolve or solve.
23. *Vandyke*: vandal.

mine. When you are more sensible of my benignity – perhaps I may be brought to encourage your addresses.

SIR LUCIUS: Mrs Malaprop, I am extremely sensible of your conde-scension; and whether you or Lucy have put this trick upon me, I am equally beholden to you. And to show you I'm not ungrateful, Captain Absolute! since you have taken that lady from me, I'll give you my Delia into the bargain.

ABSOLUTE: I am much obliged to you, Sir Lucius; but here's our friend, Fighting Bob, unprovided for.

SIR LUCIUS: Hah! little Valour – here, will you make your fortune?

ACRES: Odds wrinkles! No. But give me your hand, Sir Lucius, forget and forgive; but if ever I give you a chance of *pickling* me again, say Bob Acres is a dunce, that's all.

SIR ANTHONY: Come, Mrs Malaprop, don't be cast down – you are in your bloom yet.

MRS MALAPROP: O Sir Anthony! – men are all barbarians –

[*All retire but* JULIA *and* FAULKLAND.]

JULIA: He seems dejected and unhappy – not sullen – there was some foundation, however, for the tale he told me – O woman! how true should be your judgment, when your resolution is so weak!

FAULKLAND: Julia! – how can I sue for what I so little deserve? I dare not presume – yet hope is the child of penitence.

JULIA: Oh! Faulkland, you have not been more faulty in your unkind treatment of me, than I am now in wanting inclination to resent it. As my heart honestly bids me place my weakness to the account of love, I should be ungenerous not to admit the same plea for yours.

FAULKLAND: Now I shall be blest indeed!

[SIR ANTHONY *comes forward.*]

SIR ANTHONY: What's going on here? So you have been quarrelling too, I warrant. Come, Julia, I never interfered before; but let me have a hand in the matter at last. All the faults I have ever seen in my friend Faulkland, seemed to proceed from what he calls the *delicacy* and *warmth* of his affection for you – there, marry him directly, Julia, you'll find he'll mend surprisingly!

[*The rest come forward.*]

SIR LUCIUS: Come now, I hope there is no dissatisfied person, but what is content; for as I have been disappointed myself, it will be very hard if I have not the satisfaction of seeing other people succeed better –

ACRES: You are right, Sir Lucius. So, Jack, I wish you joy – Mr Faulkland the same. Ladies, come now, to show you I'm neither vexed nor angry, odds tabors and pipes! I'll order the fiddles in half an hour, to the New Rooms – and I insist on your all meeting me there.

SIR ANTHONY: Gad! Sir, I like your spirit; and at night we single lads will drink a health to the young couples, and a husband to Mrs Malaprop.

FAULKLAND: Our partners are stolen from us, Jack – I hope to be congratulated by each other – *yours* for having checked in time the errors of an ill-directed imagination, which might have betrayed an innocent heart; and *mine*, for having, by her gentleness and candour, reformed the unhappy temper of one, who by it made wretched whom he loved most, and tortured the heart he ought to have adored.

ABSOLUTE: Well, Faulkland,[24] we have both tasted the bitters, as well as the sweets, of love – with this difference only, that *you* always prepared the bitter cup for yourself, while I –

LYDIA: Was always obliged to *me* for it, hey! Mr Modesty? – But come, no more of that – our happiness is now as unallayed as general.

JULIA: Then let us study to preserve it so: and while hope pictures to us a flattering scene of future bliss, let us deny its pencil those colours which are too bright to be lasting. When hearts deserving happiness would unite their fortunes, virtue would crown them with an unfading garland of modest, hurtless flowers; but ill-judging passion will force the gaudier rose into the wreath, whose thorn offends them, when its leaves are dropped!

Finis

24. *Faulkland*: Jack in first and third editions; Faulkland in the Lord Chamberlain's copy.

EPILOGUE

BY THE AUTHOR
Spoken by Mrs Bulkley [1]

Ladies for you – I heard our poet say –
He'd try to coax some moral from his play:
'One moral's plain' – cried I – 'without more fuss;
Man's social happiness all rests on us –
Through all the drama – whether damned or not –
Love gilds the scene, and women guide the plot.
From every rank, obedience is our due –
D'ye doubt? – the world's great stage shall prove it true'.
The cit [2] – well skilled to shun domestic strife –
Will sup abroad; but first – he'll ask his wife:
John Trot, his friend, for once, will do the same,
But then – he'll just 'step home to tell my dame'.
The surly squire at noon resolves to rule,
And half the day – 'Zounds! Madam is a fool!'
Convinced at night – the vanquished victor says,
'Ah! Kate! you women have such coaxing ways!'
The jolly toper chides each tardy blade,
Till reeling Bacchus calls on love for aid:
Then with each toast, he sees fair bumpers swim,
And kisses Chloe on the sparkling brim!
Nay, I have heard that statesmen – great and wise –
Will sometimes counsel with a lady's eyes;
The servile suitors watch her various face,
She smiles preferment – or she frowns disgrace,
Curtsies a pension here – there nods a place.
Nor with less awe, in scenes of humbler life,

1. *Mrs Bulkley*: she played Julia.
2. *cit*: citizen or tradesman.

Is viewed the mistress, or is heard the wife.
The poorest peasant of the poorest soil,
The child of poverty, and heir to toil –
Early from radiant love's impartial light,
Steals one small spark, to cheer his world of night:
Dear spark! that oft through winter's chilling woes,
Is all the warmth his little cottage knows!
The wand'ring tar – who, not for years, has pressed
The widowed partner of his day of rest –
On the cold deck – far from her arms removed –
Still hums the ditty which his Susan loved:
And while around the cadence rude is blown,
The boatswain whistles in a softer tone.
The soldier, fairly proud of wounds and toil,
Pants for the triumph of his Nancy's smile;
But ere the battle, should he list her cries,
The lover trembles – and the hero dies!
That heart, by war and honour steeled to fear,
Droops on a sigh, and sickens at a tear!
But ye more cautious – ye nice judging few,
Who give to beauty only beauty's due,
Though friends to love – ye view with deep regret
Our conquests marred – our triumphs incomplete,
Till polished wit more lasting charms disclose,
And judgment fix the darts which beauty throws!
– In female breasts did sense and merit rule,
The lover's mind would ask no other school;
Shamed into sense – the scholars of our eyes,
Our beaux from gallantry would soon be wise;
Would gladly light, their homage to improve,
The lamp of knowledge at the torch of love!

The Critic

TO MRS GREVILLE[1]

MADAM,

In requesting your permission to address the following pages to you, which as they aim themselves to be critical, require every protection and allowance that approving taste or friendly prejudice can give them, I yet ventured to mention no other motive than the gratification of private friendship and esteem. Had I suggested a hope that your implied approbation would give a sanction to their defects, your particular reserve, and dislike to the reputation of critical taste, as well as of poetical talent, would have made you refuse the protection of your name to such a purpose. However, I am not so ungrateful as now to attempt to combat this disposition in you. I shall not here presume to argue that the present state of poetry claims and expects every assistance that taste and example can afford it: nor endeavour to prove that a fastidious concealment of the most elegant productions of judgment and fancy is an ill return for the possession of those endowments. – Continue to deceive yourself in the idea that you are known only to be eminently admired and regarded for the valuable qualities that attach private friendships, and the graceful talents that adorn conversation. Enough of what you have written, has stolen into full public notice to answer my purpose; and you will, perhaps, be the only person, conversant in elegant literature, who shall read this address and not perceive that by publishing your particular approbation of the following drama, I have a more interested object than to boast the true respect and regard with which

I have the honour to be,

MADAM,

Your very sincere,

And obedient humble servant,

R. B. SHERIDAN

1. *Mrs Greville*: Frances Greville, wife of Richard Fulke Greville.

PROLOGUE

BY THE HONORABLE RICHARD FITZPATRICK[1]

The Sister Muses, whom these realms obey,
Who o'er the Drama hold divided sway,
Sometimes, by evil counsellors, 'tis said
Like earth-born potentates have been misled:
In those gay days of wickedness and wit,
When Villiers[2] criticized what Dryden writ,
The Tragic Queen, to please a tasteless crowd,
Had learned to bellow, rant, and roar so loud,
That frightened Nature, her best friend before,
The blust'ring beldam's company forswore.
Her comic Sister, who had wit 'tis true,
With all her merits, had her failings too;
And would sometimes in mirthful moments use
A style too flippant for a well-bred Muse.
Then female modesty abashed began
To seek the friendly refuge of the fan,
Awhile behind that slight entrenchment stood,
'Till driven from thence, she left the stage for good.
In our more pious, and far chaster times!
These sure no longer are the Muse's crimes!
But some complain that, former faults to shun,
The reformation to extremes has run.
The frantic hero's wild delirium past,
Now insipidity succeeds bombast;

---

1. *Richard Fitzpatrick*: son of the Earl of Upper Ossory.
2. *Villiers*: George Villiers, 2nd Duke of Buckingham (1628–87); author, with others, of *The Rehearsal* (1671), a burlesque chiefly of John Dryden's heroic plays.

So slow Melpomene's[3] cold numbers creep, ⎞
Here dullness seems her drowsy court to keep, ⎬
And we, are scarce awake, whilst you are fast asleep. ⎠
Thalia,[4] once so ill behaved and rude,
Reformed; is now become an arrant prude,
Retailing nightly to the yawning pit,
The purest morals, undefiled by wit!
Our Author offers in these motley scenes,
A slight remonstrance to the Drama's queens,
Nor let the goddesses be over nice;
Free spoken subjects give the best advice.
Although not quite a novice in his trade,
His cause tonight requires no common aid.
To this, a friendly, just, and powerful court,
I come Ambassador to beg support.
Can he undaunted, brave the critic's rage?
In civil broils, with brother bards engage?
Hold forth their errors to the public eye,
Nay more, e'en newspapers themselves defy?
Say, must his single arm encounter all?
By numbers vanquished, e'en the brave may fall;
And though no leader should success distrust,
Whose troops are willing, and whose cause is just;
To bid such hosts of angry foes defiance,
His chief dependence must be, YOUR ALLIANCE.

3. *Melpomene*: the Muse of tragedy.
4. *Thalia*: the Muse of comedy.

DRAMATIS PERSONAE

DANGLE
SNEER
SIR FRETFUL PLAGIARY
SIGNOR PASTICCIO RITORNELLO
INTERPRETER
UNDER PROMPTER
and

PUFF
MRS DANGLE
ITALIAN GIRLS

Characters of the TRAGEDY

LORD BURLEIGH
GOVERNOR OF TILBURY FORT
EARL OF LEICESTER
SIR WALTER RALEIGH
SIR CHRISTOPHER HATTON
MASTER OF THE HORSE
BEEFEATER
JUSTICE
SON
CONSTABLE
THAMES
and

DON FEROLO WHISKERANDOS
1ST NIECE
2ND NIECE
JUSTICE'S LADY
CONFIDANTE

and

TILBURINA

Guards, Constables, Servants, Chorus, Rivers, Attendants, etc. etc.

ACT I

Scene i

[MR *and* MRS DANGLE *at breakfast, and reading newspapers.*]

DANGLE [*reading*]: 'BRUTUS tO LORD NORTH.'[1] – 'Letter the second
on the STATE OF THE ARMY' – Pshaw! 'To the first L— dash D of
the A— dash Y.'[2] – 'Genuine Extract of a letter from ST KITT'S.' –
'COXHEATH INTELLIGENCE.'[3] – 'It is now confidently asserted
that SIR CHARLES HARDY.'[4] – Pshaw! – Nothing but about the
fleet, and the nation! – and I hate all politics but theatrical politics.
– Where's the *Morning Chronicle*?

MRS DANGLE: Yes, that's your gazette.

DANGLE: So, here we have it. – '*Theatrical intelligence extraordinary*,' –
'We hear there is a new tragedy in rehearsal at Drury Lane
Theatre, called *The Spanish Armada*, said to be written by Mr Puff,
a gentleman well known in the theatrical world; if we may allow
ourselves to give credit to the report of the performers, who, truth
to say, are in general but indifferent judges, this piece abounds
with the most striking and received beauties of modern composition' – So! I am very glad my friend Puff's tragedy is in such
forwardness. – Mrs Dangle, my dear, you will be very glad to hear
that Puff's tragedy –

MRS DANGLE: Lord, Mr Dangle, why will you plague me about such
nonsense? – Now the plays are begun I shall have no peace. – Isn't

1. *Lord North*: Prime Minister, 1770–82.
2. *first L . . . dash Y*: first Lord of the Admiralty, John Montagu, Earl of Sandwich.
3. *Coxheath*: military camp in Kent.
4. *Sir Charles Hardy*: commander of the Channel Fleet.

it sufficient to make yourself ridiculous by your passion for the theatre, without continually teasing me to join you? Why can't you ride your hobby-horse without desiring to place me on a pillion behind you, Mr Dangle?

DANGLE: Nay, my dear, I was only going to read –

MRS DANGLE: No, no; you never will read anything that's worth listening to: – you hate to hear about your country; there are letters every day with Roman signatures, demonstrating the certainty of an invasion, and proving that the nation is utterly undone – But you never will read anything to entertain one.

DANGLE: What has a woman to do with politics, Mrs Dangle?

MRS DANGLE: And what have you to do with the theatre, Mr Dangle? Why should you affect the character of a critic? I have no patience with you! – haven't you made yourself the jest of all your acquaint- ance by your interference in matters where you have no business? Are not you called a theatrical Quidnunc,[5] and a mock Maecenas[6] to second-hand authors?

DANGLE: True; my power with the managers is pretty notorious; but is it no credit to have applications from all quarters for my interest? – From lords to recommend fiddlers, from ladies to get boxes, from authors to get answers, and from actors to get engagements.

MRS DANGLE: Yes, truly; you have contrived to get a share in all the plague and trouble of theatrical property, without the profit, or even the credit of the abuse that attends it.

DANGLE: I am sure, Mrs Dangle, you are no loser by it, however; *you* have all the advantages of it: mightn't you, last winter, have had the reading of the new pantomime a fortnight previous to its perform- ance? And doesn't Mr Fosbrook[7] let you take places for a play before it is advertised, and set you down for a box for every new piece through the season? And didn't my friend, Mr Smatter, dedicate his last farce to you at my particular request, Mrs Dangle?

MRS DANGLE: Yes; but wasn't the farce damned, Mr Dangle? And to be sure it is extremely pleasant to have one's house made the

---

5. *Quidnunc*: an inquisitive person; a gossip.
6. *Maecenas*: Roman statesman and patron of letters.
7. *Fosbrook*: Thomas Fosbrook, book-keeper at Drury Lane Theatre.

motley rendezvous of all the lackeys of literature! – The very high change of trading authors and jobbing critics! – Yes, my drawing-room is an absolute register-office for candidate actors, and poets without character; then to be continually alarmed with Misses and Ma'ams piping hysteric changes on Juliets and Dorindas, Pollys and Ophelias; and the very furniture trembling at the probationary starts and unprovoked rants of would-be Richards and Hamlets! – And what is worse than all, now that the manager has monopolized the opera-house,[8] haven't we the signors and signoras calling here, sliding their smooth semibreves, and gargling glib divisions in their outlandish throats – with foreign emissaries and French spies, for ought I know, disguised like fiddlers and figure dancers!

DANGLE: Mercy! Mrs Dangle!

MRS DANGLE: And to employ yourself so idly at such an alarming crisis as this too – when, if you had the least spirit, you would have been at the head of one of the Westminster associations[9] – or trailing a volunteer pike in the Artillery Ground? – But you – o' my conscience, I believe if the French were landed tomorrow, your first enquiry would be, whether they had brought a theatrical troop with them.

DANGLE: Mrs Dangle, it does not signify – I say the stage is 'the mirror of nature,' and the actors are 'the abstract, and brief chronicles of the time'[10] – and pray what can a man of sense study better? – Besides, you will not easily persuade me that there is no credit or importance in being at the head of a band of critics, who take upon them to decide for the whole town, whose opinion and patronage all writers solicit, and whose recommendation no manager dares refuse!

MRS DANGLE: Ridiculous! – Both managers and authors of the least merit, laugh at your pretensions. – The public is their critic – without whose fair approbation they know no play can rest on the stage, and with whose applause they welcome such attacks as

8. *opera-house*: Sheridan was part-purchaser of the King's Theatre which was used for operas.

9. *Westminster associations*: volunteer militia.

10. *the abstract . . . time*: see *Hamlet*, II, ii.

yours, and laugh at the malice of them, where they can't at the wit.

DANGLE: Very well, madam – very well.

[*Enter* SERVANT.]

SERVANT: Mr Sneer, sir, to wait on you.

DANGLE: Oh, shew Mr Sneer up.

[*Exit* SERVANT.]

Plague on't, now we must appear loving and affectionate, or Sneer will hitch us into a story.

MRS DANGLE: With all my heart; you can't be more ridiculous than you are.

DANGLE: You are enough to provoke –

[*Enter* MR SNEER.]

– Hah! my dear Sneer, I am vastly glad to see you. My dear, here's Mr Sneer.

MRS DANGLE: Good morning to you, sir.

DANGLE: Mrs Dangle and I have been diverting ourselves with the papers. – Pray, Sneer, won't you go to Drury Lane theatre the first night of Puff's tragedy?

SNEER: Yes; but I suppose one shan't be able to get in, for on the first night of a new piece they always fill the house with orders to support it. But here, Dangle, I have brought you two pieces, one of which you must exert yourself to make the managers accept, I can tell you that, for 'tis written by a person of consequence.

DANGLE: So! Now my plagues are beginning!

SNEER: Aye, I am glad of it, for now you'll be happy. Why, my dear Dangle, it is a pleasure to see how you enjoy your volunteer fatigue, and your solicited solicitations.

DANGLE: It's a great trouble – yet, egad, it's pleasant too. – Why, sometimes of a morning, I have a dozen people call on me at breakfast time, whose faces I never saw before, nor ever desire to see again.

SNEER: That must be very pleasant indeed!

DANGLE: And not a week but I receive fifty letters, and not a line in them about any business of my own.

SNEER: An amusing correspondence!

DANGLE [*reading*]: 'Bursts into tears, and exit.' What, is this a tragedy?

SNEER: No, that's a genteel comedy, not a translation – only *taken from the French*; it is written in a style which they have lately tried to run down; the true sentimental, and nothing ridiculous in it from the beginning to the end.

MRS DANGLE: Well, if they had kept to that, I should not have been such an enemy to the stage, there was some edification to be got from those pieces, Mr Sneer!

SNEER: I am quite of your opinion, Mrs Dangle; the theatre, in proper hands, might certainly be made the school of morality; but now, I am sorry to say it, people seem to go there principally for their entertainment!

MRS DANGLE: It would have been more to the credit of the managers to have kept it in the other line.

SNEER: Undoubtedly, madam, and hereafter perhaps to have had it recorded, that in the midst of a luxurious and dissipated age, they preserved *two* houses in the capital, where the conversation was always moral at least, if not entertaining!

DANGLE: Now, egad, I think the worst alteration is in the nicety of the audience. – No double entendre, no smart innuendo admitted; even Vanbrugh and Congreve[11] obliged to undergo a bungling reformation!

SNEER: Yes, and our prudery in this respect is just on a par with the artificial bashfulness of a courtesan, who increases the blush upon her cheek in an exact proportion to the diminution of her modesty.

DANGLE: Sneer can't even give the public a good word! – But what have we here? – This seems a very odd –

SNEER: Oh, that's a comedy, on a very new plan; replete with wit and mirth, yet of a most serious moral! You see it is called '*The Reformed Housebreaker*'; where, by the mere force of humour, housebreaking is put into so ridiculous a light, that if the piece has its proper run, I have no doubt but that bolts and bars will be entirely useless by the end of the season.

DANGLE: Egad, this is new indeed!

11. *Vanbrugh and Congreve*: Sheridan himself had produced two Congreve comedies with alterations at Drury Lane in 1776, and his adaptation of Vanbrugh's *The Relapse* in 1777.

SNEER: Yes; it is written by a particular friend of mine, who has discovered that the follies and foibles of society, are subjects unworthy the notice of the Comic Muse, who should be taught to stoop only at the greater vices and blacker crimes of humanity – gibbeting capital offences in five acts, and pillorying petty larcenies in two. – In short, his idea is to dramatize the penal laws, and make the stage a court of ease to the Old Bailey.

DANGLE: It is truly moral.

[*Enter* SERVANT.]

SERVANT: Sir Fretful Plagiary, Sir.

DANGLE: Beg him to walk up.

[*Exit* SERVANT.]

Now, Mrs Dangle, Sir Fretful Plagiary is an author to your own taste.

MRS DANGLE: I confess he is a favourite of mine, because everybody else abuses him.

SNEER: Very much to the credit of your charity, madam, if not of your judgment.

DANGLE: But, egad, he allows no merit to any author but himself, that's the truth on't – though he's my friend.

SNEER: Never. – He is as envious as an old maid verging on the desperation of six-and-thirty: and then the insiduous humility with which he seduces you to give a free opinion on any of his works, can be exceeded only by the petulant arrogance with which he is sure to reject your observations.

DANGLE: Very true, egad – though he's my friend.

SNEER: Then his affected contempt of all newspaper strictures; though, at the same time, he is the sorest man alive, and shrinks like scorched parchment from the fiery ordeal of true criticism: yet is he so covetous of popularity, that he had rather be abused than not mentioned at all.

DANGLE: There's no denying it – though he is my friend.

SNEER: You have read the tragedy he has just finished, haven't you?

DANGLE: Oh yes; he sent it to me yesterday.

SNEER: Well, and you think it execrable, don't you?

DANGLE: Why between ourselves, egad I must own – though he's my friend – that it is one of the most – [*Aside*] He's here – finished and most admirable perform –

[SIR FRETFUL, *without.*]: Mr Sneer with him, did you say?

[*Enter* SIR FRETFUL.]

Ah, my dear friend! – Egad, we were just speaking of your tragedy. – Admirable, Sir Fretful, admirable!

SNEER: You never did anything beyond it, Sir Fretful – never in your life.

SIR FRETFUL: You make me extremely happy; – for without a compliment, my dear Sneer, there isn't a man in the world whose judgment I value as I do yours. – And Mr Dangle's.

MRS DANGLE: They are only laughing at you, Sir Fretful; for it was but just now that –

DANGLE: Mrs Dangle! – Ah, Sir Fretful, you know Mrs Dangle. – My friend Sneer was rallying just now – He knows how she admires you, and –

SIR FRETFUL: O Lord – I am sure Mr Sneer has more taste and sincerity than to – [*Aside*] A damned double-faced fellow!

DANGLE: Yes, yes, – Sneer will jest – but a better humoured –

SIR FRETFUL: Oh, I know –

DANGLE: He has a ready turn for ridicule – his wit costs him nothing. –

SIR FRETFUL: No, egad, [*aside*] or I should wonder how he came by it.

MRS DANGLE: Because his jest is always at the expense of his friend.

DANGLE: But, Sir Fretful, have you sent your play to the managers yet? – or can I be of any service to you?

SIR FRETFUL: No, no, I thank you; I believe the piece had sufficient recommendation with it. – I thank you though. – I sent it to the manager of Covent Garden Theatre this morning.

SNEER: I should have thought now, that it might have been cast (as the actors call it) better at Drury Lane.

SIR FRETFUL: O lud! no – never send a play there while I live – harkee!

[*Whispers* SNEER.]

SNEER: *Writes himself*! – I know he does –

SIR FRETFUL: I say nothing – I take away from no man's merit – am hurt at no man's good fortune – I say nothing – But this I will say –

through all my knowledge of life, I have observed – that there is not a passion so strongly rooted in the human heart as envy!

SNEER: I believe you have reason for what you say, indeed.

SIR FRETFUL: Besides – I can tell you it is not always so safe to leave a play in the hands of those who write themselves.

SNEER: What, they may steal from them, hey, my dear Plagiary?

SIR FRETFUL: Steal! – to be sure they may; and, egad, serve your best thoughts as gypsies do stolen children, disfigure them to make 'em pass for their own.

SNEER: But your present work is a sacrifice to Melpomene, and He, you know, never –

SIR FRETFUL: That's no security. – A dexterous plagiarist may do anything. – Why, sir, for ought I know, he might take out some of the best things in my tragedy, and put them into his own comedy.

SNEER: That might be done, I dare be sworn.

SIR FRETFUL: And then, if such a person gives you the least hint or assistance, he is devilish apt to take the merit of the whole. –

DANGLE: If it succeeds.

SIR FRETFUL: Aye, – but with regard to this piece, I think I can hit that gentleman, for I can safely swear he never read it.

SNEER: I'll tell you how you may hurt him more –

SIR FRETFUL: How? –

SNEER: Swear he wrote it.

SIR FRETFUL: Plague on't now, Sneer, I shall take it ill. – I believe you want to take away my character as an author!

SNEER: Then I am sure you ought to be very much obliged to me.

SIR FRETFUL: Hey! – Sir! –

DANGLE: Oh you know, he never means what he says.

SIR FRETFUL: Sincerely then – you do like the piece?

SNEER: Wonderfully!

SIR FRETFUL: But come now, there must be something that you think might be mended, hey? – Mr Dangle, has nothing struck you?

DANGLE: Why faith, it is but an ungracious thing for the most part to –

SIR FRETFUL: With most authors it is just so indeed; they are in general strangely tenacious! – But, for my part, I am never so well pleased as when a judicious critic points out any defect to me; for what is the purpose of showing a work to a friend, if you don't mean to profit by his opinion?

SNEER: Very true. – Why then, though I seriously admire the piece upon the whole, yet there is one small objection; which, if you'll give me leave, I'll mention.

SIR FRETFUL: Sir, you can't oblige me more.

SNEER: I think it wants incident.

SIR FRETFUL: Good God! – you surprise me! – wants incident! –

SNEER: Yes; I own I think the incidents are too few.

SIR FRETFUL: Good God! – Believe me, Mr Sneer, there is no person for whose judgment I have a more implicit deference. – But I protest to you, Mr Sneer, I am only apprehensive that the incidents are too crowded. – My dear Dangle, how does it strike you?

DANGLE: Really I can't agree with my friend Sneer. – I think the plot quite sufficient; and the four first acts by many degrees the best I ever read or saw in my life. If I might venture to suggest anything, it is that the interest rather falls off in the fifth. –

SIR FRETFUL: Rises; I believe you mean, sir.

DANGLE: No; I don't upon my word.

SIR FRETFUL: Yes, yes, you do upon my soul – it certainly don't fall off, I assure you – No, no, it don't fall off.

DANGLE: Now, Mrs Dangle, didn't you say it struck you in the same light?

MRS DANGLE: No, indeed, I did not – I did not see a fault in any part of the play from the beginning to the end.

SIR FRETFUL: Upon my soul the women are the best judges after all!

MRS DANGLE: Or if I made any objection, I am sure it was to nothing in the piece; but that I was afraid it was, on the whole, a little too long.

SIR FRETFUL: Pray, madam, do you speak as to duration of time; or do you mean that the story is tediously spun out?

MRS DANGLE: O lud! no. – I speak only with reference to the usual length of acting plays.

SIR FRETFUL: Then I am very happy – very happy indeed, – because the play is a short play, a remarkably short play: – I should not venture to differ with a lady on a point of taste; but, on these occasions, the watch, you know, is the critic.

MRS DANGLE: Then, I suppose, it must have been Mr Dangle's drawling manner of reading it to me.

SIR FRETFUL: Oh, if Mr Dangle read it! that's quite another affair! – But I assure you, Mrs Dangle, the first evening you can spare me three hours and an half, I'll undertake to read you the whole from beginning to end, with the prologue and epilogue, and allow time for the music between the acts.

MRS DANGLE: I hope to see it on the stage next.

DANGLE: Well, Sir Fretful, I wish you may be able to get rid as easily of the newspaper criticisms as you do of ours. –

SIR FRETFUL: The newspapers! – Sir, they are the most villainous – licentious – abominable – infernal – Not that I ever read them – No – I make it a rule never to look into a newspaper.

DANGLE: You are quite right – for it certainly must hurt an author of delicate feelings to see the liberties they take.

SIR FRETFUL: No! – quite the contrary; – their abuse is, in fact, the best panegyric – I like it of all things. – An author's reputation is only in danger from their support.

SNEER: Why that's true – and that attack now on you the other day –

SIR FRETFUL: What? where?

DANGLE: Aye, you mean in a paper of Thursday; it was completely ill-natured to be sure.

SIR FRETFUL: Oh, so much the better. – Ha! ha! ha! – I wouldn't have it otherwise.

DANGLE: Certainly it is only to be laughed at; for –

SIR FRETFUL: You don't happen to recollect what the fellow said, do you?

SNEER: Pray, Dangle – Sir Fretful seems a little anxious –

SIR FRETFUL: O lud, no! – anxious, – not I, – not the least. – I – But one may as well hear you know.

DANGLE: Sneer, do *you* recollect? [*Aside*] Make out something.

SNEER [*to* DANGLE]: I will. – Yes, yes, I remember perfectly.

SIR FRETFUL: Well, and pray now – not that it signifies – what might the gentleman say?

SNEER: Why, he roundly asserts that you have not the slightest invention, or original genius whatever; though you are the greatest traducer of all other authors living.

SIR FRETFUL: Ha! ha! ha! – very good!

SNEER: That as to comedy, you have not one idea of your own, he believes, even in your commonplace-book – where stray jokes, and pilfered witticisms are kept with as much method as the ledger of the lost-and-stolen office.

SIR FRETFUL: Ha! ha! ha! – very pleasant!

SNEER: Nay, that you are so unlucky as not to have the skill even to *steal* with taste. – But that you glean from the refuse of obscure volumes, where more judicious plagiarists have been before you; so that the body of your work is a composition of dregs and sediments – like a bad tavern's worst wine.

SIR FRETFUL: Ha! ha!

SNEER: In your more serious efforts, he says, your bombast would be less intolerable, if the thoughts were ever suited to the expression; but the homeliness of the sentiment stares through the fantastic encumbrance of its fine language, like a clown in one of the new uniforms!

SIR FRETFUL: Ha! ha!

SNEER: That your occasional tropes and flowers suit the general coarseness of your style, as tambour sprigs would a ground of linsey-wolsey;[12] while your imitations of Shakespeare resemble the mimicry of Falstaff's page,[13] and are about as near the standard of the original.

SIR FRETFUL: Ha! –

SNEER: In short, that even the finest passages you steal are of no service to you; for the poverty of your own language prevents their assimilating; so that they lie on the surface like lumps of a marl[14] on a barren moor, encumbering what it is not in their power to fertilize! –

SIR FRETFUL [*after great agitation*]: Now another person would be vexed at this.

SNEER: Oh! but I wouldn't have told you, only to divert you.

12. *tambour . . . linsey-wolsey*: elaborate decoration embroidered on coarse, inferior background.

13. *Falstaff's page*: see 2 *Henry IV*, II, ii.

14. *marl*: 'clay mixed with carbonate of lime, valuable as a fertilizer' (*O.E.D.*).

SIR FRETFUL: I know it – I *am* diverted, – Ha! ha! ha! – not the least invention! – Ha! ha! ha! very good! – very good!

SNEER: Yes – no genius! Ha! ha! ha!

DANGLE: A severe rogue! Ha! ha! ha! But you are quite right, Sir Fretful, never to read such nonsense.

SIR FRETFUL: To be sure – for if there is anything to one's praise, it is a foolish vanity to be gratified at it, and if it is abuse, – why one is always sure to hear of it from one damned good natured friend or another!

[*Enter* SERVANT.]

SERVANT: Sir, there is an Italian gentleman, with a French interpreter, and three young ladies, and a dozen musicians, who say they are sent by Lady Rondeau and Mrs Fuge.

DANGLE: Gadso! they come by appointment. Dear Mrs Dangle do let them know I'll see them directly.

MRS DANGLE: You know, Mr Dangle, I shan't understand a word they say.

DANGLE: But you hear there's an interpreter.

MRS DANGLE: Well, I'll try to endure their complaisance till you come.

[*Exit.*]

SERVANT: And Mr Puff, sir, has sent word that the last rehearsal is to be this morning, and that he'll call on you presently.

DANGLE: That's true – I shall certainly be at home.

[*Exit* SERVANT.]

Now, Sir Fretful, if you have a mind to have justice done you in the way of answer – Egad, Mr Puff's your man.

SIR FRETFUL: Pshaw! Sir, why should I wish to have it answered, when I tell you I am pleased at it?

DANGLE: True, I had forgot that. – But I hope you are not fretted at what Mr Sneer –

SIR FRETFUL: Zounds! no, Mr Dangle, don't I tell you these things never fret me in the least.

DANGLE: Nay, I only thought –

SIR FRETFUL: And let me tell you, Mr Dangle, 'tis damned affronting in you to suppose that I am hurt, when I tell you I am not.

SNEER: But why so warm, Sir Fretful?

SIR FRETFUL: Gadslife! Mr Sneer, you are as absurd as Dangle; how often must I repeat it to you, that nothing can vex me but your supposing it possible for me to mind the damned nonsense you have been repeating to me! – and let me tell you, if you continue to believe this, you must mean to insult me, gentlemen – and then your disrespect will affect me no more than the newspaper criticisms – and I shall treat it – with exactly the same calm indifference and philosophic contempt – and so your servant.
[*Exit.*]

SNEER: Ha! ha! ha! Poor Sir Fretful! Now will he go and vent his philosophy in anonymous abuse of all modern critics and authors – But, Dangle, you must get your friend Puff to take me to the rehearsal of his tragedy.

DANGLE: I'll answer for't, he'll thank you for desiring it. But come and help me to judge of this musical family; they are recommended by people of consequence, I assure you.

SNEER: I am at your disposal the whole morning – but I thought you had been a decided critic in music, as well as in literature?

DANGLE: So I am – but I have a bad ear. – I'faith, Sneer, though, I am afraid we were a little too severe on Sir Fretful – though he is my friend.

SNEER: Why, 'tis certain, that unnecessarily to mortify the vanity of any writer, is a cruelty which mere dullness never can deserve; but where a base and personal malignity usurps the place of literary emulation, the aggressor deserves neither quarter nor pity.

DANGLE: That's true egad! – though he's my friend!

Scene ii

A drawing room, harpsichord, etc. Italian family, French interpreter.

[MRS DANGLE *and* SERVANTS *discovered.*]

INTERPRETER: Je dis madame, j'ai l'honneur to *introduce* et de vous demander votre protection pour le Signor Pasticcio Retornello et pour sa charmante famille.

SIGNOR PASTICCIO: Ah! Vosignoria noi vi preghiamo di favoritevi colla vostra protezione.

1ST DAUGHTER: Vosignoria fatevi questi grazzie.

2ND DAUGHTER: Si Signora.

INTERPRETER: Madame – *me interpret.* – C'est à dire – in English – qu'ils vous prient de leur faire l'honneur –

MRS DANGLE: I say again, gentlemen, I don't understand a word you say.

SIGNOR PASTICCIO: Questo Signore spiegheró.

INTERPRETER: Oui – *me interpret* – nous avons les lettres de recommendation pour Monsieur Dangle de –

MRS DANGLE: Upon my word, sir, I don't understand you.

SIGNOR PASTICCIO: La Contessa Rondeau e nostra padrona.

3RD DAUGHTER: Si, padre, & mi Ladi Fuge.

INTERPRETER: Oh! – *me interpret.* – Madame, ils disent – *in English* – qu'ils ont l'honneur d'etre protegés de ces dames. – *You understand?*

MRS DANGLE: No, sir, – no understand!

[*Enter* DANGLE *and* SNEER.]

INTERPRETER: Ah voici Monsieur Dangle!

ALL ITALIANS: A! Signor Dangle!

MRS DANGLE: Mr Dangle, here are two very civil gentlemen trying to make themselves understood, and I don't know which is the interpreter.

DANGLE: Eh bien!

[*Speaking together*]

INTERPRETER: Monsieur Dangle – le grand bruit de vos talents pour la critique & de votre interest avec Messieurs les Directeurs a tous les théâtres.

SIGNOR PASTICCIO: Vosignoria siete si famoso par la vostra conoscensa e vostra interessa colla le Direttore da –

DANGLE: Egad I think the interpreter is the hardest to be understood of the two!

SNEER: Why I thought, Dangle, you had been an admirable linguist!

DANGLE: So I am, if they would not talk so damned fast.

SNEER: Well I'll explain that – the less time we lose in hearing them the better, – for that I suppose is what they are brought here for.

[SNEER *speaks to* SIGNOR PASTICCIO. – *They sing trios, etc.*
DANGLE *beating out of time.* SERVANT *enters and whispers*
DANGLE.]

[*Exit* SERVANT.]

DANGLE: Show him up.

Bravo! admirable! bravissimo! admirablissimo! – Ah! Sneer!
where will you find such as these voices in England?

SNEER: Not easily.

DANGLE: But Puff is coming. – Signor and little Signoras – obligatis-
simo! – Sposa Signora Danglena – Mrs Dangle, shall I beg you to
offer them some refreshments, and take their address in the next
room.

[*Exit* MRS DANGLE *with the* ITALIANS *and* INTERPRETER
ceremoniously.]

[*Re-enter* SERVANT.]

SERVANT: Mr Puff, Sir.

[*Enter* PUFF.]

DANGLE: My dear Puff!

PUFF: My dear Dangle, how is it with you?

DANGLE: Mr Sneer, give me leave to introduce Mr Puff to you.

PUFF: Mr Sneer is this? Sir, he is a gentleman whom I have long
panted for the honour of knowing – a gentleman whose critical
talents and transcendent judgment –

SNEER: – Dear sir –

DANGLE: Nay, don't be modest, Sneer, my friend Puff only talks to
you in the style of his profession.

SNEER: His profession!

PUFF: Yes, sir; I make no secret of the trade I follow – among friends
and brother authors, Dangle knows I love to be frank on the
subject, and to advertise myself *viva voce.* – I am, sir, a practitioner
in panegyric, or to speak more plainly – a Professor of the Art of
Puffing, at your service – or anybody else's.

SNEER: Sir, you are very obliging! – I believe, Mr Puff, I have often
admired your talents in the daily prints.

PUFF: Yes, sir, I flatter myself I do as much business in that way as any
six of the fraternity in town. – Devilish hard work all the summer –
friend Dangle? never worked harder! – But harkee, – the winter

managers were a little sore I believe.

DANGLE: No – I believe they took it all in good part.

PUFF: Aye! – Then that must have been affectation in them, for egad, there were some of the attacks which there was no laughing at!

SNEER: Aye, the humorous ones. – But I should think Mr Puff, that authors would in general be able to do this sort of work for themselves.

PUFF: Why yes – but in a clumsy way. – Besides, we look on that as an encroachment, and so take the opposite side. – I dare say now you conceive half the very civil paragraphs and advertisements you see, to be written by the parties concerned, or their friends? – No such thing – Nine out of ten, manufactured by me in the way of business.

SNEER: Indeed! –

PUFF: Even the auctioneers now, – the auctioneers I say, though the rogues have lately got some credit for their language – not an article of the merit theirs! – take them out of their pulpits, and they are as dull as catalogues. – No, sir; – 'twas I first enriched their style – 'twas I first taught them to crowd their advertisements with panegyrical superlatives, each epithet rising above the other – like the bidders in their own auction-rooms! From me they learned to enlay their phraseology with variegated chips of exotic metaphor: by me too their inventive faculties were called forth. – Yes sir, by me they were instructed to clothe ideal walls with gratuitous fruits – to insinuate obsequious rivulets into visionary groves – to teach courteous shrubs to nod their approbation of the grateful soil! or on emergencies to raise upstart oaks, where there never had been an acorn; to create a delightful vicinage without the assistance of a neighbour; or fix the temple of Hygeia[15] in the fens of Lincolnshire!

DANGLE: I am sure, you have done them infinite service; for now, when a gentleman is ruined, he parts with his house with some credit.

SNEER: Service! if they had any gratitude, they would erect a statue to him, they would figure him as a presiding Mercury, the god of

15. *Hygeia*: goddess of health.

traffic and fiction, with a hammer in his hand instead of a caduceus.[16] But pray, Mr Puff, what first put you on exercising your talents in this way?

PUFF: Egad sir, – sheer necessity – the proper parent of an art so nearly allied to invention: you must know Mr Sneer, that from the first time I tried my hand at an advertisement, my success was such, that for sometime after, I led a most extraordinary life indeed!

SNEER: How, pray?

PUFF: Sir, I supported myself two years entirely by my misfortunes.

SNEER: By your misfortunes!

PUFF: Yes sir, assisted by long sickness, and other occasional disorders; and a very comfortable living I had of it.

SNEER: From sickness and misfortunes! – You practised as a doctor, and an attorney at once?

PUFF: No egad, both maladies and miseries were my own.

SNEER: Hey! – what the plague!

DANGLE: 'Tis true, i' faith.

PUFF: Harkee! – By advertisements – 'To the charitable and humane!' and 'to those whom Providence hath blessed with affluence!'

SNEER: Oh, – I understand you.

PUFF: And in truth, I deserved what I got, for I suppose never man went through such a series of calamities in the same space of time! – Sir, I was five times made a bankrupt, and reduced from a state of affluence, by a train of unavoidable misfortunes! then sir, though a very industrious tradesman, I was twice burnt out, and lost my little all, both times! – I lived upon those fires a month. – I soon after was confined by a most excruciating disorder, and lost the use of my limbs! – That told very well, for I had the case strongly attested, and went about to collect the subscriptions myself.

DANGLE: Egad, I believe that was when you first called on me. –

PUFF: – In November last? Oh no! – I was at that time, a close prisoner in the Marshalsea,[17] for a debt benevolently contracted to

16. *caduceus*: the wand carried by Mercury.
17. *Marshalsea*: debtor's prison.

serve a friend! – I was afterwards twice tapped for a dropsy, which declined into a very profitable consumption! – I was then reduced to – Oh no – then, I became a widow with six helpless children, – after having had eleven husbands pressed, and being left every time eight months gone with child, and without money to get me into an hospital!

SNEER: And you bore all with patience, I make no doubt?

PUFF: Why, yes, – though I made some occasional attempts at felo-de-se;[18] but as I did not find those rash actions answer, I left off killing myself very soon. – Well, sir, – at last, what with bankruptcies, fires, gouts, dropsies, imprisonments, and other valuable calamities, having got together a pretty handsome sum, I determined to quit a business which had always gone rather against my conscience, and in a more liberal way still to indulge my talents for fiction and embellishment, through my favourite channels of diurnal communication – and so, sir, you have my history.

SNEER: Most obligingly communicative indeed; and your confession if published, might certainly serve the cause of true charity, by rescuing the most useful channels of appeal to benevolence from the cant of imposition. – But surely, Mr Puff, there is no great *mystery* in your present profession?

PUFF: Mystery! Sir, I will take upon me to say the matter was never scientifically treated, nor reduced to rule before.

SNEER: Reduced to rule?

PUFF: O lud, sir! you are very ignorant, I am afraid. – Yes sir, – PUFFING is of various sorts – the principal are, The PUFF DIRECT – the PUFF PRELIMINARY – the PUFF COLLATERAL – the PUFF COLLUSIVE, and the PUFF OBLIQUE, or PUFF by IMPLICATION. – These all assume, as circumstances require, the various forms of LETTER TO THE EDITOR – OCCASIONAL ANECDOTE – IMPARTIAL CRITIQUE – OBSERVATION from CORRESPONDENT, – or ADVERTISEMENT FROM THE PARTY.

SNEER: The puff direct, I can conceive –

PUFF: O yes, that's simple enough, – for instance – A new comedy or

18. *felo-de-se*: suicide.

farce is to be produced at one of the theatres (though by the by they don't bring out half what they ought to do). The author, suppose Mr Smatter, or Mr Dapper – or any particular friend of mine – very well; the day before it is to be performed, I write an account of the manner in which it was received – I have the plot from the author, – and only add – Characters strongly drawn – highly coloured – hand of a master – fund of genuine humour – mine of invention – neat dialogue – attic salt! Then for the performance – Mr Dodd[19] was astonishingly great in the character of Sir Harry! That universal and judicious actor Mr Palmer,[20] perhaps never appeared to more advantage than in the Colonel; – but it is not in the power of language to do justice to Mr King![21] – Indeed he more than merited those repeated bursts of applause which he drew from a most brilliant and judicious audience! As to the scenery – The miraculous powers of Mr de Loutherbourg's[22] pencil are universally acknowledged! – In short, we are at a loss which to admire most, – the unrivalled genius of the author, the great attention and liberality of the managers – the wonderful abilities of the painter, or the incredible exertions of all the performers! –

SNEER: That's pretty well indeed, sir.

PUFF: Oh cool – quite cool – to what I sometimes do.

SNEER: And do you think there are any who are influenced by this.

PUFF: O, lud! yes, sir; – the number of those who go through the fatigue of judging for themselves is very small indeed!

SNEER: Well, sir, – the PUFF PRELIMINARY?

PUFF: Oh that, sir, does well in the form of a *caution*. – In a matter of gallantry now – Sir Flimsy Gossimer, wishes to be well with Lady Fanny Fete – He applies to me – I open trenches for him with a paragraph in the *Morning Post*. – It is recommended to the beautiful and accomplished Lady F four stars F dash E to be on her guard against that dangerous character, Sir F dash G; who,

19. *Mr Dodd*: James Dodd (1740?–96) played Dangle.
20. *Mr Palmer*: John Palmer (1742–98) played Sneer.
21. *Mr King*: Thomas King (1730–1805) played Puff.
22. *Mr de Loutherbourg*: Philippe de Loutherbourg (1730–1812) designed the sets.

however pleasing and insinuating his manners may be, is certainly not remarkable for the *constancy of his attachments!* – in italics. – Here you see, Sir Flimsy Gossimer is introduced to the particular notice of Lady Fanny – who, perhaps never thought of him before – she finds herself publicly cautioned to avoid him, which naturally makes her desirous of seeing him; – the observation of their acquaintance causes a pretty kind of mutual embarrassment, this produces a sort of sympathy of interest – which, if Sir Flimsy is unable to improve effectually, he at least gains the credit of having their names mentioned together, by a particular set, and in a particular way, – which nine times out of ten is the full accomplishment of modern gallantry!

DANGLE: Egad, Sneer, you will be quite an adept in the business.

PUFF: Now, sir, the PUFF COLLATERAL is much used as an appendage to advertisements, and may take the form of anecdote. – Yesterday as the celebrated George Bon-Mot was sauntering down St James's Street, he met the lively Lady Mary Myrtle, coming out of the Park, – 'Good God, Lady Mary, I'm surprised to meet you in a white jacket, – for I expected never to have seen you, but in a full-trimmed uniform, and a light horseman's cap!' – 'Heavens, George, where could you have learned that?' – 'Why, replied the wit, I just saw a print of you, in a new publication called the *Camp Magazine*, which, by the by, is a devilish clever thing, – and is sold at No. 3, on the right hand of the way, two doors from the printing-office, the corner of Ivy-lane, Paternoster-row, price only one shilling!'

SNEER: Very ingenious indeed!

PUFF: But the PUFF COLLUSIVE is the newest of any; for it acts in the disguise of determined hostility. – It is much used by bold booksellers and enterprising poets. – An indignant correspondent observes – that the new poem called *Beelzebub's Cotillion*, or *Proserpine's Fête Champêtre*, is one of the most unjustifiable performances he ever read! The severity with which certain characters are handled is quite shocking! And as there are many descriptions in it too warmly coloured for female delicacy, the shameful avidity with which this piece is bought by all people of fashion, is a reproach on the taste of the times, and a disgrace to the delicacy of the age! – Here you see the two strongest inducements are held forth; – First, that nobody ought to read it; – and secondly, that everybody buys it; on the strength of which, the publisher boldly prints the tenth edition, before he had sold ten of the first; and then establishes it by threatening himself with the pillory, or absolutely indicting himself for Scan. Mag.![23]

DANGLE: Ha! ha! ha! – 'gad I know it is so.

PUFF: As to the PUFF OBLIQUE, or PUFF BY IMPLICATION, it is too various and extensive to be illustrated by an instance; – it attracts in titles, and presumes in patents; it lurks in the *limitation* of a subscription, and invites in the assurance of crowd and incommodation at public places; it delights to draw forth concealed merit, with a most disinterested assiduity; and sometimes wears a countenance of smiling censure and tender reproach. – It has a wonderful memory for Parliamentary debates, and will often give the whole speech of a favoured member, with the most flattering accuracy. But, above all, it is a great dealer in reports and suppositions. – It has the earliest intelligence of intended preferments that will reflect honour on the patrons; and embryo promotions of modest gentlemen – who know nothing of the matter themselves. It can hint a riband for implied services, in the air of a common report; and with the carelessness of a casual paragraph, suggest officers into commands – to which they have no pretension but their wishes. This, sir, is the last principal class in the ART OF PUFFING – An art which I hope you will now agree with me, is of the highest dignity – yielding a tablature of benevolence and public spirit; befriending equally trade, gallantry, criticism, and politics: the applause of genius! the register of charity! the triumph of heroism! the self defence of contractors! the fame of orators! – and the gazette of ministers!

SNEER: Sir, I am completely a convert both to the importance and ingenuity of your profession; and now, sir, there is but one thing which can possibly increase my respect for you, and that is, your permitting me to be present this morning at the rehearsal of your new trage–

23. *Scan. Mag.*: scandalum magnatum, defamation of somebody holding high office.

PUFF: – Hush, for heaven's sake. – *My* tragedy! – Egad, Dangle, I take this very ill – you know how apprehensive I am of being known to be the author.

DANGLE: I'faith I would not have told – but it's in the papers, and your name at length – in the *Morning Chronicle*.

PUFF: Ah! those damned editors never can keep a secret! – Well, Mr Sneer – no doubt you will do me great honour – I shall be infinitely happy – highly flattered –

DANGLE: I believe it must be near the time – shall we go together.

PUFF: No; it will not be yet this hour, for they are always late at that theatre: besides, I must meet you there, for I have some little matters here to send to the papers, and a few paragraphs to scribble before I go.

[*Looking at memorandums.*]

– Here is 'a Conscientious Baker, on the Subject of the Army Bread;' and 'a Detester of Visible Brickwork, in favour of the new invented Stucco;' both in the style of Junius,[24] and promised for tomorrow. – The Thames navigation too is at a stand. – Misomud or Anti-shoal must go to work again directly. – Here too are some political memorandums I see; aye – To take Paul Jones,[25] and get the Indiamen out of the Shannon – reinforce Byron[26] – compel the Dutch to – so! – I must do that in the evening papers, or reserve it for the *Morning Herald*, for I know that I have undertaken tomorrow, besides, to establish the unanimity of the fleet in the *Public Advertiser*, and to shoot Charles Fox[27] in the *Morning Post*. – So, egad, I ha'n't a moment to lose!

DANGLE: Well! – we'll meet in the green room.[28]

[*Exeunt severally.*]

---

24. *Junius*: the pen-name of (probably) Sir Philip Francis (1740–1818), whose letters, critical of George III and his ministers, were published in the *Public Advertiser* between 1769 and 1772.

25. *Paul Jones*: John Paul Jones (1747–92), privateer.

26. *Byron*: John Byron, commander of the West Indies fleet.

27. *Charles Fox*: Charles James Fox (1749–1806), politician.

28. *green room*: backstage assembly room.

ACT II

Scene i

The Theatre

[*Enter* DANGLE, PUFF, *and* SNEER, *as before the curtain.*]

PUFF: No, no, sir; what Shakespeare says of actors may be better applied to the purpose of plays; *they* ought to be 'the abstract and brief chronicles of the times.' Therefore when history, and particularly the history of our own country, furnishes anything like a case in point, to the time in which an author writes, if he knows his own interest, he will take advantage of it; so, sir, I call my tragedy *The Spanish Armada*; and have laid the scene before Tilbury Fort.

SNEER: A most happy thought certainly!

DANGLE: Egad it was – I told you so. – But pray now I don't understand how you have contrived to introduce any love into it.

PUFF: Love! – Oh nothing so easy; for it is a received point among poets, that where history gives you a good heroic outline for a play, you may fill up with a little love at your own discretion; in doing which, nine times out of ten, you only make up a deficiency in the private history of the times. – Now I rather think I have done this with some success.

SNEER: No scandal about Queen Elizabeth, I hope?

PUFF: O lud! no, no. – I only suppose the Governor of Tilbury Fort's daughter to be in love with the son of the Spanish Admiral.

SNEER: Oh, is that all?

DANGLE: Excellent, i'faith! – I see it at once. – But won't this appear rather improbable?

PUFF: To be sure it will – but what the plague! a play is not to shew occurrences that happen every day, but things just so strange, that though they never *did*, they *might* happen.

SNEER: Certainly nothing is unnatural, that is not physically impossible.

PUFF: Very true – and for that matter Don Ferolo Whiskerandos – for that's the lover's name, might have been over here in the train of the Spanish Ambassador; or Tilburina, for that is the lady's name, might have been in love with him, from having heard his character, or seen his picture; or from knowing that he was the last man in the world she ought to be in love with – or for any other good female reason. – However, sir, the fact is, that though she is but a Knight's daughter, egad! she is in love like any Princess!

DANGLE: Poor young lady! I feel for her already! for I can conceive how great the conflict must be between her passion and her duty; her love for her country, and her love for Don Ferolo Whiskerandos!

PUFF: Oh amazing! – her poor susceptible heart is swayed to and fro, by contending passions like –

[*Enter* UNDER PROMPTER.]

UNDER PROMPTER: Sir, the scene is set, and everything is ready to begin if you please. –

PUFF: Egad; then we'll lose no time.

UNDER PROMPTER: Though I believe, sir, you will find it very short, for all the performers have profited by the kind permission you granted them.

PUFF: Hey! what!

UNDER PROMPTER: You know, sir, you gave them leave to cut out or omit whatever they found heavy or unnecessary to the plot, and I must own they have taken very liberal advantage of your indulgence.

PUFF: Well, well. – They are in general very good judges; and I know I am luxuriant. – Now, Mr Hopkins,[1] as soon as you please.

UNDER PROMPTER [*to the music*]: Gentlemen, will you play a few bars of something, just to –

PUFF: Aye, that's right, – for as we have the scenes, and dresses, egad,

1. *Mr Hopkins*: William Hopkins, prompter at Drury Lane Theatre.

we'll go to't, as if it was the first night's performance; – but you
need not mind stopping between the acts.

[*Exit* UNDER PROMPTER.]

[*Orchestra play. Then the bell rings.*]

Soh! stand clear gentlemen. – Now you know there will be a cry of
down! – down! – hats off! silence! – Then up curtain, – and let us
see what our painters have done for us.

Scene ii

[*The curtain rises and discovers Tilbury Fort.*]

[*Two Sentinels asleep.*]

DANGLE: Tilbury Fort! – very fine indeed!

PUFF: Now, what do you think I open with?

SNEER: Faith, I can't guess –

PUFF: A clock. – Hark! – [*clock strikes.*] I open with a clock striking, to
beget an awful attention in the audience – it also marks the time,
which is four o'clock in the morning, and saves a description of the
rising sun, and a great deal about gilding the eastern hemisphere.

DANGLE: But pray, are the sentinels to be asleep?

PUFF: Fast as watchmen.

SNEER: Isn't that odd though at such an alarming crisis?

PUFF: To be sure it is, – but smaller things must give way to a striking
scene at the opening; that's a rule. – And the case is, that two great
men are coming to this very spot to begin the piece; now, it is not to
be supposed they would open their lips, if these fellows were
watching them, so, egad, I must either have sent them off their
posts, or set them asleep.

SNEER: O that accounts for it! – But tell us, who are these coming? –

PUFF: These are they – Sir Walter Raleigh, and Sir Christopher
Hatton. – You'll know Sir Christopher, by his turning out his toes –
famous you know for his dancing. I like to preserve all the little
traits of character. – Now attend.

Enter SIR WALTER RALEIGH *and* SIR CHRISTOPHER HATTON.

SIR CHRISTOPHER:
True, gallant Raleigh! –

DANGLE: What, they had been talking before?

PUFF: Oh, yes; all the way as they came along. – [*To the actors*] I beg pardon gentlemen but these are particular friends of mine, whose remarks may be of great service to us. [*To* SNEER *and* DANGLE] Don't mind interrupting them whenever anything strikes you.

SIR CHRISTOPHER:
                    True, gallant Raleigh!
But O, thou champion of thy country's fame,
There *is* a question which I yet must ask;
A question, which I never asked before –
What mean these mighty armaments?
This general muster? and this throng of chiefs?

SNEER: Pray, Mr Puff, how came Sir Christopher Hatton never to ask that question before?

PUFF: What, before the play began? How the plague could he?

DANGLE: That's true i'faith!

PUFF: But you will hear what he thinks of the matter.

SIR CHRISTOPHER:
Alas, my noble friend, when I behold
Yon tented plains in martial symmetry
Arrayed. – When I count o'er yon glittering lines
Of crested warriors, where the proud steeds neigh,
And valour-breathing trumpet's shrill appeal,
Responsive vibrate on my list'ning ear;
When virgin majesty herself I view,
Like her protecting Pallas veiled in steel,
With graceful confidence exhort to arms!
When briefly all I hear or see bears stamp
Of martial vigilance, and stern defence,
I cannot but surmise. – Forgive, my friend,
If the conjecture's rash – I cannot but
Surmise. – The state some danger apprehends!

SNEER: A very cautious conjecture that.

PUFF: Yes, that's his character; not to give an opinion, but on secure grounds – now then.

SIR WALTER:
O, most accomplished Christopher. –

PUFF: He calls him by his Christian name, to show that they are on the most familiar terms.

SIR WALTER:
O most accomplished Christopher, I find
Thy staunch sagacity still tracks the future,
In the fresh print of the o'ertaken past.

PUFF: Figurative!

SIR WALTER:
Thy fears are just.

SIR CHRISTOPHER:
But where? whence? when? and what
The danger is – Methinks I fain would learn.

SIR WALTER:
You know, my friend, scarce two revolving suns,
And three revolving moons, have closed their course,
Since haughty Philip,[2] in despite of peace,
With hostile hand hath struck at England's trade.

SIR CHRISTOPHER:
I know it well.

SIR WALTER:
Philip you know is proud, Iberia's king!

SIR CHRISTOPHER:
He is.

SIR WALTER:
– His subjects in base bigotry
And Catholic oppression held, – while we
You know, the Protestant persuasion hold.

SIR CHRISTOPHER:
We do.

SIR WALTER.
You know beside, – his boasted armament,

2. *Philip*: Philip II, King of Spain.

The famed Armada, – by the Pope baptized,
With purpose to invade these realms –

SIR CHRISTOPHER:
– Is sailed,
Our last advices so report.

SIR WALTER:
While the Iberian Admiral's chief hope,
His darling son –

SIR CHRISTOPHER:
– Ferolo Whiskerandos hight –

SIR WALTER:
The same – by chance a pris'ner hath been ta'en,
And in this fort of Tilbury –

SIR CHRISTOPHER:
– Is now
Confined, – 'tis true, and oft from yon tall turret's top
I've marked the youthful Spaniard's haughty mien
Unconquered, though in chains!

SIR WALTER:
You also know –

DANGLE: Mr Puff, as he *knows* all this, why does Sir Walter go on
telling him?

PUFF: But the audience are not supposed to know anything of the
matter, are they?

SNEER: True, but I think you manage ill: for there certainly appears
no reason why Sir Walter should be so communicative.

PUFF: 'Fore Gad now, that is one of the most ungrateful observations
I ever heard – for the less inducement he has to tell all this, the
more I think, you ought to be obliged to him; for I am sure you'd
know nothing of the matter without it.

DANGLE: That's very true, upon my word.

PUFF: But you will find he was *not* going on.

SIR CHRISTOPHER:
Enough, enough, – 'tis plain – and I no more
Am in amazement lost! –

PUFF: Here, now you see, Sir Christopher did not in fact ask any one question for his own information.

SNEER: No indeed: – his has been a most disinterested curiosity!

DANGLE: Really, I find we are very much obliged to them both.

PUFF: To be sure you are. Now then for the Commander in Chief, the Earl of Leicester! who, you know, was no favourite but of the Queen's. – We left off – 'in amazement lost!' –

SIR CHRISTOPHER:
                    Am in amazement lost. –
But, see where noble Leicester comes! supreme
In honours and command.

SIR WALTER:
                    And yet methinks,
At such a time, so perilous, so feared,
That staff might well become an abler grasp.

SIR CHRISTOPHER:
And so by heaven! think I; but soft, he's here!

PUFF: Aye, they envy him.

SNEER: But who are these with him?

PUFF: Oh, very valiant knights; one is the Governor of the fort, the other the Master of the horse. – And now, I think you shall hear some better language: I was obliged to be plain and intelligible in the first scene, because there was so much matter of fact in it; but now, i'faith, you have trope, figure, and metaphor, as plenty as noun-substantives.

Enter EARL OF LEICESTER, THE GOVERNOR, *and others.*

LEICESTER:
How's this my friends! is't thus your new fledged zeal
And plumed valour moults in roosted sloth?
Why dimly glimmers that heroic flame,
Whose red'ning blaze by patriot spirit fed,
Should be the beacon of a kindling realm?
Can the quick current of a patriot heart,
Thus stagnate in a cold and weedy converse,
Or freeze in tideless inactivity?
No! rather let the fountain of your valour
Spring through each stream of enterprise,

> Each petty channel of conducive daring,
> Till the full torrent of your foaming wrath
> O'erwhelm the flats of sunk hostility!

PUFF: There it is, – followed up!

SIR WALTER:
> No more! the fresh'ning breath of thy rebuke
> Hath filled the swelling canvas of our souls!
> And thus, though fate should cut the cable of   *[All take hands.]*
> Our topmost hopes, in friendship's closing line
> We'll grapple with despair, and if we fall,
> We'll fall in Glory's wake!

EARL OF LEICESTER:
> There spoke Old England's genius!
> Then, are we all resolved?

ALL:
> We are – all resolved.

EARL OF LEICESTER:
> To conquer – or be free?

ALL:
> To conquer, or be free.

EARL OF LEICESTER:
> All?

ALL:
> All.

DANGLE: *Nem. con.*[3] egad!

PUFF: Oh yes, where they *do* agree on the stage, their unanimity is wonderful!

EARL OF LEICESTER:
> Then, let's embrace – and now –

SNEER: What the plague, is he going to pray?

PUFF: Yes, hush! – in great emergencies, there is nothing like a prayer!

EARL OF LEICESTER:
> O mighty Mars!

3. *Nem. con.*: *nemine contradicente*, without opposition.

DANGLE: But why should he pray to *Mars*?

PUFF: Hush!

> EARL OF LEICESTER:
>
>   If in thy homage bred,
> Each point of discipline I've still observed;
> Nor but by due promotion, and the right
> Of service, to the rank of Major-General
> Have risen; assist thy votary now!

> GOVERNOR:
>
> Yet do not rise, – hear me!

> MASTER OF HORSE:
>
> And me!

> KNIGHT:
>
> And me!

> SIR WALTER:
>
> And me!

> SIR CHRISTOPHER:
>
> And me!

PUFF: Now, pray all together.

> ALL:
>
> Behold thy votaries submissive beg,
> That thou will deign to grant them all they ask;
> Assist them to accomplish all their ends,
> And sanctify whatever means they use
> To gain them!

SNEER: A very orthodox quintetto!

PUFF: Vastly well, gentlemen. – Is that well managed or not? Have you such a prayer as that on the stage?

SNEER: Not exactly.

> [EARL OF LEICESTER *to* PUFF.]
>
> But, sir, you haven't settled how we are to get off here.

PUFF: You could not go off kneeling, could you?

> [SIR WALTER *to* PUFF.]
>
> Oh no, sir! impossible!

PUFF: It would have a good effect i'faith, if you could! exeunt praying! – Yes, and would vary the established mode of springing off with a glance at the pit.

SNEER: Oh never mind, so as you get them off, I'll answer for it the audience won't care how.

PUFF: Well then, repeat the last line standing, and go off the old way.

ALL:
And sanctify whatever means we use to gain them.   [*Exeunt.*]

DANGLE: Bravo! a fine exit.

SNEER: Well, really Mr Puff. –

PUFF: Stay a moment. –

THE SENTINELS *get up.*

1ST SENTINEL:
All this shall to Lord Burleigh's ear.

2ND SENTINEL:
'Tis meet it should.   [*Exeunt* SENTINELS.]

DANGLE: Hey! – why, I thought those fellows had been asleep?

PUFF: Only a pretence, there's the art of it; they were spies of Lord Burleigh's.

SNEER: But isn't it odd, they were never taken notice of, not even by the commander in chief.

PUFF: Oh lud, sir, if people who want to listen, or overhear, were not always connived at in a tragedy, there would be no carrying on any plot in the world.

DANGLE: That's certain!

PUFF: But take care, my dear Dangle, the morning gun is going to fire.

     [*Cannon fires.*]

DANGLE: Well, that will have a fine effect.

PUFF: I think so, and helps to realize the scene. –

     [*Cannon twice.*]

What the plague! – *three* morning guns! – there never is but one! – aye, this is always the way at the theatre – give these fellows a good thing, and they never know when to have done with it. You have no more cannon to fire?

PROMPTER [*from within*]: No sir.

PUFF: Now then, for soft music.

SNEER: Pray what's that for?

PUFF: It shows that Tilburina is coming; nothing introduces you a heroine like soft music. – Here she comes.

DANGLE: And her confidante, I suppose?

PUFF: To be sure: here they are – inconsolable to the minuet in *Ariadne*![4]

[*Soft music.*]

Enter TILBURINA *and* CONFIDANTE.

TILBURINA:

Now has the whispering breath of gentle morn,
Bade Nature's voice, and Nature's beauty rise;
While orient Phoebus with unborrowed hues,
Clothes the waked loveliness which all night slept
In heavenly drapery! Darkness is fled.
Now flowers unfold their beauties to the sun,
And blushing, kiss the beam he sends to wake them,
The striped carnation, and the guarded rose,
The vulgar wallflower, and smart gillyflower,
The polyanthus mean – the dapper daisy,
Sweet William, and sweet marjoram, – and all
The tribe of single and of double pinks!
Now too, the feathered warblers tune their notes
Around, and charm the list'ning grove. – The lark!
The linnet! chaffinch! bullfinch! goldfinch! greenfinch!
– But O to me, no joy can they afford!
Nor rose, nor wallflower, nor smart gillyflower,
Nor polyanthus mean, nor dapper daisy,
Nor William sweet, nor marjoram – nor lark,
Linnet, nor all the finches of the grove!

PUFF: Your white handkerchief madam –

TILBURINA: I thought, sir, I wasn't to use that till, 'heart rending woe'.

PUFF: Oh yes madam – at 'the finches of the grove', if you please.

---

4. *Ariadne*: Handel's *Ariadne in Crete* (1734).

TILBURINA:
Nor lark,
Linnet, nor all the finches of the grove! [*Weeps.*]

PUFF: Vastly well madam!
DANGLE: Vastly well indeed!

TILBURINA:
For, O too sure, heart rending woe is now
The lot of wretched Tilburina!

DANGLE: Oh! – 'tis too much.
SNEER: Oh! – it is indeed.

CONFIDANTE:
Be comforted sweet lady – for who knows,
But Heaven has yet some milk-white day in store.

TILBURINA:
Alas, my gentle Nora,
Thy tender youth, as yet hath never mourned
Love's fatal dart. – Else wouldst thou know, that when
The soul is sunk in comfortless despair,
It cannot taste of merriment!

DANGLE: That's certain.

CONFIDANTE:
But see where your stern father comes;
It is not meet that he should find you thus.

PUFF: Hey, what the plague! – what a cut is here! – why, what is
become of the description of her first meeting with Don Whiskerandos? His gallant behaviour in the sea fight, and the simile of the
canary bird?
TILBURINA: Indeed sir, you'll find they will not be missed.
PUFF: Very well. – Very well!
TILBURINA: The cue ma'am if you please.

CONFIDANTE:
It is not meet that he should find you thus.

TILBURINA:
Thou counsel'st right, but 'tis no easy task
For barefaced grief to wear a mask of joy.

Enter GOVERNOR.

How's this – in tears? – O Tilburina, shame!
Is this a time for maudling tenderness,
And Cupid's baby woes? – hast thou not heard
That haughty Spain's Pope-consecrated fleet
Advances to our shores, while England's fate,
Like a clipped guinea, trembles in the scale!

TILBURINA:

Then, is the crisis of *my* fate at hand!
I see the fleets approach – I see –

PUFF: Now, pray gentlemen mind. – This is one of the most useful figures we tragedy writers have, by which a hero or heroine, in consideration of their being often obliged to overlook things that *are* on the stage, is allowed to hear and see a number of things that are not.

SNEER: Yes – a kind of poetical second-sight!

PUFF: Yes – now then madam.

TILBURINA:

I see their decks
Are cleared! – I see the signal made!
The line is formed! – a cable's length asunder!
I see the frigates stationed in the rear;
And now, I hear the thunder of the guns!
I hear the victor's shouts – I also hear
The vanquished groan! – and now 'tis smoke – and now
I see the loose sails shiver in the wind!
I see – I see – what soon you'll see –

GOVERNOR:

Hold daughter! peace! this love hath turned thy brain:
The Spanish fleet thou *canst* not see – because
– It is not yet in sight!

DANGLE: Egad though, the governor seems to make no allowance for this poetical figure you talk of.

PUFF: No, a plain matter-of-fact man – that's his character.

TILBURINA:

But will you then refuse his offer?

GOVERNOR:
I must – I will – I can – I ought – I do.

TILBURINA:
Think what a noble price. –

GOVERNOR:
No more – you urge in vain.

TILBURINA:
His liberty is all he asks.

SNEER: All *who* asks Mr Puff? Who is –

PUFF: Egad sir, I can't tell. – Here has been such cutting and slashing, I don't know where they have got to myself.

TILBURINA: Indeed sir, you will find it will connect very well.

– And your reward secure.

PUFF: O, – if they hadn't been so devilish free with their cutting here, you would have found that Don Whiskerandos has been tampering for his liberty, and has persuaded Tilburina to make this proposal to her father – and now pray observe the conciseness with which the argument is conducted. Egad, the *pro* and *con* goes as smart as hits in a fencing match. It is indeed a sort of small-sword logic, which we have borrowed from the French.

TILBURINA:
A retreat in Spain!

GOVERNOR:
Outlawry here!

TILBURINA:
Your daughter's prayer!

GOVERNOR:
Your father's oath!

TILBURINA:
My lover!

GOVERNOR:
My country!

TILBURINA:
Tilburina!

GOVERNOR:
 England!

TILBURINA:
 A title!

GOVERNOR:
 Honour!

TILBURINA:
 A pension!

GOVERNOR:
 Conscience!

TILBURINA:
 A thousand pounds!

GOVERNOR:
 Hah! thou hast touched me nearly!

PUFF: There you see – she threw in *Tilburina*, quick, parry cart with *England!* – Hah! thrust in tierce a title! – parried by honour. – Hah! a pension over the arm! – put by by conscience. – Then flankonade[5] with a thousand pounds – and a palpable hit egad!

TILBURINA:
 Canst thou –
 Reject the *suppliant*, and the *daughter* too?

GOVERNOR:
 No more; I would not hear thee plead in vain,
 The *father* softens – but the *governor*
 Is fixed!   [*Exit.*]

DANGLE: Aye, that antithesis of persons – is a most established figure.

TILBURINA:
 'Tis well, – hence then fond hopes, – fond passion hence;
 Duty, behold I am all over thine –

WHISKERANDOS [*without*]:
 Where is my love – my –

TILBURINA:
 Ha!

5. *parry cart . . . thrust in tierce . . . flankonade*: fencing terms.

WHISKERANDOS [*entering*]:
My beauteous enemy –

PUFF: Oh dear ma'am, you must start a great deal more than that; consider you had just determined in favour of duty – when in a moment the sound of his voice revives your passion, – overthrows your resolution, destroys your obedience. – If you don't express all that in your start – you do nothing at all.

TILBURINA: Well, we'll try again!

DANGLE: Speaking from within, has always a fine effect.

SNEER: Very.

WHISKERANDOS:
My conquering Tilburina! How! is't thus
We meet? Why are thy looks averse! What means
That falling tear – that frown of boding woe?
Hah! now indeed I am a prisoner!
Yes, now I feel the galling weight of these
Disgraceful chains – which, cruel Tilburina!
Thy doting captive gloried in before. –
But thou art false, and Whiskerandos is undone!

TILBURINA:
O no; how little dost thou know thy Tilburina!

WHISKERANDOS:
Art thou then true? Begone cares, doubts and fears,
I make you all a present to the winds;
And if the winds reject you – try the waves.

PUFF: The wind you know, is the established receiver of all stolen sighs, and cast off griefs and apprehensions.

TILBURINA:
Yet must we part? – stern duty seals our doom:
Though here I call yon conscious clouds to witness,
Could I pursue the bias of my soul,
All friends, all right of parents I'd disclaim,
And thou, my Whiskerandos, should'st be father
And mother, brother, cousin, uncle, aunt,
And friend to me!

WHISKERANDOS:
O matchless excellence! – and must we part?
Well, if – we must – we must – and in that case,
The less is said the better.

PUFF: Hey day! here's a cut! – What, are all the mutual protestations out?

TILBURINA: Now, pray sir, don't interrupt us just here, you ruin our feelings.

PUFF: *Your* feelings! – but zounds, *my* feelings, ma'am!

SNEER: No; pray don't interrupt them.

WHISKERANDOS:
One last embrace. –

TILBURINA:
Now, – farewell, for ever.

WHISKERANDOS:
For ever!

TILBURINA:
Aye, for ever. [*Going.*]

PUFF: 'Sdeath and fury! – Gadslife! Sir! Madam! if you go out without the parting look, you might as well dance out – Here, here!

CONFIDANTE: But pray sir, how am *I* to get off here?

PUFF: *You*, pshaw! what the devil signifies how *you* get off! edge away at the top, or where you will – [*Pushes the confidante off.*] Now ma'am you see –

TILBURINA: We understand you sir.

Aye for ever.

BOTH:
Ohh! – [*Turning back and exeunt.*]
[*Scene closes.*]

DANGLE: O charming!

PUFF: Hey! – 'tis pretty well I believe – you see I don't attempt to strike out anything new – but I take it I improve on the established modes.

SNEER: You do indeed. – But pray is not Queen Elizabeth to appear?

PUFF: No not once – but she is to be talked of for ever; so that egad you'll think a hundred times that she is on the point of coming in.

SNEER: Hang it, I think it's a pity to keep *her* in the green room all the night.

PUFF: Oh no, that always has a fine effect – it keeps up expectation.

DANGLE: But are we not to have a battle?

PUFF: Yes, yes, you will have a battle at last, but, egad, it's not to be by land – but by sea – and that is the only quite new thing in the piece.

DANGLE: What, Drake at the Armada, hey?

PUFF: Yes, i'faith – fire ships and all – then we shall end with the procession. – Hey! that will do I think.

SNEER: No doubt on't.

PUFF: Come, we must not lose time – so now for the under plot.

SNEER: What the plague, have you another plot?

PUFF: Oh lord, yes – ever while you live, have two plots to your tragedy. – The grand point in managing them, is only to let your under plot have as little connection with your main plot as possible. – I flatter myself nothing can be more distinct than mine, for as in my chief plot, the characters are all great people – I have laid my under plot in low life – and as the former is to end in deep distress, I make the other end as happy as a farce. – Now Mr Hopkins, as soon as you please.

[*Enter* UNDER PROMPTER.]

UNDER PROMPTER: Sir, the carpenter says it is impossible you can go to the Park scene yet.

PUFF: The Park scene! No – I mean the description scene here, in the wood.

UNDER PROMPTER: Sir, the performers have cut it out.

PUFF: Cut it out!

UNDER PROMPTER: Yes sir.

PUFF: What! the whole account of Queen Elizabeth?

UNDER PROMPTER: Yes sir.

PUFF: And the description of her horse and side-saddle?

UNDER PROMPTER: Yes sir.

PUFF: So, so, this is very fine indeed! Mr Hopkins, how the plague could you suffer this?

HOPKINS [*from within*]: Sir, indeed the pruning knife –

PUFF: The pruning knife – zounds the axe! why, here has been such lopping and topping, I shan't have the bare trunk of my play left presently. – Very well, sir – the performers must do as they please, but upon my soul, I'll print it every word.

SNEER: That I would indeed.

PUFF: Very well – sir – then we must go on – zounds! I would not have parted with the description of the horse! – Well, sir, go on – sir, it was one of the finest and most laboured things – Very well, sir, let them go on – there you had him and his accoutrements from the bit to the crupper – very well, sir, we must go to the Park scene.

UNDER PROMPTER: Sir, there is the point, the carpenters say, that unless there is some business put in here before the drop, they shan't have time to clear away the fort, or sink Gravesend and the river.

PUFF: So! this is a pretty dilemma truly! – Gentlemen – you must excuse me, these fellows will never be ready, unless I go and look after them myself.

SNEER: Oh dear sir – these little things will happen –

PUFF: To cut out this scene! – but I'll print it – egad, I'll print it every word!

[*Exeunt.*]

ACT III

Scene i

Before the curtain.

[*Enter* PUFF, SNEER, *and* DANGLE.]

PUFF: Well, we are ready – now then for the justices.
[*Curtain rises; Justices, Constables, etc. discovered.*]

SNEER: This, I suppose, is a sort of senate scene.

PUFF: To be sure – there has not been one yet.

DANGLE: It is the under plot, isn't it?

PUFF: Yes. What, gentlemen, do you mean to go at once to the discovery scene?

JUSTICE: If you please, sir.

PUFF: Oh very well – harkee, I don't choose to say anything more, but i'faith, they have mangled my play in a most shocking manner!

DANGLE: It's a great pity!

PUFF: Now then, Mr Justice, if you please.

JUSTICE:
Are all the volunteers without?

CONSTABLE:
They are.
Some ten in fetters, and some twenty drunk.

JUSTICE:
Attends the youth, whose most opprobrious fame
And clear convicted crimes have stamped him soldier?

CONSTABLE:
He waits your pleasure; eager to repay
The blest reprieve that sends him to the fields

Of glory, there to raise his branded hand
In honour's cause.

JUSTICE:
'Tis well – 'tis Justice arms him!
O! may he now defend his country's laws
With half the spirit he has broke them all!
If 'tis your worship's pleasure, bid him enter.

CONSTABLE:
I fly, the herald of your will. [*Exit* CONSTABLE.]

PUFF: Quick, sir! –

SNEER: But, Mr Puff, I think not only the Justice, but the clown seems
to talk in as high a style as the first hero among them.

PUFF: Heaven forbid they should not in a free country! – Sir, I am not
for making slavish distinctions, and giving all the fine language to
the upper sort of people.

DANGLE: That's very noble in you indeed.

[*Enter* JUSTICE'S LADY.]

PUFF: Now pray mark this scene.

LADY:
Forgive this interruption, good my love;
But as I just now passed, a pris'ner youth
Whom rude hands hither led, strange bodings seized
My fluttering heart, and to myself I said,
An if our Tom had lived, he'd surely been
This stripling's height!

JUSTICE:
Ha! sure some powerful sympathy directs
Us both –

Enter SON *and* CONSTABLE.

JUSTICE:
What is thy name?

SON:
My name's Tom Jenkins – *alias*, have I none –
Though orphaned, and without a friend!

JUSTICE:
Thy parents?

SON:
My father dwelt in Rochester – and was,
As I have heard – a fishmonger – no more.

PUFF: What, sir, do you leave out the account of your birth, parentage
and education?

SON: They have settled it so, sir, here.

PUFF: Oh! oh!

LADY:
How loudly nature whispers to my heart!
Had he no other name?

SON:
I've seen a bill
Of his, signed *Tomkins*, creditor.

JUSTICE:
This does indeed confirm each circumstance
The gypsy told! – Prepare!

SON:
I do.

JUSTICE:
No orphan, nor without a friend art thou –
I am thy father, *here's* thy mother, *there*
Thy uncle – this thy first cousin, and those
Are all your near relations!

MOTHER:
O ecstasy of bliss!

SON:
O most unlooked for happiness!

JUSTICE:
O wonderful event!
[*They faint alternately in each others' arms.*]

PUFF: There, you see relationship, like murder, will out.

JUSTICE:
Now let's revive – else were this joy too much!
But come – and we'll unfold the rest within,
And thou my boy must needs want rest and food.
Hence may each orphan hope, as chance directs,
To find a father – where he least expects!   [*Exeunt.*]

PUFF: What do you think of that?

DANGLE: One of the finest discovery-scenes I ever saw. – Why, this under plot would have made a tragedy itself.

SNEER: Aye, or a comedy either.

PUFF: And keeps quite clear you see of the other.

[*Enter* SCENEMEN, *taking away the seats.*]

PUFF: The scene remains, does it?

SCENEMAN: Yes, sir.

PUFF: You are to leave one chair you know. – But it is always awkward in a tragedy, to have you fellows coming in in your playhouse liveries to remove things – I wish that could be managed better. – So now for my mysterious yeoman.

Enter A BEEFEATER.

BEEFEATER:
Perdition catch my soul but *I* do love thee.

SNEER: Haven't I heard that line before?

PUFF: No, I fancy not – where pray?

DANGLE: Yes, I think there is something like it in *Othello*.

PUFF: Gad! now you put me in mind on't, I believe there is – but that's of no consequence – all that can be said is, that two people happened to hit on the same thought – and Shakespeare made use of it first, that's all.

SNEER: Very true.

PUFF: Now, sir, your soliloquy – but speak more to the pit, if you please – the soliloquy always to the pit – that's a rule.

BEEFEATER:
Though hopeless love finds comfort in despair,
It never can endure a rival's bliss!
But soft – I am observed.   [*Exit* BEEFEATER.]

DANGLE: That's a very short soliloquy.

PUFF: Yes – but it would have been a great deal longer if he had not been observed.

SNEER: A most sentimental Beefeater that, Mr Puff.

PUFF: Hark'ee – I would not have you be too sure that he *is* a Beefeater.

SNEER: What! a hero in disguise?

PUFF: No matter – I only give you a hint. – But now for my principal character – here he comes – Lord Burleigh in person! Pray, gentlemen, step this way – softly – I only hope the Lord High Treasurer is perfect – if he is but perfect!

[*Enter* BURLEIGH, *goes slowly to a chair and sits.*]

SNEER: Mr Puff!

PUFF: Hush! – vastly well, sir! vastly well! a most interesting gravity!

DANGLE: What, isn't he to speak at all?

PUFF: Egad, I thought you'd ask me that – yes it is a very likely thing – that a Minister in his situation, with the whole affairs of the nation on his head, should have time to talk! – but hush! or you'll put him out.

SNEER: Put him out! How the plague can that be, if he's not going to say anything?

PUFF: There's a reason! – why, his part is to *think*, and how the plague! do you imagine he can *think* if you keep talking?

DANGLE: That's very true upon my word!

[BURLEIGH *comes forward, shakes his head and exit.*]

SNEER: He is very perfect indeed. – Now, pray what did he mean by that?

PUFF: You don't take it?

SNEER: No; I don't upon my soul.

PUFF: Why, by that shake of the head, he gave you to understand that even though they had more justice in their cause and wisdom in their measures – yet, if there was not a greater spirit shown on the part of the people – the country would at last fall a sacrifice to the hostile ambition of the Spanish monarchy.

SNEER: The devil! – did he mean all that by shaking his head?

PUFF: Every word of it – if he shook his head as I taught him.

DANGLE: Ah! there certainly is a vast deal to be done on the stage by dumb show, and expression of face, and a judicious author knows how much he may trust to it.

SNEER: Oh, here are some of our old acquaintance.

Enter HATTON *and* RALEIGH.

SIR CHRISTOPHER:
My niece, and *your* niece too!

By heaven! there's witchcraft in't – He could not else
Have gained their hearts – But see where they approach;
Some horrid purpose low'ring on their brows!

SIR WALTER:
Let us withdraw and mark them. [*They withdraw.*]

SNEER: What is all this?

PUFF: Ah! here has been more pruning! – but the fact is, these two young ladies are also in love with Don Whiskerandos. – Now, gentlemen, this scene goes entirely for what we call SITUATION and STAGE EFFECT, by which the greatest applause may be obtained, without the assistance of language, sentiment or character: pray mark!

Enter the TWO NIECES.

1ST NIECE:
Ellena here!
She is his scorn as much as I – that is
Some comfort still.

PUFF: Oh dear madam, you are not to say that to her face! – *aside*, ma'am, *aside*. – The whole scene is to be *aside*.

1ST NIECE:
She is his scorn as much as I – that is
Some comfort still!   [*Aside.*]

2ND NIECE:
I know he prizes not Pollina's love,
But Tilburina lords it o'er his heart.   [*Aside.*]

1ST NIECE:
But see the proud destroyer of my peace.
Revenge is all the good I've left.   [*Aside.*]

2ND NIECE:
He comes, the false disturber of my quiet.
Now vengeance do thy worst –   [*Aside.*]

Enter WHISKERANDOS.
O hateful liberty – if thus in vain
I seek my Tilburina!

BOTH NIECES:
And ever shalt!

SIR CHRISTOPHER AND SIR WALTER *come forward.*
Hold! we will avenge you.

WHISKERANDOS:
Hold *you* – or see your nieces bleed!

[*The two nieces draw their two daggers to strike* WHISKERANDOS, *the two uncles at the instant with their two swords drawn, catch their two nieces' arms, and turn the points of their swords to* WHISKERANDOS, *who immediately draws two daggers, and holds them to the two nieces' bosoms.*]

PUFF: There's situation for you! – there's an heroic group! – You see the ladies can't stab Whiskerandos – he durst not strike them for fear of their uncles – the uncles durst not kill him, because of their nieces – I have them all at a dead lock! – for every one of them is afraid to let go first.

SNEER: Why, then they must stand there for ever.

PUFF: So they would, if I hadn't a very fine contrivance for't. – Now mind –

Enter BEEFEATER *with his halberd.*
In the Queen's name I charge you all to drop
Your swords and daggers!
[*They drop their swords and daggers.*]

SNEER: That is a contrivance indeed.

PUFF: Aye – in the Queen's name.

SIR CHRISTOPHER:
Come niece!

SIR WALTER:
Come niece! [*Exeunt with the two nieces.*]

WHISKERANDOS:
What's he, who bids us thus renounce our guard?

BEEFEATER:
Thou must do more, renounce thy love!

WHISKERANDOS:
Thou liest – base Beefeater!

BEEFEATER:
Ha! Hell! the lie!
By heaven thou'st roused the lion in my heart!

Off yeoman's habit! – base disguise! – off! off!
> [*Discovers himself, by throwing off his upper dress,
> and appearing in a very fine waistcoat.*]

Am I a Beefeater now?
Or beams my crest as terrible as when
In Biscay's Bay I took thy captive sloop.

PUFF: There, egad! he comes out to be the very Captain of the privateer who had taken Whiskerandos prisoner – and was himself an old lover of Tilburina's.

DANGLE: Admirably managed indeed.

PUFF: Now, stand out of their way.

WHISKERANDOS:
I thank thee fortune! that hast thus bestowed
A weapon to chastise this insolent.   [*Takes up one of the swords.*]

BEEFEATER:
I take thy challenge, Spaniard, and I thank
Thee Fortune too! –   [*Takes up the other sword.*]

DANGLE: That's excellently contrived! – it seems as if the two uncles had left their swords on purpose for them.

PUFF: No, egad, they could not help leaving them.

WHISKERANDOS:
Vengeance and Tilburina!

BEEFEATER:
Exactly so –
> [*They fight – and after the usual number
> of wounds given,* WHISKERANDOS *falls.*]

WHISKERANDOS:
O cursed parry! – that last thrust in tierce
Was fatal – Captain, thou hast fenced well!
And Whiskerandos quits this bustling scene
For all eter–

BEEFEATER:
–nity – He would have added, but stern death
Cut short his being, and the noun at once!

PUFF: Oh, my dear sir, you are too slow, now mind me. – Sir, shall I trouble you to die again?

WHISKERANDOS:
And Whiskerandos quits this bustling scene
For all eter–

BEEFEATER:
–nity – He would have added –

PUFF: No, sir – that's not it – once more if you please –

WHISKERANDOS: I wish, sir – you would practise this without me – I can't stay dying here all night.

PUFF: Very well, we'll go over it by and by – I must humour these gentlemen!

[*Exit* WHISKERANDOS.]

BEEFEATER:
Farewell – brave Spaniard! and when next –

PUFF: Dear sir, you needn't speak that speech as the body has walked off.

BEEFEATER: That's true, sir – then I'll join the fleet.

[*Exit* BEEFEATER.]

PUFF: If you please.

Now, who comes on?

Enter GOVERNOR, *with his hair properly disordered.*

GOVERNOR:
A hemisphere of evil planets reign!
And every planet sheds contagious frenzy!
My Spanish prisoner is slain! my daughter,
Meeting the dead corse borne along – has gone
Distract!   [*A loud flourish of trumpets.*]
         But hark! I am summoned to the fort,
Perhaps the fleets have met! amazing crisis!
O Tilburina! from thy aged father's beard
Thou'st plucked the few brown hairs which time had left!

[*Exit* GOVERNOR.]

SNEER: Poor gentleman!

PUFF: Yes – and no one to blame but his daughter!

DANGLE: And the planets –

PUFF: True. – Now enter Tilburina! –

SNEER: Egad, the business comes on quick here.

PUFF: Yes, sir – now she comes in stark mad in white satin.

SNEER: Why in white satin?

PUFF: O Lord, sir – when a heroine goes mad, she always goes into white satin – don't she, Dangle?

DANGLE: Always – it's a rule.

PUFF: Yes – here it is – [*looking at the book*]: 'Enter Tilburina stark mad in white satin, and her confidante stark mad in white linen.'

[*Enter* TILBURINA *and* CONFIDANT *mad, according to custom.*]

SNEER: But what the deuce, is the confidante to be mad too?

PUFF: To be sure she is, the confidante is always to do whatever her mistress does; weep when she weeps, smile when she smiles, go mad when she goes mad. – Now madam confidante – but – keep your madness in the background, if you please.

TILBURINA:
    The wind whistles – the moon rises – see
    They have killed my squirrel in his cage!
    Is this a grasshopper! – Ha! no, it is my
    Whiskerandos – you shall not keep him –
    I know you have him in your pocket –
    An oyster may be crossed in love! – Who says
    A whale's a bird? – Ha! did you call, my love?
    – He's here! He's there! – He's everywhere!
    Ah me! He's nowhere!   [*Exit* TILBURINA.]

PUFF: There, do you ever desire to see anybody madder than that?

SNEER: Never while I live!

PUFF: You observed how she mangled the metre?

DANGLE: Yes – egad, it was the first thing made me suspect she was out of her senses.

SNEER: And pray what becomes of her?

PUFF: She is gone to throw herself into the sea to be sure – and that brings us at once to the scene of action, and so to my catastrophe – my sea-fight, I mean.

SNEER: What, you bring that in at last?

PUFF: Yes – yes – you know my play is called *The Spanish Armada*, otherwise, egad, I have no occasion for the battle at all. – Now then for my magnificence! – my battle! – my noise! – and my procession! – You are all ready?

PROMPTER [*within*]: Yes, sir.

PUFF: Is the Thames dressed?

[*Enter* THAMES *with two Attendants.*]

THAMES: Here I am, sir.

PUFF: Very well indeed. – See, gentlemen, there's a river for you! – This is blending a little of the masque with my tragedy – a new fancy you know – and very useful in my case; for as there must be a procession, I suppose Thames and all his tributary rivers to compliment Britannia with a fete in honour of the victory.

SNEER: But pray, who are these gentlemen in green with him.

PUFF: Those? – those are his banks.

SNEER: His banks?

PUFF: Yes, one crowned with alders and the other with a villa! – you take the allusions? – but hey! what the plague! you have got both your banks on one side – Here sir, come round – Ever while you live, Thames, go between your banks. [*Bell rings.*] – There, soh! now for't! – Stand aside my dear friends! – away Thames!

[*Exit* THAMES *between his banks.*]

[*Flourish of drums – trumpets – cannon, etc. etc. Scene changes to the sea – the fleets engage – the music plays 'Britons strike home'.*[1] *Spanish fleet destroyed by fire-ships, etc. – English fleet advances – music plays 'Rule Britannia'. – The procession of all the English rivers and their tributaries with their emblems, etc. begins with Handel's water music – ends with a chorus, to the march in* Judas Maccabeus.[2] *– During this scene, Puff directs and applauds everything – then*]

PUFF: Well, pretty well – but not quite perfect – so ladies and gentlemen, if you please, we'll rehearse this piece again to-morrow.

CURTAIN DROPS

FINIS

1. '*Britons strike home*': from *Bonduca* (1696, music by Henry Purcell), and incorporated into a revision of the original John Fletcher play (also called *Bonduca*) by George Colman the Elder in 1778.

2. *Judas Maccabeus*: oratorio by Handel.

The School for Scandal

PROLOGUE

A School for Scandal! Tell me, I beseech you,
Needs there a school this modish art to teach you?
No need of lesson now, the knowing think;
We might as well be taught to eat and drink.
Caused by a dearth of scandal, should the vapours
Distress our fair ones – let them read the papers.
Their powerful mixtures such disorders hit;
Crave what you will – there's *quantum sufficit.*[1]
'Lord!' cries my Lady Wormwood (who loves tattle,
And puts much salt and pepper in her prattle),
Just risen at noon, all night at cards when threshing
Strong tea and scandal – 'Bless me, how refreshing!
Give me the papers, Lisp – how bold and free! (*sips*)
Last night Lord L. (sips) *was caught with Lady D.*
For aching heads what charming sal volatile![2] (*sips*)
If Mrs B. will still continue flirting,
We hope she'll draw, *or we'll* undraw *the curtain.*
Fine satire, poz[3] – in public all abuse it,
But, by ourselves, (*sips*) our praise we can't refuse it.
Now, Lisp, read you – there; at that dash and star.'
'Yes, ma'am: *A certain lord had best beware,*
Who lives not twenty miles from Grosvenor Square;
For should he Lady W. find willing,
Wormwood is bitter' – 'Oh! that's me, the villain!
Throw it behind the fire and never more

1. *quantum sufficit*: appropriate quantity.
2. *sal volatile*: solution of ammonium carbonate used as a restorative.
3. *poz*: abbreviation of *positively*.

Let that vile paper come within my door.'
Thus at our friends we laugh, who feel the dart;
To reach our feelings, we ourselves must smart.
Is our young bard so young to think that he
Can stop the full spring-tide of calumny?
Knows he the world so little, and its trade?
Alas! the devil's sooner raised than laid.
So strong, so swift, the monster there's no gagging;
Cut Scandal's head off, still the tongue is wagging.
Proud of your smiles once lavishly bestowed,
Again our young Don Quixote takes the road;
To show his gratitude he draws his pen
And seeks this hydra, Scandal, in his den.
For your applause all perils he would through –
He'll fight – that's write – a cavalliero true,
Till every drop of blood – that's ink – is spilt for you.

DRAMATIS PERSONAE

Men

SIR PETER TEAZLE
SIR OLIVER SURFACE
JOSEPH SURFACE
CHARLES SURFACE
CRABTREE
SIR BENJAMIN BACKBITE
ROWLEY
MOSES
TRIP
SNAKE
CARELESS
SIR TOBY BUMPER

Women

LADY TEAZLE
MARIA
LADY SNEERWELL
MRS CANDOUR

ACT I

Scene i

LADY SNEERWELL's *house.*

[LADY SNEERWELL *at the dressing-table;* SNAKE *drinking chocolate.*]

LADY SNEERWELL: The paragraphs, you say, Mr Snake, were all inserted?

SNAKE: They were, madam, and as I copied them myself in a feigned hand, there can be no suspicion whence they came.

LADY SNEERWELL: Did you circulate the report of Lady Brittle's intrigue with Captain Boastall?

SNAKE: That's in as fine a train as your ladyship could wish. In the common course of things, I think it must reach Mrs Clackitt's ears within four and twenty hours; and then, you know, the business is as good as done.

LADY SNEERWELL: Why, truly, Mrs Clackitt has a very pretty talent, and a great deal of industry.

SNAKE: True, madam, and has been tolerably successful in her day. To my knowledge she has been the cause of six matches being broken off and three sons disinherited; of four forced elopements, and as many close confinements; nine separate maintenances, and two divorces. Nay, I have more than once traced her causing a *tête-à-tête*[1] in the *Town and Country Magazine,* when the parties

---

1. *tête-à-tête*: a scandalous story that formed a regular part of the *Town and Country Magazine.*

perhaps had never seen each other's face before in the course of their lives.

LADY SNEERWELL: She certainly has talents, but her manner is gross.

SNAKE: 'Tis very true. She generally designs well, has a free tongue, and a bold invention; but her colouring is too dark and her outlines often extravagant. She wants that delicacy of hint and mellowness of sneer which distinguishes your ladyship's scandal.

LADY SNEERWELL: You are partial, Snake.

SNAKE: Not in the least. Everybody allows that Lady Sneerwell can do more with a word or a look than many can with the most laboured detail, even when they happen to have a little truth on their side to support it.

LADY SNEERWELL: Yes, my dear Snake, and I am no hypocrite to deny the satisfaction I reap from the success of my efforts. Wounded myself in the early part of my life by the envenomed tongue of slander, I confess I have since known no pleasure equal to the reducing others to the level of my own injured reputation.

SNAKE: Nothing can be more natural. But, Lady Sneerwell, there is one affair in which you have lately employed me, wherein, I confess, I am at a loss to guess your motives.

LADY SNEERWELL: I conceive you mean with respect to my neighbour, Sir Peter Teazle, and his family?

SNAKE: I do. Here are two young men, to whom Sir Peter has acted as a kind of guardian since their father's death; the eldest possessing the most amiable character and universally well spoken of, the youngest the most dissipated and extravagant young fellow in the kingdom, without friends or character – the former an avowed admirer of your ladyship and apparently your favourite; the latter attached to Maria, Sir Peter's ward, and confessedly beloved by her. Now on the face of these circumstances, it is utterly unaccountable to me why you, the widow of a City knight with a good jointure, should not close with the passion of a man of such character and expectations as Mr Surface; and more so why you should be so uncommonly earnest to destroy the mutual attachment subsisting between his brother Charles and Maria.

LADY SNEERWELL: Then at once to unravel this mystery, I must inform you that love has no share whatever in the intercourse between Mr Surface and me.

SNAKE: No!

LADY SNEERWELL: His real attachment is to Maria, or her fortune. But finding in his brother a favoured rival, he has been obliged to mask his pretensions and profit by my assistance.

SNAKE: Yet still I am more puzzled why you should interest yourself in his success.

LADY SNEERWELL: How dull you are! Cannot you surmise the weakness which I hitherto through shame have concealed even from you? Must I confess that Charles, that libertine, that extravagant, that bankrupt in fortune and reputation, that he it is for whom I'm thus anxious and malicious, and to gain whom I would sacrifice everything?

SNAKE: Now, indeed, your conduct appears consistent; but how came you and Mr Surface so confidential?

LADY SNEERWELL: For our mutual interest. I have found him out a long time since. I know him to be artful, selfish, and malicious – in short, a sentimental[2] knave, while with Sir Peter, and indeed with all his acquaintance, he passes for a youthful miracle of prudence, good sense, and benevolence.

SNAKE: Yes, yet Sir Peter vows he has not his equal in England; and above all, he praises him as a man of sentiment.

LADY SNEERWELL: True; and with the assistance of his sentiment and hypocrisy he has brought Sir Peter entirely into his interest with regard to Maria, while poor Charles has no friend in the house, though I fear he has a powerful one in Maria's heart, against whom we must direct our schemes.

[*Enter* SERVANT.]

SERVANT: Mr Surface.

LADY SNEERWELL: Show him up.

[*Exit* SERVANT.]

He generally calls about this time. I don't wonder at people's giving him to me for a lover.

[*Enter* JOSEPH SURFACE.]

2. *sentimental*: given to aphoristic moral reflections.

JOSEPH: My dear Lady Sneerwell, how do you do today? Mr Snake, your most obedient.

LADY SNEERWELL: Snake has just been arraigning me on our mutual attachment; but I have informed him of our real views. You know how useful he has been to us, and, believe me, the confidence is not ill placed.

JOSEPH: Madam, it is impossible for me to suspect a man of Mr Snake's sensibility and discernment.

LADY SNEERWELL: Well, well, no compliments now; but tell me when you saw your mistress, Maria – or what is more material to me, your brother.

JOSEPH: I have not seen either since I left you; but I can inform you that they never meet. Some of your stories have taken a good effect on Maria.

LADY SNEERWELL: Ah, my dear Snake, the merit of this belongs to you. But do your brother's distresses increase?

JOSEPH: Every hour. I am told he has had another execution[3] in the house yesterday. In short, his dissipation and extravagance exceed anything I have ever heard of.

LADY SNEERWELL: Poor Charles!

JOSEPH: True, madam; notwithstanding his vices, one can't help feeling for him. Poor Charles! I'm sure I wish it were in my power to be of any essential service to him; for the man who does not share in the distresses of a brother, even though merited by his own misconduct, deserves –

LADY SNEERWELL: O lud, you are going to be moral and forget that you are among friends.

JOSEPH: Egad, that's true; I'll keep that sentiment till I see Sir Peter. However, it is certainly a charity to rescue Maria from such a libertine, who, if he is to be reclaimed, can be so only by a person of your ladyship's superior accomplishments and understanding.

SNAKE: I believe, Lady Sneerwell, here's company coming. I'll go and copy the letter I mentioned to you. Mr Surface, your most obedient.

---

3. *execution*: goods seized for non-payment of debt.

JOSEPH: Sir, your very devoted.

[*Exit* SNAKE.]

Lady Sneerwell, I am very sorry you have put any further confidence in that fellow.

LADY SNEERWELL: Why so?

JOSEPH: I have lately detected him in frequent conference with old Rowley, who was formerly my father's steward and has never, you know, been a friend of mine.

LADY SNEERWELL: And do you think he would betray us?

JOSEPH: Nothing more likely. Take my word for 't, Lady Sneerwell, that fellow hasn't virtue enough to be faithful even to his own villainy. Ah, Maria!

[*Enter* MARIA.]

LADY SNEERWELL: Maria, my dear, how do you do? What's the matter?

MARIA: Oh, there's that disagreeable lover of mine, Sir Benjamin Backbite, has just called at my guardian's with his odious uncle, Crabtree; so I slipped out and ran hither to avoid them.

LADY SNEERWELL: Is that all?

JOSEPH: If my brother Charles had been of the party, madam, perhaps you would not have been so much alarmed.

LADY SNEERWELL: Nay, now you are severe; for I dare swear the truth of the matter is, Maria heard you were here. But, my dear, what has Sir Benjamin done that you should avoid him so?

MARIA: Oh, he has done nothing; but 'tis for what he has said. His conversation is a perpetual libel on all his acquaintance.

JOSEPH: Aye, and the worst of it is, there is no advantage in not knowing him, for he'll abuse a stranger just as soon as his best friend; and his uncle's as bad.

LADY SNEERWELL: Nay, but we should make allowance. Sir Benjamin is a wit and a poet.

MARIA: For my part, I confess, madam, wit loses its respect with me when I see it in company with malice. What do you think, Mr Surface?

JOSEPH: Certainly, madam. To smile at the jest which plants a thorn in another's breast is to become a principal in the mischief.

LADY SNEERWELL: Pshaw, there's no possibility of being witty without a little ill nature. The malice of a good thing is the barb that makes it stick. What's your opinion, Mr Surface?

JOSEPH: To be sure, madam, that conversation where the spirit of raillery is suppressed will ever appear tedious and insipid.

MARIA: Well, I'll not debate how far scandal may be allowable; but in a man, I am sure, it is always contemptible. We have pride, envy, rivalship, and a thousand motives to depreciate each other; but the male slanderer must have the cowardice of a woman before he can traduce one.

[*Enter* SERVANT.]

SERVANT: Madam, Mrs Candour is below, and if your ladyship's at leisure, will leave her carriage.

LADY SNEERWELL: Beg her to walk in.

[*Exit* SERVANT.]

Now, Maria, here is a character to your taste, for though Mrs Candour is a little talkative, everybody allows her to be the best-natured and best sort of woman.

MARIA: Yes, with a very gross affectation of good nature and benevolence, she does more mischief than the direct malice of old Crabtree.

JOSEPH: I'faith that's true, Lady Sneerwell. Whenever I hear the current running against the characters of my friends, I never think them in such danger as when Candour undertakes their defence.

LADY SNEERWELL: Hush! Here she is.

[*Enter* MRS CANDOUR.]

MRS CANDOUR: My dear Lady Sneerwell, how have you been this century? Mr Surface, what news do you hear? Though indeed it is no matter, for I think one hears nothing else but scandal.

JOSEPH: Just so, indeed, ma'am.

MRS CANDOUR: Ah, Maria, child! What, is the whole affair off between you and Charles? His extravagance, I presume? The town talks of nothing else.

MARIA: Indeed! I am very sorry, ma'am, the town is not better employed.

MRS CANDOUR: True, true, child; but there's no stopping people's tongues. I own I was hurt to hear it, as indeed I was to learn from the same quarter that your guardian, Sir Peter, and Lady Teazle have not agreed lately as well as could be wished.

MARIA: 'Tis strangely impertinent for people to busy themselves so.

MRS CANDOUR: Very true, child, but what's to be done? People will talk; there's no preventing it. Why, it was but yesterday I was told that Miss Gadabout had eloped with Sir Filigree Flirt. But, Lord, there's no minding what one hears; though to be sure, I had this from very good authority.

MARIA: Such reports are highly scandalous.

MRS CANDOUR: So they are, child – shameful, shameful! But the world is so censorious, no character escapes. Lord, now who would have suspected your friend, Miss Prim, of an indiscretion? Yet such is the ill nature of people that they say her uncle stopped her last week, just as she was stepping into the York diligence[4] with her dancing-master.

MARIA: I'll answer for't there are no grounds for that report.

MRS CANDOUR: Oh, no foundation in the world, I dare swear. No more, probably, than for the story circulated last month of Mrs Festino's affair with Colonel Cassino – though, to be sure, that matter was never rightly cleared up.

JOSEPH: The licence of invention some people take is monstrous indeed.

MARIA: 'Tis so – but in my opinion those who report such things are equally culpable.

MRS CANDOUR: To be sure they are. Tale-bearers are as bad as the tale-makers – 'tis an old observation, and a very true one. But what's to be done, as I said before? How will you prevent people from talking? Today Mrs Clackitt assured me, Mr and Mrs Honeymoon were at last become mere man and wife, like the rest of their acquaintance. She likewise hinted that a certain widow in the next street had got rid of her dropsy and recovered her shape in a most surprising manner. And at the same time Miss Tattle, who was by, affirmed that Lord Buffalo had discovered his lady at a house of no extraordinary fame – and that Sir Harry Bouquet and Tom Saunter were to measure swords on a similar provocation.

4. *diligence*: fast stage-coach.

But, Lord, do you think I would report these things? No, no, tale-bearers, as I said before, are just as bad as the tale-makers.

JOSEPH: Ah, Mrs Candour, if everybody had your forbearance and good nature!

MRS CANDOUR: I confess, Mr Surface, I cannot bear to hear people attacked behind their backs, and when ugly circumstances come out against one's acquaintance, I own I always love to think the best. By the by, I hope 'tis not true your brother is absolutely ruined?

JOSEPH: I am afraid his circumstances are very bad indeed, ma'am.

MRS CANDOUR: Ah, I heard so – but you must tell him to keep up his spirits. Everybody almost is in the same way – Lord Spindle, Sir Thomas Splint, Captain Quinze, and Mr Nickit – all up, I hear, within this week. So if Charles is undone, he'll find half his acquaintance ruined too, and that, you know, is a consolation.

JOSEPH: Doubtless, ma'am, a very great one.

[*Enter* SERVANT.]

SERVANT: Mr Crabtree and Sir Benjamin Backbite.

[*Exit* SERVANT.]

LADY SNEERWELL: So, Maria, you see your lover pursues you; positively you shan't escape.

[*Enter* CRABTREE *and* SIR BENJAMIN BACKBITE.]

CRABTREE: Lady Sneerwell, I kiss your hand. Mrs Candour, I don't believe you are acquainted with my nephew, Sir Benjamin Backbite? Egad! ma'am, he has a pretty wit, and is a pretty poet too, isn't he, Lady Sneerwell?

SIR BENJAMIN: Oh, fie, uncle!

CRABTREE: Nay, egad, it's true. I'll back him at a rebus[5] or a charade[6] against the best rhymer in the kingdom. Has your ladyship heard the epigram he wrote last week on Lady Frizzle's feather catching fire? Do, Benjamin, repeat it, or the charade you made last night extempore at Mrs Drowzie's conversazione. Come now: your first

5. *rebus*: 'an enigmatical representation of a name, word or phrase by figures, pictures, arrangement of letters etc. which suggests the syllables of which it is made up' (*O.E.D.*).

6. *charade*: 'riddle, in which each syllable of the word to be guessed ... is enigmatically described' (*O.E.D.*).

is the name of a fish, your second a great naval commander, and –

SIR BENJAMIN: Uncle, now, prithee –

CRABTREE: I'faith, ma'am, 'twould surprise you to hear how ready he is at all these fine sort of things.

LADY SNEERWELL: I wonder, Sir Benjamin, you never publish anything.

SIR BENJAMIN: To say truth, ma'am, 'tis very vulgar to print. And as my little productions are mostly satires and lampoons on particular people, I find they circulate more by giving copies in confidence to the friends of the parties. However, I have some love elegies, which, when favoured with this lady's smiles, I mean to give the public.

CRABTREE: 'Fore heaven, ma'am, they'll immortalize you! You will be handed down to posterity, like Petrarch's Laura, or Waller's Sacharissa.[7]

SIR BENJAMIN: Yes, madam, I think you will like them when you shall see them on a beautiful quarto page, where a neat rivulet of text shall meander through a meadow of margin. 'Fore Gad, they will be the most elegant things of their kind!

CRABTREE: But, ladies, that's true. Have you heard the news?

MRS CANDOUR: What, sir, do you mean the report of –

CRABTREE: No, ma'am, that's not it. Miss Nicely is going to be married to her own footman!

MRS CANDOUR: Impossible!

CRABTREE: Ask Sir Benjamin.

SIR BENJAMIN: 'Tis very true, ma'am. Everything is fixed and the wedding liveries bespoke.

CRABTREE: Yes, and they do say there were pressing reasons for it.

LADY SNEERWELL: Why, I have heard something of this before.

MRS CANDOUR: It can't be. And I wonder anyone should believe such a story of so prudent a lady as Miss Nicely.

SIR BENJAMIN: O lud, ma'am, that's the very reason 'twas believed at once. She has always been so cautious and so reserved that everybody was sure there was some reason for it at bottom.

---

7. *Petrarch* ... *Sacharissa*: Petrarch (1304–74) wrote sonnets to 'Laura' and Edmund Waller (1606–87) composed verses for 'Sacharissa'.

MRS CANDOUR: Why, to be sure, a tale of scandal is as fatal to the credit of a prudent lady of her stamp, as a fever is generally to those of the strongest constitutions. But there is a sort of puny, sickly reputation that is always ailing, yet will outlive the robuster characters of a hundred prudes.

SIR BENJAMIN: True, madam, there are valetudinarians in reputation as well as in constitution, who, being conscious of their weak part, avoid the least breath of air, and supply their want of stamina by care and circumspection.

MRS CANDOUR: Well, but this may be all a mistake. You know, Sir Benjamin, very trifling circumstances often give rise to the most injurious tales.

CRABTREE: That they do, I'll be sworn, ma'am. Did you ever hear how Miss Piper came to lose her lover and her character last summer at Tunbridge? Sir Benjamin, you remember it?

SIR BENJAMIN: Oh, to be sure – the most whimsical circumstance.

LORD SNEERWELL: How was it, pray?

CRABTREE: Why, one evening at Mrs Ponto's assembly, the conversation happened to turn on the difficulty of breeding Nova Scotia sheep in this country. Says a young lady in company, 'I have known instances of it, for Miss Letitia Piper, a first cousin of mine, had a Nova Scotia sheep that produced her twins'. 'What', cries the Lady Dowager Dundizzy, who you know is as deaf as a post, 'has Miss Piper had twins?' This mistake, as you may imagine, threw the whole company into a fit of laughter. However, 'twas next morning everywhere reported, and in a few days believed by the whole town, that Miss Letitia Piper had actually been brought to bed of a fine boy and a girl; and in less than a week there were some people who could name the father, and the farm-house where the babies were put to nurse.

LADY SNEERWELL: Strange indeed!

CRABTREE: Matter of fact, I assure you. O lud, Mr Surface, pray is it true that your uncle Sir Oliver is coming home?

JOSEPH: Not that I know of, indeed, sir.

CRABTREE: He has been in the East Indies a long time. You can scarcely remember him, I believe? Sad comfort, whenever he returns, to hear how your brother has gone on.

JOSEPH: Charles has been imprudent, sir, to be sure; but I hope no busy people have already prejudiced Sir Oliver against him. He may reform.

SIR BENJAMIN: To be sure, he may. For my part, I never believed him to be so utterly void of principle as people say, and, though he has lost all his friends, I am told nobody is better spoken of by the Jews.

CRABTREE: That's true, egad, nephew. If the Old Jewry[8] was a ward, I believe Charles would be an alderman – no man more popular there, 'fore Gad! I hear he pays as many annuities as the Irish tontine[9] – and that whenever he is sick, they have prayers for the recovery of his health in the Synagogue.

SIR BENJAMIN: Yet no man lives in greater splendour. They tell me when he entertains his friends he will sit down to dinner with a dozen of his own securities, have a score of tradesmen waiting in the antechamber, and an officer[10] behind every guest's chair.

JOSEPH: This may be entertainment to you, gentlemen, but you pay very little regard to the feelings of a brother.

MARIA: Their malice is intolerable. Lady Sneerwell, I must wish you a good morning; I'm not very well.

[*Exit* MARIA.]

MRS CANDOUR: Oh dear, she changes colour very much.

LADY SNEERWELL: Do, Mrs Candour, follow her; she may want assistance.

MRS CANDOUR: That I will, with all my soul, ma'am. Poor dear girl, who knows what her situation may be!

[*Exit* MRS CANDOUR.]

LADY SNEERWELL: 'Twas nothing but that she could not bear to hear Charles reflected on, notwithstanding their difference.

SIR BENJAMIN: The young lady's *penchant* is obvious.

CRABTREE: But, Benjamin, you must not give up the pursuit for that. – Follow her, and put her into good humour. Repeat her some of your own verses. Come, I'll assist you.

---

8. *Old Jewry*: street in the City of London.
9. *tontine*: a financial lottery invented by Lorenzo Tonti, a Neapolitan banker.
10. *officer*: bailiff.

SIR BENJAMIN: Mr Surface, I did not mean to hurt you; but depend on't your brother is utterly undone.

CRABTREE: O lud, aye! Undone as ever man was. Can't raise a guinea!

SIR BENJAMIN: And everything sold, I'm told, that was movable.

CRABTREE: I have seen one that was at his house. – Not a thing left but some empty bottles that were overlooked, and the family pictures, which I believe are framed in the wainscots.

SIR BENJAMIN: And I'm very sorry, also, to hear some bad stories against him. [*Going.*]

CRABTREE: Oh, he has done many mean things, that's certain.

SIR BENJAMIN: But, however, as he's your brother – [*Going.*]

CRABTREE: We'll tell you all another opportunity.

[*Exeunt* CRABTREE *and* SIR BENJAMIN.]

LADY SNEERWELL: Ha, ha! 'tis very hard for them to leave a subject they have not quite run down.

JOSEPH: And I believe the abuse was no more acceptable to your ladyship than Maria.

LADY SNEERWELL: I doubt her affections are farther engaged than we imagined. But the family are to be here this evening, so you may as well dine where you are, and we shall have an opportunity of observing farther. In the meantime I'll go and plot mischief – and you shall study sentiment.

[*Exeunt.*]

Scene ii

SIR PETER TEAZLE's *house.*

[*Enter* SIR PETER.]

SIR PETER: When an old bachelor marries a young wife, what is he to expect? 'Tis now six months since Lady Teazle made me the happiest of men – and I have been the miserablest dog ever since! We tifted a little going to church, and fairly quarrelled before the bells had done ringing. I was more than once nearly choked with gall during the honeymoon, and had lost all comfort in life before my friends had done wishing me joy. Yet I chose with caution – a girl bred wholly in the country, who never knew luxury beyond one silk gown, nor dissipation above the annual gala of a race ball. Yet now she plays her part in all the extravagant fopperies of the fashion and the town, with as ready a grace as if she had never seen a bush nor a grass-plot out of Grosvenor Square! I am sneered at by all my acquaintance and paragraphed in the newspapers. She dissipates my fortune and contradicts all my humours. Yet the worst of it is, I doubt I love her, or I should never bear all this. However, I'll never be weak enough to own it.

[*Enter* ROWLEY.]

ROWLEY: Oh, Sir Peter, your servant. How is it with you, sir?

SIR PETER: Very bad, Master Rowley, very bad. I meet with nothing but crosses and vexations.

ROWLEY: What can have happened to trouble you since yesterday?

SIR PETER: A good question to a married man!

ROWLEY: Nay, I'm sure your lady, Sir Peter, can't be the cause of your uneasiness.

SIR PETER: Why, has anybody told you she was dead?

ROWLEY: Come, come, Sir Peter, you love her, notwithstanding your tempers don't exactly agree.

SIR PETER: But the fault is entirely hers, Master Rowley. I am myself the sweetest-tempered man alive and hate a teasing temper – and so I tell her a hundred times a day.

ROWLEY: Indeed!

SIR PETER: Aye – and what is very extraordinary, in all our disputes she is always in the wrong! But Lady Sneerwell, and the set she meets at her house, encourage the perverseness of her disposition. Then, to complete my vexations, Maria, my ward, whom I ought to have the power of a father over, is determined to turn rebel too, and absolutely refuses the man whom I have long resolved on for her husband; – meaning, I suppose, to bestow herself on his profligate brother.

ROWLEY: You know, Sir Peter, I have always taken the liberty to differ with you on the subject of these two young gentlemen. I only wish you may not be deceived in your opinion of the elder. For

Charles (my life on't!), he will retrieve his errors yet. Their worthy father, once my honoured master, was at his years, nearly as wild a spark; yet, when he died, he did not leave a more benevolent heart to lament his loss.

SIR PETER: You are wrong, Master Rowley. On their father's death, you know, I acted as a kind of guardian to them both, till their uncle Sir Oliver's eastern liberality gave them an early independence. Of course, no person could have more opportunities of judging of their hearts, and I was never mistaken in my life. Joseph is indeed a model for the young men of the age. He is a man of sentiment, and acts up to the sentiments he professes; but for the other, take my word for't, if he had any grain of virtue by descent, he has dissipated it with the rest of his inheritance. Ah, my old friend Sir Oliver will be deeply mortified when he finds how part of his bounty has been misapplied.

ROWLEY: I am sorry to find you so violent against the young man, because this may be the most critical period of his fortune. I came hither with news that will surprise you.

SIR PETER: What? Let me hear.

ROWLEY: Sir Oliver *is* arrived and at this moment in town.

SIR PETER: How? You astonish me! I thought you did not expect him this month.

ROWLEY: I did not; but his passage has been remarkably quick.

SIR PETER: Egad, I shall rejoice to see my old friend. 'Tis fifteen years since we met. We have had many a day together. But does he still enjoin us not to inform his nephews of his arrival?

ROWLEY: Most strictly. He means, before it is known, to make some trial of their dispositions.

SIR PETER: Ah, there needs no art to discover their merits; however, he shall have his way. But pray does he know I am married?

ROWLEY: Yes, and will soon wish you joy.

SIR PETER: What, as we drink health to a friend in a consumption? Ah, Oliver will laugh at me. We used to rail at matrimony together, and he has been steady to his text. Well, he must be soon at my house, though! I'll instantly give orders for his reception. But, Master Rowley, don't drop a word that Lady Teazle and I ever disagree.

ROWLEY: By no means.

SIR PETER: For I should never be able to stand Noll's jokes. So I'd have him think, Lord forgive me, that we are a very happy couple.

ROWLEY: I understand you. – But then you must be very careful not to differ while he is in the house with you.

SIR PETER: Egad, and so we must – and that's impossible. Ah, Master Rowley, when an old bachelor marries a young wife, he deserves – no, the crime carries its punishment along with it.

[*Exeunt.*]

ACT II

Scene i

[*Enter* SIR PETER *and* LADY TEAZLE.]

SIR PETER: Lady Teazle, Lady Teazle, I'll not bear it!

LADY TEAZLE: Sir Peter, Sir Peter, you may bear it or not as you please; but I ought to have my own way in everything – and what's more I will too. What, though I was educated in the country, I know very well that women of fashion in London are accountable to nobody after they are married.

SIR PETER: Very well, ma'am, very well. So a husband is to have no influence, no authority?

LADY TEAZLE: Authority! No, to be sure: if you wanted authority over me, you should have adopted me and not married me. I am sure you were old enough.

SIR PETER: Old enough! Aye – there it is. Well, well, Lady Teazle, though my life may be made unhappy by your temper, I'll not be ruined by your extravagance.

LADY TEAZLE: My extravagance! I'm sure I'm not more extravagant than a woman of fashion ought to be.

SIR PETER: No, no, madam, you shall throw away no more sums on such unmeaning luxury. 'Slife, to spend as much to furnish your dressing-room with flowers in winter as would suffice to turn the Pantheon[1] into a greenhouse and give a *fête champêtre* at Christmas!

---

1. *Pantheon*: fashionable meeting place in Oxford Street.

LADY TEAZLE: Lord, Sir Peter, am I to blame because flowers are dear in cold weather? You should find fault with the climate and not with me. For my part, I'm sure I wish it was spring all the year round and that roses grew under our feet!

SIR PETER: Oons, madam, if you had been born to this, I shouldn't wonder at your talking thus; but you forget what your situation was when I married you.

LADY TEAZLE: No, no, I don't. 'Twas a very disagreeable one, or I should never have married you.

SIR PETER: Yes, yes, madam, you were then in somewhat an humbler style – the daughter of a plain country squire. Recollect, Lady Teazle, when I saw you first, sitting at your tambour[2] in a pretty figured linen gown, with a bunch of keys at your side, your hair combed smooth over a roll, and your apartment hung round with fruits in worsted of your own working.

LADY TEAZLE: Oh, yes! I remember it very well, and a curious life I led – my daily occupation to inspect the dairy, superintend the poultry, make extracts from the family receipt-book, and comb my aunt Deborah's lap-dog.

SIR PETER: Yes, yes, ma'am, 'twas so indeed.

LADY TEAZLE: And then, you know, my evening amusements – to draw patterns for ruffles which I had not the materials to make up; to play Pope Joan[3] with the curate; to read a sermon to my aunt; or to be stuck down to an old spinet to strum my father to sleep after a fox-chase.

SIR PETER: I am glad you have so good a memory. Yes, madam, these were the recreations I took you from; but now you must have your coach – *vis-à-vis*[4] – and three powdered footmen before your chair,[5] and in the summer a pair of white cats[6] to draw you to Kensington Gardens. No recollection, I suppose, when you were content to ride double behind the butler on a docked coach-horse.

---

2. *tambour*: embroidery frame.
3. *Pope Joan*: a card game.
4. *vis-à-vis*: 'a light carriage for two persons sitting face to face' (*O.E.D.*).
5. *chair*: sedan chair.
6. *cats*: probably ponies.

LADY TEAZLE: No – I swear I never did that: I deny the butler and the coach-horse.

SIR PETER: This, madam, was your situation; and what have I done for you? I have made you a woman of fashion, of fortune, of rank – in short, I have made you my wife.

LADY TEAZLE: Well, then – and there is but one thing more you can make me to add to the obligation, and that is –

SIR PETER: My widow, I suppose?

LADY TEAZLE: Hem! Hem!

SIR PETER: Thank you, madam. But don't flatter yourself; for though your ill conduct may disturb my peace, it shall never break my heart, I promise you. However, I am equally obliged to you for the hint.

LADY TEAZLE: Then why will you endeavour to make yourself so disagreeable to me, and thwart me in every little elegant expense?

SIR PETER: 'Slife, madam, I say, had you any of these little elegant expenses when you married me?

LADY TEAZLE: Lud, Sir Peter, would you have me be out of the fashion?

SIR PETER: The fashion, indeed! What had you to do with the fashion before you married me?

LADY TEAZLE: For my part, I should think you would like to have your wife thought a woman of taste.

SIR PETER: Aye! There again! Taste! Zounds, madam, you had no taste when you married me.

LADY TEAZLE: That's very true, indeed, Sir Peter; and after having married you, I should never pretend to taste again, I allow. But now, Sir Peter, if we have finished our daily jangle, I presume I may go to my engagement at Lady Sneerwell's.

SIR PETER: Aye, there's another precious circumstance: a charming set of acquaintance you have made there!

LADY TEAZLE: Nay, Sir Peter, they are all people of rank and fortune, and remarkably tenacious of reputation.

SIR PETER: Yes, egad, they are tenacious of reputation with a vengeance; for they don't choose anybody should have a character but themselves. Such a crew! Ah, many a wretch has rid on a hurdle[7] who has done less mischief than these utterers of forged tales, coiners of scandal, and clippers of reputation.

LADY TEAZLE: What, would you restrain the freedom of speech?

SIR PETER: Ah, they have made you just as bad as any one of the society.

LADY TEAZLE: Why, I believe I do bear a part with a tolerable grace. But I vow I bear no malice against the people I abuse. When I say an ill-natured thing, 'tis out of pure good humour; and I take it for granted they deal exactly in the same manner with me. But, Sir Peter, you know you promised to come to Lady Sneerwell's too.

SIR PETER: Well, well, I'll call in just to look after my own character.

LADY TEAZLE: Then, indeed, you must make haste after me, or you'll be too late. So good-bye to ye!

[Exit.]

SIR PETER: So I have gained much by my intended expostulation. Yet with what a charming air she contradicts everything I say, and how pleasingly she shows her contempt for my authority! Well, though I can't make her love me, there is great satisfaction in quarrelling with her; and I think she never appears to such advantage as when she is doing everything in her power to plague me.

[Exit.]

Scene ii

At LADY SNEERWELL's.

[LADY SNEERWELL, MRS CANDOUR, CRABTREE, SIR BENJAMIN BACKBITE, and JOSEPH SURFACE.]

LADY SNEERWELL: Nay, positively, we will hear it.

JOSEPH SURFACE: Yes, yes, the epigram, by all means.

SIR BENJAMIN: Oh, plague on't, uncle! 'Tis mere nonsense.

CRABTREE: No, no; 'fore Gad, very clever for an extempore.

7. hurdle: a wooden device on which prisoners were dragged to the gallows.

SIR BENJAMIN: But, ladies, you should be acquainted with the circumstance. You must know that one day last week, as Lady Betty Curricle was taking the dust in Hyde Park in a sort of duodecimo phaeton,[8] she desired me to write some verses on her ponies; upon which I took out my pocket-book and in one moment produced the following:

> Sure never were seen two such beautiful ponies;
> Other horses are clowns, but these macaronies.[9]
> To give 'em this title I'm sure isn't wrong,
> Their legs are so slim and their tails are so long.

CRABTREE: There, ladies, done in the smack of a whip, and on horseback too.

JOSEPH SURFACE: A very Phoebus[10] mounted – indeed, Sir Benjamin!

SIR BENJAMIN: Oh, dear sir! Trifles, trifles.

[*Enter* LADY TEAZLE *and* MARIA.]

MRS CANDOUR: I must have a copy.

LADY SNEERWELL: Lady Teazle! I hope we shall see Sir Peter?

LADY TEAZLE: I believe he'll wait on your ladyship presently.

LADY SNEERWELL: Maria, my love, you look grave. Come, you shall sit down to piquet with Mr Surface.

MARIA: I take very little pleasure in cards; however, I'll do as your ladyship pleases.

LADY TEAZLE [*aside*]: I am surprised Mr Surface should sit down with her; I thought he would have embraced this opportunity of speaking to me before Sir Peter came.

MRS CANDOUR: Now, I'll die; but you are so scandalous I'll forswear your society.

LADY TEAZLE: What's the matter, Mrs Candour?

MRS CANDOUR: They'll not allow our friend Miss Vermilion to be handsome.

LADY SNEERWELL: Oh, surely she is a pretty woman.

CRABTREE: I am very glad you think so, ma'am.

---

8. *duodecimo phaeton*: small open carriage.
9. *macaronies*: fops.
10. *Phoebus*: Phoebus Apollo, god of poetry.

MRS CANDOUR: She has a charming fresh colour.

LADY TEAZLE: Yes, when it is fresh put on.

MRS CANDOUR: Oh, fie! I'll swear her colour is natural: I have seen it come and go.

LADY TEAZLE: I daresay you have, ma'am: it goes off at night and comes again in the morning.

SIR BENJAMIN: True, ma'am, it not only comes and goes, but, what's more, egad – her maid can fetch and carry it.

MRS CANDOUR: Ha, ha, ha! How I hate to hear you talk so! But surely now, her sister is – or *was* – very handsome.

CRABTREE: Who – Mrs Evergreen? Oh, Lord, she's six and fifty if she's an hour.

MRS CANDOUR: Now positively you wrong her. Fifty-two or fifty-three is the utmost – and I don't think she looks more.

SIR BENJAMIN: Ah, there is no judging by her looks unless one could see her face.

LADY SNEERWELL: Well, well, if Mrs Evergreen does take some pains to repair the ravages of time, you must allow she effects it with great ingenuity; and surely that's better than the careless manner in which the widow Ochre chalks her wrinkles.

SIR BENJAMIN: Nay, now, Lady Sneerwell, you are severe upon the widow. Come, come, 'tis not that she paints so ill – but when she has finished her face, she joins it on so badly to her neck that she looks like a mended statue, in which the connoisseur sees at once that the head's modern, though the trunk's antique.

CRABTREE: Ha, ha, ha! Well said, nephew!

MRS CANDOUR: Ha, ha, ha! Well, you make me laugh, but I vow I hate you for it. What do you think of Miss Simper?

SIR BENJAMIN: Why, she has very pretty teeth.

LADY TEAZLE: Yes, and on that account, when she is neither speaking nor laughing (which very seldom happens), she never absolutely shuts her mouth, but leaves it always on a jar, as it were, thus.

[*Shows her teeth.*]

MRS CANDOUR: How can you be so ill-natured?

LADY TEAZLE: Nay, I allow even that's better than the pains Mrs Prim takes to conceal her losses in front. She draws her mouth till it positively resembles the aperture of a poor's-box and all her words appear to slide out edgewise, as it were thus, *How do you do, madam? – Yes, madam.*

LADY SNEERWELL: Very well, Lady Teazle; I see you can be a little severe.

LADY TEAZLE: In defence of a friend it is but justice. But here comes Sir Peter to spoil our pleasantry.

[*Enter* SIR PETER TEAZLE.]

SIR PETER: Ladies, your most obedient. [*Aside*] Mercy on me, here is the whole set! A character dead at every word, I suppose.

MRS CANDOUR: I am rejoiced you are come, Sir Peter. They have been so censorious – and Lady Teazle as bad as anyone.

SIR PETER: It must be very distressing to you, Mrs Candour, I dare swear.

MRS CANDOUR: Oh, they will allow good qualities to nobody – not even good nature to our friend Mrs Pursy.

LADY TEAZLE: What, the fat dowager who was at Mrs Quadrille's last night?

MRS CANDOUR: Nay, her bulk is her misfortune; and when she takes such pains to get rid of it, you ought not to reflect on her.

LADY SNEERWELL: That's very true, indeed.

LADY TEAZLE: Yes, I know she almost lives on acids and small whey; laces herself by pulleys; and often in the hottest noon in summer, you may see her on a little squat pony, with her hair plaited up behind like a drummer's, and puffing round the Ring[11] on a full trot.

MRS CANDOUR: I thank you, Lady Teazle, for defending her.

SIR PETER: Yes, a good defence truly!

MRS CANDOUR: Truly, Lady Teazle is as censorious as Miss Sallow.

CRABTREE: Yes, and she is a curious being to pretend to be censorious – an awkward gawky, without any one good point under heaven!

MRS CANDOUR: Positively you shall not be so very severe. Miss Sallow is a near relation of mine by marriage, and as for her person, great allowance is to be made; for, let me tell you, a woman labours

11. *the Ring*: in Hyde Park.

under many disadvantages who tries to pass for a girl at six and thirty.

LADY SNEERWELL: Though surely she is handsome still – and for the weakness in her eyes, considering how much she reads by candle-light, it is not to be wondered at.

MRS CANDOUR: True, and then as to her manner – upon my word I think it is particularly graceful, considering she never had the least education. For you know her mother was a Welsh milliner and her father a sugar-baker at Bristol.

SIR BENJAMIN: Ah, you are both of you too good-natured!

SIR PETER [aside]: Yes, damned good-natured! This their own relation! Mercy on me!

MRS CANDOUR: For my part, I own I cannot bear to hear a friend ill spoken of.

SIR PETER: No, to be sure!

SIR BENJAMIN: Oh, you are of a moral turn. Mrs Candour and I can sit for an hour and hear Lady Stucco talk sentiment.

LADY TEAZLE: Nay, I vow Lady Stucco is very well with the dessert after dinner; for she's just like the French fruit one cracks for mottoes – made up of paint and proverb.

MRS CANDOUR: Well, I never will join in ridiculing a friend – and so I constantly tell my cousin Ogle, and you all know what pretensions she has to be critical on beauty.

CRABTREE: Oh, to be sure. She has herself the oddest countenance that ever was seen: 'tis a collection of features from all the different countries of the globe.

SIR BENJAMIN: So she has indeed. An Irish front –

CRABTREE: Caledonian locks –

SIR BENJAMIN: Dutch nose –

CRABTREE: Austrian lip –

SIR BENJAMIN: Complexion of a Spaniard –

CRABTREE: And teeth à la Chinoise!

SIR BENJAMIN: In short, her face resembles a *table d'hôte* at Spa,[12] where no two guests are of a nation –

12. *Spa*: health resort in Belgium.

CRABTREE: Or a Congress at the close of a general war – wherein all the members, even to her eyes, appear to have a different interest, and her nose and chin are the only parties likely to join issue.

MRS CANDOUR: Ha, ha, ha!

SIR PETER [aside]: Mercy on my life – a person they dine with twice a week!

LADY SNEERWELL: Go, go; you are a couple of provoking toads.

MRS CANDOUR: Nay, but I vow you shall not carry the laugh off so. For give me leave to say that Mrs Ogle –

SIR PETER: Madam, madam, I beg your pardon – there's no stopping these good gentlemen's tongues. But when I tell you, Mrs Candour, that the lady they are abusing is a particular friend of mine, I hope you'll not take her part.

LADY SNEERWELL: Ha, ha, ha! Well said, Sir Peter! But you are a cruel creature, too phlegmatic yourself for a jest, and too peevish to allow wit in others.

SIR PETER: Ah, madam, true wit is more nearly allied to good nature than your ladyship is aware of.

LADY TEAZLE: True, Sir Peter: I believe they are so near akin that they can never be united.

SIR BENJAMIN: Or rather, madam, suppose them to be man and wife, because one seldom sees them together.

LADY TEAZLE: But Sir Peter is such an enemy to scandal, I believe he would have it put down by Parliament.

SIR PETER: 'Fore heaven, madam, if they were to consider the sporting with reputation of as much importance as poaching on manors, and pass an Act for the Preservation of Fame, I believe there are many would thank them for the Bill.

LADY SNEERWELL: O lud, Sir Peter, would you deprive us of our privileges?

SIR PETER: Aye, madam; and then no person should be permitted to kill characters and run down reputations, but qualified old maids and disappointed widows.

LADY SNEERWELL: Go, you monster!

MRS CANDOUR: But surely you would not be quite so severe on those who only report what they hear?

SIR PETER: Yes, madam, I would have law merchant[13] for them too; and in all cases of slander currency, whenever the drawer of the lie was not to be found, the injured parties should have a right to come on any of the endorsers.

CRABTREE: Well, for my part I believe there never was a scandalous tale without some foundation.

SIR PETER: Oh, nine out of ten of the malicious inventions are founded on some ridiculous misrepresentation.

LADY SNEERWELL: Come, ladies, shall we sit down to cards in the next room?

[*Enter a* SERVANT, *who whispers* SIR PETER.]

SIR PETER: I'll be with them directly.

[*Exit* SERVANT.]

[*Aside*] I'll get away unperceived.

LADY SNEERWELL: Sir Peter, you are not leaving us?

SIR PETER: Your ladyship must excuse me; I'm called away by particular business. But I leave my character behind me.

[*Exit* SIR PETER.]

SIR BENJAMIN: Well, certainly, Lady Teazle, that lord of yours is a strange being. I could tell you some stories of him would make you laugh heartily if he were not your husband.

LADY TEAZLE: Oh, pray don't mind that. Come, do let's hear them.

[*They join the rest of the company, all talking as they are going into the next room.*]

JOSEPH [*rising with* MARIA]: Maria, I see you have no satisfaction in this society.

MARIA: How is it possible I should? If to raise malicious smiles at the infirmities or misfortunes of those who have never injured us be the province of wit or humour, heaven grant me a double portion of dullness!

JOSEPH: Yet they appear more ill-natured than they are – they have no malice at heart.

MARIA: Then is their conduct still more contemptible, for, in my opinion, nothing could excuse the intemperance of their tongues but a natural and ungovernable bitterness of mind.

13. *law merchant*: law applying to merchants.

JOSEPH: Undoubtedly, madam; and it has always been a sentiment of mine, that to propagate a malicious truth wantonly is more despicable than to falsify from revenge. But can you, Maria, feel thus for others, and be unkind to me alone? Is hope to be denied the tenderest passion?

MARIA: Why will you distress me by renewing the subject?

JOSEPH: Ah, Maria, you would not treat me thus, and oppose your guardian Sir Peter's will, but that I see that profligate Charles is still a favoured rival.

MARIA: Ungenerously urged! But whatever my sentiments are of that unfortunate young man, be assured I shall not feel more bound to give him up because his distresses have lost him the regard even of a brother.

JOSEPH: Nay, but Maria, do not leave me with a frown. By all that's honest I swear – [*Kneels.*]

    [*Enter* LADY TEAZLE.]

    [*Aside*] Gad's life, here's Lady Teazle. [*Aloud*] You must not – no, you shall not – for though I have the greatest regard for Lady Teazle –

MARIA: Lady Teazle!

JOSEPH: Yet were Sir Peter to suspect –

    [LADY TEAZLE *comes forward.*]

LADY TEAZLE: What is this, pray? Do you take her for me? – Child, you are wanted in the next room.

    [*Exit* MARIA.]

What is all this, pray?

JOSEPH: Oh, the most unlucky circumstance in nature! Maria has somehow suspected the tender concern I have for your happiness and threatened to acquaint Sir Peter with her suspicions, and I was just endeavouring to reason with her when you came in.

LADY TEAZLE: Indeed! But you seemed to adopt a very tender mode of reasoning. Do you usually argue on your knees?

JOSEPH: Oh, she's a child and I thought a little bombast – but, Lady Teazle, when are you to give me your judgment on my library, as you promised?

LADY TEAZLE: No, no; I begin to think it would be imprudent, and you know I admit you as a lover no farther than fashion sanctions.

JOSEPH: True – a mere Platonic cicisbeo[14] – what every wife is entitled to.

LADY TEAZLE: Certainly one must not be out of the fashion. However, I have so much of my country prejudices left that, though Sir Peter's ill humour may vex me ever so, it shall never provoke me to –

JOSEPH: The only revenge in your power. Well, I applaud your moderation.

LADY TEAZLE: Go! You are an insinuating wretch! But we shall be missed. Let us join the company.

JOSEPH: But we had best not return together.

LADY TEAZLE: Well, don't stay, for Maria shan't come to hear any more of your reasoning, I promise you.

[*Exit.*]

JOSEPH: A curious dilemma my politics have run me into! I wanted at first only to ingratiate myself with Lady Teazle that she might not be my enemy with Maria; and I have, I don't know how, become her serious lover. Sincerely I begin to wish I had never made such a point of gaining so very good a character, for it has led me into so many cursed rogueries that I doubt I shall be exposed at last.

[*Exit.*]

Scene iii

SIR PETER TEAZLE's *house.*

[*Enter* SIR OLIVER SURFACE *and* ROWLEY.]

SIR OLIVER: Ha, ha, ha! So my old friend is married, hey? A young wife out of the country. Ha, ha, ha! That he should have stood bluff[15] to old bachelor so long and sink into a husband at last.

ROWLEY: But you must not rally him on the subject, Sir Oliver. 'Tis a tender point, I assure you, though he has been married only seven months.

14. *cicisbeo*: companion.
15. *bluff*: stood firm.

SIR OLIVER: Then he has been just half a year on the stool of repentance! Poor Peter! But you say he has entirely given up Charles – never sees him, hey?

ROWLEY: His prejudice against him is astonishing, and I am sure greatly increased by a jealousy of him with Lady Teazle, which he has industriously been led into by a scandalous society in the neighbourhood, who have contributed not a little to Charles's ill name; whereas the truth is, I believe, if the lady is partial to either of them, his brother is the favourite.

SIR OLIVER: Aye, I know there are a set of malicious, prating, prudent gossips, both male and female, who murder characters to kill time, and will rob a young fellow of his good name before he has years to know the value of it. But I am not to be prejudiced against my nephew by such, I promise you. No, no, if Charles has done nothing false or mean, I shall compound for his extravagance.

ROWLEY: Then, my life on't, you will reclaim him. Ah, sir, it gives me new life to find that your heart is not turned against him, and that the son of my good old master has one friend, however, left.

SIR OLIVER: What, shall I forget, Master Rowley, when I was at his years myself? Egad, my brother and I were neither of us very prudent youths – and yet, I believe, you have not seen many better men than your old master was.

ROWLEY: Sir, 'tis this reflection gives me assurance that Charles may yet be a credit to his family. But here comes Sir Peter.

SIR OLIVER: Egad, so he does! Mercy on me, he's greatly altered, and seems to have a settled married look. One may read husband in his face at this distance!

[*Enter* SIR PETER TEAZLE.]

SIR PETER: Hah! Sir Oliver – my old friend. Welcome to England a thousand times!

SIR OLIVER: Thank you – thank you, Sir Peter! And i'faith I am as glad to find you well, believe me.

SIR PETER: Oh! 'tis a long time since we met – fifteen years, I doubt, Sir Oliver, and many a cross accident in the time.

SIR OLIVER: Aye, I have had my share. But what – I find you are married, hey? Well, well, it can't be helped, and so I wish you joy with all my heart.

SIR PETER: Thank you, thank you, Sir Oliver. Yes, I have entered into the happy state. But we'll not talk of that now.

SIR OLIVER: True, true, Sir Peter: old friends should not begin on grievances at first meeting. No, no, no.

ROWLEY [*to* SIR OLIVER]: Take care, pray, sir.

SIR OLIVER: Well – so one of my nephews is a wild rogue, hey?

SIR PETER: Wild! Ah, my old friend, I grieve for your disappointment there; he's a lost young man, indeed. However, his brother will make you amends; Joseph is, indeed, what a youth should be. Everybody in the world speaks well of him.

SIR OLIVER: I am sorry to hear it; he has too good a character to be an honest fellow. Everybody speaks well of him! Pshaw! Then he has bowed as low to knaves and fools as to the honest dignity of genius and virtue.

SIR PETER: What, Sir Oliver, do you blame him for not making enemies?

SIR OLIVER: Yes, if he has merit enough to deserve them.

SIR PETER: Well, well – you'll be convinced when you know him. 'Tis edification to hear him converse; he professes the noblest sentiments.

SIR OLIVER: Oh, plague of his sentiments! If he salutes me with a scrap of morality in his mouth, I shall be sick directly. But, however, don't mistake me, Sir Peter; I don't mean to defend Charles's errors. But before I form my judgment of either of them, I intend to make a trial of their hearts; and my friend Rowley and I have planned something for the purpose.

ROWLEY: And Sir Peter shall own for once he has been mistaken.

SIR PETER: Oh, my life on Joseph's honour!

SIR OLIVER: Well, come, give us a bottle of good wine, and we'll drink the lads' health, and tell you our scheme.

SIR PETER: *Allons*, then!

SIR OLIVER: And don't, Sir Peter, be so severe against your old friend's son. Odds my life! I am not sorry that he has run out of the course a little. For my part, I hate to see prudence clinging to the green suckers of youth; 'tis like ivy round a sapling and spoils the growth of the tree.

[*Exeunt.*]

ACT III

Scene i

SIR PETER TEAZLE'*s house.*

[*Enter* SIR PETER TEAZLE, SIR OLIVER SURFACE, *and* ROWLEY.]

SIR PETER: Well then, we will see this fellow first and have our wine afterwards. But how is this, Master Rowley? I don't see the jet[1] of your scheme.

ROWLEY: Why, sir, this Mr Stanley, who I was speaking of, is nearly related to them by their mother. He was once a merchant in Dublin but has been ruined by a series of undeserved misfortunes. He has applied by letter since his confinement both to Mr Surface and Charles. From the former he has received nothing but evasive promises of future service, while Charles has done all that his extravagance has left him power to do; and he is, at this time, endeavouring to raise a sum of money, part of which, in the midst of his own distresses, I know he intends for the service of poor Stanley.

SIR OLIVER: Ah, he is my brother's son.

SIR PETER: Well, but how is Sir Oliver personally to –

ROWLEY: Why, sir, I will inform Charles and his brother that Stanley has obtained permission to apply personally to his friends; and, as they have neither of them ever seen him, let Sir Oliver assume his character, and he will have a fair opportunity of judging at least of the benevolence of their dispositions. And believe me, sir, you will

---

1. *jet*: point, gist.

find in the younger brother one who, in the midst of folly and dissipation, has still, as our immortal bard expresses it,

a tear for pity and a hand
Open as day for melting charity.[2]

SIR PETER: Pshaw! What signifies his having an open hand, or purse either, when he has nothing left to give? Well, well, make the trial if you please. But where is the fellow whom you brought for Sir Oliver to examine relative to Charles's affairs?

ROWLEY: Below, waiting his commands, and no one can give him better intelligence. This, Sir Oliver, is a friendly Jew, who, to do him justice, has done everything in his power to bring your nephew to a proper sense of his extravagance.

SIR PETER: Pray, let us have him in.

ROWLEY [*apart to* SERVANT]: Desire Mr Moses to walk upstairs.

SIR PETER: But, pray, why should you suppose he will speak the truth?

ROWLEY: Oh, I have convinced him that he has no chance of recovering certain sums advanced to Charles but through the bounty of Sir Oliver, who he knows has arrived, so that you may depend on his fidelity to his own interests. I have also another evidence in my power, one Snake, whom I have detected in a matter little short of forgery and shall speedily produce him to remove some of your prejudices.

SIR PETER: I have heard too much on that subject.

ROWLEY: Here comes the honest Israelite.

[*Enter* MOSES.]

This is Sir Oliver.

SIR OLIVER: Sir, I understand you have lately had great dealings with my nephew, Charles.

MOSES: Yes, Sir Oliver, I have done all I could for him; but he was ruined before he came to me for assistance.

SIR OLIVER: That was unlucky truly, for you have had no opportunity of showing your talents.

MOSES: None at all. I hadn't the pleasure of knowing his distresses till he was some thousands worse than nothing.

2. *a . . . charity*: see *2 Henry IV*, IV, iv.

SIR OLIVER: Unfortunate, indeed! But I suppose you have done all in your power for him, honest Moses?

MOSES: Yes, he knows that. This very evening I was to have brought him a gentleman from the City, who does not know him, and will, I believe, advance him some money.

SIR PETER: What – one Charles has never had money from before?

MOSES: Yes. Mr Premium of Crutched Friars,[3] formerly a broker.

SIR PETER: Egad, Sir Oliver, a thought strikes me. Charles, you say, does not know Mr Premium?

MOSES: Not at all.

SIR PETER: Now then, Sir Oliver, you may have a better opportunity of satisfying yourself than by an old romancing tale of a poor relation. Go with my friend Moses and represent Mr Premium, and then, I'll answer for it, you'll see your nephew in all his glory.

SIR OLIVER: Egad, I like this idea better than the other, and I may visit Joseph afterwards as old Stanley.

SIR PETER: True, so you may.

ROWLEY: Well, this is taking Charles rather at a disadvantage, to be sure. However, Moses, you understand Sir Peter and will be faithful?

MOSES: You may depend upon me. This is near the time I was to have gone.

SIR OLIVER: I'll accompany you as soon as you please, Moses. But hold, I have forgot one thing. How the plague shall I be able to pass for a Jew?

MOSES: There's no need – the principal is Christian.

SIR OLIVER: Is he? I'm very sorry to hear it. But then again, a'n't I rather too smartly dressed to look like a money-lender?

SIR PETER: Not at all; 'twould not be out of character, if you went in your own carriage. Would it, Moses?

MOSES: Not in the least.

SIR OLIVER: Well, but how must I talk? There's certainly some cant of usury and mode of treating that I ought to know.

SIR PETER: Oh, there's not much to learn. The great point, as I take it, is to be exorbitant enough in your demands – hey, Moses?

3. *Crutched Friars*: in the City of London.

MOSES: Yes, that's a very great point.

SIR OLIVER: I'll answer for't I'll not be wanting in that. I'll ask him eight or ten per cent on the loan – at least.

MOSES: If you ask him no more than that, you'll be discovered immediately.

SIR OLIVER: Hey, what the plague! How much then?

MOSES: That depends upon the circumstances. If he appears not very anxious for the supply, you should require only forty or fifty per cent. But if you find him in great distress and want the moneys very bad, you may ask double.

SIR PETER: A good honest trade you're learning, Sir Oliver.

SIR OLIVER: Truly, I think so – and not unprofitable.

MOSES: Then, you know, you haven't the moneys yourself, but are forced to borrow them for him of an old friend.

SIR OLIVER: Oh, I borrow it of a friend, do I?

MOSES: Yes, and your friend is an unconscionable dog; but you can't help that.

SIR OLIVER: My friend is an unconscionable dog, is he?

MOSES: Yes, and he himself has not the moneys by him, but is forced to sell stock at a great loss.

SIR OLIVER: He is forced to sell stock at a great loss, is he? Well, that's very kind of him.

SIR PETER: I'faith, Sir Oliver – Mr Premium, I mean – you'll soon be master of the trade. But, Moses, wouldn't you have him run out a little against the Annuity Bill?[4] That would be in character, I should think.

MOSES: Very much.

ROWLEY: And lament that a young man now must be at years of discretion before he is suffered to ruin himself?

MOSES: Aye, great pity!

SIR PETER: And abuse the public for allowing merit to an Act whose only object is to snatch misfortune and imprudence from the rapacious relief of usury, and give the minor a chance of inheriting his estate without being undone by coming into possession.

---

4. *Annuity Bill*: an Act for the financial protection of minors that became law on 12 May 1777.

SIR OLIVER: So – so. Moses shall give me further instructions as we go together.

SIR PETER: You will not have much time, for your nephew lives hard by.

SIR OLIVER: Oh, never fear: my tutor appears so able, that though Charles lived in the next street, it must be my own fault if I am not a complete rogue before I turn the corner.

[*Exeunt* SIR OLIVER SURFACE *and* MOSES.]

SIR PETER: So now I think Sir Oliver will be convinced. You are partial, Rowley, and would have prepared Charles for the other plot.

ROWLEY: No, upon my word, Sir Peter.

SIR PETER: Well, go bring me this Snake, and I'll hear what he has to say presently. I see Maria and want to speak with her.

[*Exit* ROWLEY.]

I should be glad to be convinced my suspicions of Lady Teazle and Charles were unjust. I have never yet opened my mind on this subject to my friend Joseph. I am determined I will do it; he will give me his opinion sincerely.

[*Enter* MARIA.]

So, child, has Mr Surface returned with you?

MARIA: No, sir; he was engaged.

SIR PETER: Well, Maria, do you not reflect, the more you converse with that amiable young man, what return his partiality for you deserves?

MARIA: Indeed, Sir Peter, your frequent importunity on this subject distresses me extremely. You compel me to declare that I know no man who has ever paid me a particular attention whom I would not prefer to Mr Surface.

SIR PETER: So – here's perverseness! No, no, Maria, 'tis Charles only whom you would prefer. 'Tis evident his vices and follies have won your heart.

MARIA: This is unkind, sir. You know I have obeyed you in neither seeing nor corresponding with him. I have heard enough to convince me that he is unworthy my regard. Yet I cannot think it culpable, if, while my understanding severely condemns his vices, my heart suggests some pity for his distresses.

SIR PETER: Well, well, pity him as much as you please, but give your heart and hand to a worthier object.

MARIA: Never to his brother.

SIR PETER: Go, perverse and obstinate! But take care, madam; you have never yet known what the authority of a guardian is. Don't compel me to inform you of it.

MARIA: I can only say, you shall not have just reason. 'Tis true, by my father's will, I am for a short period bound to regard you as his substitute, but must cease to think you so when you would compel me to be miserable.

[*Exit.*]

SIR PETER: Was ever man so crossed as I am? – everything conspiring to fret me! I had not been involved in matrimony a fortnight before her father, a hale and hearty man, died, on purpose I believe, for the pleasure of plaguing me with the care of his daughter. But here comes my helpmate. She appears in great good humour. How happy I should be if I could tease her into loving me, though but a little!

[*Enter* LADY TEAZLE.]

LADY TEAZLE: Lud, Sir Peter, I hope you haven't been quarrelling with Maria? It is not using me well to be ill-humoured when I am not by.

SIR PETER: Ah, Lady Teazle, you might have the power to make me good-humoured at all times.

LADY TEAZLE: I am sure I wish I had, for I want you to be in a charming sweet temper at this moment. Do be good-humoured now, and let me have two hundred pounds, will you?

SIR PETER: Two hundred pounds! What, a'n't I to be in a good humour without paying for it? But speak to me thus and i'faith there's nothing I could refuse you. You shall have it; but seal me a bond for the repayment.

LADY TEAZLE: Oh, no. There – my note of hand will do as well.

SIR PETER [*kissing her hand*]: And you shall no longer reproach me with not giving you an independent settlement. I mean shortly to surprise you. But shall we always live thus, hey?

LADY TEAZLE: If you please. I'm sure I don't care how soon we leave off quarrelling, provided you'll own you were tired first.

SIR PETER: Well, then let our future contest be, who shall be most obliging.

LADY TEAZLE: I assure you, Sir Peter, good nature becomes you. You look now as you did before we were married, when you used to walk with me under the elms and tell me stories of what a gallant you were in your youth and chuck me under the chin, you would, and ask me if I thought I could love an old fellow who would deny me nothing – didn't you?

SIR PETER: Yes, yes, and you were as kind and attentive –

LADY TEAZLE: Aye, so I was, and would always take your part, when my acquaintance used to abuse you and turn you into ridicule.

SIR PETER: Indeed!

LADY TEAZLE: Aye, and when my cousin Sophy has called you a stiff, peevish old bachelor and laughed at me for thinking of marrying one who might be my father, I have always defended you and said I didn't think you so ugly by any means – and I dared say you'd make a very good sort of a husband.

SIR PETER: And you prophesied right; and we shall certainly now be the happiest couple –

LADY TEAZLE: And never differ again?

SIR PETER: No, never. Though at the same time indeed, my dear Lady Teazle, you must watch your temper very narrowly, for in all our quarrels, my dear, if you recollect, my love, you always began first.

LADY TEAZLE: I beg your pardon, my dear Sir Peter: indeed you always gave the provocation.

SIR PETER: Now see, my angel! Take care – contradicting isn't the way to keep friends.

LADY TEAZLE: Then don't you begin it, my love.

SIR PETER: There, now, you – you – are going on. You don't perceive, my life, that you are just doing the very thing which you know always makes me angry.

LADY TEAZLE: Nay, you know if you will be angry without any reason, my dear –

SIR PETER: There! now you want to quarrel again.

LADY TEAZLE: No, I'm sure I don't; but if you will be so peevish –

SIR PETER: There now! who begins first?

LADY TEAZLE: Why you, to be sure. I said nothing; but there's no bearing your temper.

SIR PETER: No, no, madam: the fault's in your own temper.

LADY TEAZLE: Aye, you are just what my cousin Sophy said you would be.

SIR PETER: Your cousin Sophy is a forward, impertinent gipsy.

LADY TEAZLE: You are a great bear, I'm sure, to abuse my relations.

SIR PETER: Now may all the plagues of marriage be doubled on me if ever I try to be friends with you any more!

LADY TEAZLE: So much the better.

SIR PETER: No, no, madam. 'Tis evident you never cared a pin for me and I was a madman to marry you – a pert, rural coquette, that had refused half the honest squires in the neighbourhood.

LADY TEAZLE: And I am sure I was a fool to marry you – an old dangling bachelor, who was single at fifty only because he never could meet with anyone who would have him.

SIR PETER: Aye, aye, madam; but you were pleased enough to listen to me. You never had such an offer before.

LADY TEAZLE: No? Didn't I refuse Sir Tivy Terrier, who everybody said would have been a better match, for his estate is just as good as yours and he has broke his neck since we have married?

SIR PETER: I have done with you, madam! You are an unfeeling, ungrateful – but there's an end of everything. I believe you capable of everything that is bad. Yes, madam, I now believe the reports relative to you and Charles, madam. Yes, madam, you and Charles are, not without grounds –

LADY TEAZLE: Take care, Sir Peter! You had better not insinuate any such thing. I'll not be suspected without cause, I promise you.

SIR PETER: Very well, madam, very well! A separate maintenance as soon as you please. Yes, madam, or a divorce! I'll make an example of myself for the benefit of all old bachelors. Let us separate, madam.

LADY TEAZLE: Agreed, agreed! And now, my dear Sir Peter, we are of a mind once more, we may be the happiest couple and never differ again, you know. Ha, ha, ha! Well, you are going to be in a passion, I see, and I shall only interrupt you; so bye, bye!

[*Exit.*]

SIR PETER: Plagues and tortures! Can't I make her angry either? Oh, I am the miserablest fellow! But I'll not bear her presuming to keep her temper. No, she may break my heart, but she shan't keep her temper.

[*Exit.*]

Scene ii

CHARLES SURFACE's *house.*

[*Enter* TRIP, MOSES, *and* SIR OLIVER SURFACE.]

TRIP: Here, Master Moses! If you'll stay a moment, I'll try whether – what's the gentleman's name?

SIR OLIVER [*aside to* MOSES]: Mr Moses, what is my name?

MOSES: Mr Premium.

TRIP: Premium. Very well.

[*Exit, taking snuff.*]

SIR OLIVER: To judge by the servants, one wouldn't believe the master was ruined. But what – sure, this was my brother's house?

MOSES: Yes, sir; Mr Charles bought it of Mr Joseph, with the furniture, pictures, etc., just as the old gentleman left it. Sir Peter thought it a great piece of extravagance in him.

SIR OLIVER: In my mind the other's economy in selling it to him was more reprehensible by half.

[*Enter* TRIP.]

TRIP: My master says you must wait, gentlemen; he has company and can't speak with you yet.

SIR OLIVER: If he knew who it was wanted to see him, perhaps he wouldn't have sent such a message.

TRIP: Yes, yes, sir; he knows you are here. I didn't forget little Premium, no, no, no.

SIR OLIVER: Very well. And I pray, sir, what may be your name?

TRIP: Trip, sir. My name is Trip, at your service.

SIR OLIVER: Well, then, Mr Trip, you have a pleasant sort of place here, I guess?

TRIP: Why, yes. Here are three or four of us pass our time agreeably enough, but then our wages are sometimes a little in arrear – and not very great either – but fifty pounds a year, and find our own bags[5] and bouquets.

SIR OLIVER [*aside*]: Bags and bouquets! Halters and bastinadoes!

TRIP: But *à propos*, Moses, have you been able to get me that little bill discounted?

SIR OLIVER [*aside*]: Wants to raise money – mercy on me! Has his distresses too, I warrant, like a lord – and affects creditors and duns.

MOSES: 'Twas not to be done, indeed, Mr Trip.
    [*Gives the note.*]

TRIP: Good lack, you surprise me! My friend Brush has endorsed it, and I thought when he put his name at the back of a bill 'twas as good as cash.

MOSES: No, 'twouldn't do.

TRIP: A small sum – but twenty pounds. Hark'ee, Moses, do you think you could get it me by way of annuity?

SIR OLIVER [*aside*]: An annuity! Ha, ha! A footman raise money by way of annuity! Well done, luxury, egad!

MOSES: Well, but you must insure your place.

TRIP: Oh, with all my heart! I'll insure my place, and my life too, if you please.

SIR OLIVER [*aside*]: It's more than I would your neck.

MOSES: But is there nothing you could deposit?

TRIP: Why, nothing capital of my master's wardrobe has dropped lately; but I could give you a mortgage on some of his winter clothes, with equity of redemption before November. Or you shall have the reversion of the French velvet, or a post-obit[6] on the blue and silver. These, I should think, Moses, with a few pair of point ruffles, as a collateral security – hey, my little fellow?

MOSES: Well, well.
    [*Bell rings.*]

TRIP: Egad, I heard the bell. I believe, gentlemen, I can now

5. *bags*: silk pouches for back-hair of a wig.
6. *post-obit*: a bond which takes effect after death.

introduce you. Don't forget the annuity, little Moses! This way, gentlemen. Insure my place, you know.

SIR OLIVER [*aside*]: If the man be a shadow of the master, this is the temple of dissipation indeed.

[*Exeunt.*]

Scene iii

[CHARLES SURFACE, CARELESS, *etc., at a table with wine, etc.*]

CHARLES: 'Fore heaven, 'tis true – there's the great degeneracy of the age! Many of our acquaintance have taste, spirit, and politeness; but plague on't, they won't drink.

CARELESS: It is so, indeed, Charles. They give in to all the substantial luxuries of the table, and abstain from nothing but wine and wit.

CHARLES: Oh, certainly society suffers by it intolerably; for now, instead of the social spirit of raillery that used to mantle over a glass of bright burgundy, their conversation is become just like the Spa-water they drink, which has all the pertness and flatulence of champagne, without its spirit or flavour.

1ST GENTLEMAN: But what are they to do who love play better than wine?

CARELESS: True: there's Harry diets himself for gaming, and is now under a hazard[7] regimen.

CHARLES: Then he'll have the worst of it. What! You wouldn't train a horse for the course by keeping him from corn. For my part, egad, I am now never so successful as when I am a little merry: let me throw on a bottle of champagne, and I never lose – at least I never feel my losses, which is exactly the same thing.

2ND GENTLEMAN: Aye, that I believe.

CHARLES: And then what man can pretend to be a believer in love, who is an abjurer of wine? 'Tis the test by which the lover knows his

7. *hazard*: dice game.

own heart. Fill a dozen bumpers to a dozen beauties, and she that floats atop is the maid that has bewitched you.

CARELESS: Now then, Charles, be honest, and give us your real favourite.

CHARLES: Why, I have withheld her only in compassion to you. If I toast her, you must give a round of her peers, which is impossible – on earth.

CARELESS: Oh, then we'll find some canonized vestals or heathen goddesses that will do, I warrant.

CHARLES: Here then, bumpers, you rogues! Bumpers! Maria! Maria!

SIR TOBY: Maria who?

CHARLES: Oh, damn the surname – 'tis too formal to be registered in love's calendar. But now, Sir Toby, beware! We must have beauty superlative.

CARELESS: Nay, never study, Sir Toby: we'll stand to the toast though your mistress should want an eye, and you know you have a song will excuse you.

SIR TOBY: Egad, so I have, and I'll give him the song instead of the lady.

    [*Sings.*]

SONG

Here's to the maiden of bashful fifteen;
Here's to the widow of fifty;
Here's to the flaunting, extravagant quean,[8]
And here's to the housewife that's thrifty.

CHORUS Let the toast pass,
          Drink to the lass,
I'll warrant she'll prove an excuse for the glass!

Here's to the charmer whose dimples we prize;
Now to the maid who has none, sir!
Here's to the girl with a pair of blue eyes,
And here's to the nymph with but *one*, sir!

CHORUS Let the toast pass, etc.

8. *quean*: impudent woman or harlot.

Here's to the maid with a bosom of snow;
Now to her that's brown as a berry:
Here's to the wife with a face full of woe,
And now to the girl that is merry.

CHORUS Let the toast pass, etc.

For let 'em be clumsy, or let 'em be slim,
Young or ancient, I care not a feather;
So fill a pint bumper quite up to the brim,
And let us e'en toast them together.

CHORUS Let the toast pass, etc.

ALL: Bravo! bravo!

[*Enter* TRIP *and whispers* CHARLES SURFACE.]

CHARLES: Gentlemen, you must excuse me a little. Careless, take the chair, will you?

CARELESS: Nay, prithee, Charles, what now? This is one of your peerless beauties, I suppose, has dropped in by chance?

CHARLES: No, faith! To tell you the truth, 'tis a Jew and a broker, who are come by appointment.

CARELESS: Oh, damn it, let's have the Jew in.

1ST GENTLEMAN: Aye, and the broker too, by all means.

2ND GENTLEMAN: Yes, yes, the Jew and the broker!

CHARLES: Egad, with all my heart! Trip, bid the gentlemen walk in.

[*Exit* TRIP.]

Though there's one of them a stranger, I can tell you.

CARELESS: Charles, let us give them some generous burgundy and perhaps they'll grow conscientious.

CHARLES: Oh, hang 'em, no! Wine does but draw forth a man's natural qualities, and to make them drink would only be to whet their knavery.

[*Enter* TRIP, SIR OLIVER, *and* MOSES.]

CHARLES: So, honest Moses, walk in: walk in, pray, Mr Premium – that's the gentleman's name, isn't it, Moses?

MOSES: Yes, sir.

CHARLES: Set chairs, Trip. Sit down, Mr Premium. Glasses, Trip. Sit down, Moses. Come, Mr Premium, I'll give you a sentiment: here's *Success to usury!* Moses, fill the gentleman a bumper.

MOSES: *Success to usury!*
  [*Drinks.*]

CARELESS: Right, Moses! Usury is prudence and industry, and deserves to succeed.

SIR OLIVER: Then here's – *all the success it deserves!*
  [*Drinks.*]

CARELESS: No, no, that won't do. Mr Premium, you have demurred at the toast and must drink it in a pint bumper.

1ST GENTLEMAN: A pint bumper at least.

MOSES: Oh, pray, sir, consider: Mr Premium's a gentleman.

CARELESS: And therefore loves good wine.

2ND GENTLEMAN: Give Moses a quart glass: this is mutiny and a high contempt for the chair.

CARELESS: Here, now for't. I'll see justice done to the last drop of my bottle.

SIR OLIVER: Nay, pray, gentlemen; I did not expect this usage.

CHARLES: No, hang it, you shan't. Mr Premium's a stranger.

SIR OLIVER (*aside*): Odd! I wish I was well out of their company.

CARELESS: Plague on 'em, then! If they don't drink, we'll not sit down with 'em. Come, Harry, the dice are in the next room. Charles, you'll join us when you have finished your business with these gentlemen?

CHARLES: I will! I will!
  [*Exeunt.*]
  Careless!

CARELESS (*returning*): Well?

CHARLES: Perhaps I may want you.

CARELESS: Oh, you know I am always ready: word, note, or bond, 'tis all the same to me.
  [*Exit.*]

MOSES: Sir, this is Mr Premium, a gentleman of the strictest honour and secrecy – and always performs what he undertakes. Mr Premium, this is –

CHARLES: Pshaw! have done. Sir, my friend Moses is a very honest fellow, but a little slow at expression: he'll be an hour giving us our titles. Mr Premium, the plain state of the matter is this: I am an extravagant young fellow who wants to borrow money; you I take to be a prudent old fellow, who has got money to lend. I am blockhead enough to give fifty per cent sooner than not have it; and you, I presume, are rogue enough to take a hundred if you can get it. Now, sir, you see we are acquainted at once and may proceed to business without further ceremony.

SIR OLIVER: Exceeding frank, upon my word. I see, sir, you are not a man of many compliments.'

CHARLES: Oh, no, sir. Plain dealing in business I always think best.

SIR OLIVER: Sir, I like you the better for it. However, you are mistaken in one thing. I have no money to lend, but I believe I could procure some of a friend; but then he's an unconscionable dog, isn't he, Moses?

MOSES: But you can't help that.

SIR OLIVER: And must sell stock to accommodate you – mustn't he, Moses?

MOSES: Yes, indeed! You know I always speak the truth, and scorn to tell a lie!

CHARLES: Right. People that speak the truth generally do: but these are trifles, Mr Premium. What! I know money isn't to be bought without paying for't.

SIR OLIVER: Well – but what security could you give? You have no land, I suppose?

CHARLES: Not a mole-hill, nor a twig, but what's in beau-pots[9] out of the window!

SIR OLIVER: Nor any stock, I presume?

CHARLES: Nothing but live stock – and that's only a few pointers and ponies. But pray, Mr Premium, are you acquainted at all with any of my connections?

SIR OLIVER: Why, to say truth, I am.

CHARLES: Then you must know that I have a dev'lish rich uncle in the East Indies, Sir Oliver Surface, from whom I have the greatest expectations.

SIR OLIVER: That you have a wealthy uncle I have heard, but how your expectations will turn out is more, I believe, than you can tell.

CHARLES: Oh, no – there can be no doubt. They tell me I'm a

9. *beau-pots*: flower-pots.

prodigious favourite and that he talks of leaving me everything.

SIR OLIVER: Indeed! This is the first I've heard on't.

CHARLES: Yes, yes, 'tis just so. Moses knows 'tis true, don't you, Moses?

MOSES: Oh, yes! I'll swear to't.

SIR OLIVER [*aside*]: Egad, they'll persuade me presently I'm at Bengal.

CHARLES: Now I propose, Mr Premium, if it's agreeable to you, a post-obit on Sir Oliver's life; though at the same time the old fellow has been so liberal to me that I give you my word I should be very sorry to hear that anything had happened to him.

SIR OLIVER: Not more than *I* should, I assure you. But the bond you mention happens to be just the worst security you could offer me – for I might live to a hundred and never recover the principal.

CHARLES: Oh, yes, you would. The moment Sir Oliver dies, you know, you would come on me for the money.

SIR OLIVER: Then I believe I should be the most unwelcome dun you ever had in your life.

CHARLES: What? I suppose you are afraid now that Sir Oliver is too good a life?

SIR OLIVER: No, indeed I am not – though I have heard he is as hale and healthy as any man of his years in Christendom.

CHARLES: There again you are misinformed. No, no, the climate has hurt him considerably, poor Uncle Oliver. Yes, yes, he breaks apace, I'm told – and so much altered lately that his nearest relations don't know him.

SIR OLIVER: No? Ha, ha, ha! – so much altered lately that his nearest relations don't know him! Ha, ha, ha! That's droll, egad, ha, ha, ha!

CHARLES: Ha, ha! You're glad to hear that, little Premium.

SIR OLIVER: No, no, I'm not.

CHARLES: Yes, yes, you are. Ha, ha, ha! You know that mends your chance.

SIR OLIVER: But I'm told Sir Oliver is coming over. Nay, some say he is actually arrived.

CHARLES: Pshaw! Sure I must know better than you whether he's come or not. No, no, rely on't, he's at this moment at Calcutta, isn't he, Moses?

THE SCHOOL FOR SCANDAL

MOSES: Oh, yes, certainly.

SIR OLIVER: Very true, as you say, you must know better than I, though I have it from pretty good authority, haven't I, Moses?

MOSES: Yes, most undoubted!

SIR OLIVER: But, sir, as I understand you want a few hundreds immediately, is there nothing you could dispose of?

CHARLES: How do you mean?

SIR OLIVER: For instance now, I have heard that your father left behind him a great quantity of massy old plate.

CHARLES: Oh, lud, that's gone long ago. Moses can tell you how better than I can.

SIR OLIVER (*aside*): Good lack, all the family race-cups and corporation bowls! [*Aloud*] Then it was also supposed that his library was one of the most valuable and complete –

CHARLES: Yes, yes, so it was – vastly too much so for a private gentleman. For my part, I was always of a communicative disposition, so I thought it a shame to keep so much knowledge to myself.

SIR OLIVER [*aside*]: Mercy upon me! Learning that had run in the family like an heirloom! [*Aloud*] Pray, what are become of the books?

CHARLES: You must inquire of the auctioneer, Master Premium, for I don't believe even Moses can direct you.

MOSES: I know nothing of books.

SIR OLIVER: So, so, nothing of the family property left, I suppose?

CHARLES: Not much, indeed, unless you have a mind to the family pictures. I have got a room full of ancestors above, and if you have a taste for paintings, egad, you shall have 'em a bargain.

SIR OLIVER: Hey! What the devil! Sure, you wouldn't sell your forefathers, would you?

CHARLES: Every man of them to the best bidder.

SIR OLIVER: What! Your great-uncles and aunts?

CHARLES: Aye, and my great-grandfathers and grandmothers too.

SIR OLIVER [*aside*]: Now I give him up! [*Aloud*] What the plague, have you no bowels for your own kindred? Odd's life, do you take me for Shylock in the play, that you would raise money of me on your own flesh and blood?

CHARLES: Nay, my little broker, don't be angry: what need you care if you have your money's worth?

SIR OLIVER: Well, I'll be the purchaser: I think I can dispose of the family canvas. [*Aside*] Oh, I'll never forgive him this – never!
    [*Enter* CARELESS.]

CARELESS: Come, Charles, what keeps you?

CHARLES: I can't come yet. I'faith, we are going to have a sale above stairs. Here's little Premium will buy all my ancestors.

CARELESS: Oh, burn your ancestors!

CHARLES: No, he may do that afterwards if he pleases. Stay, Careless, we want you. Egad, you shall be auctioneer; so come along with us.

CARELESS: Oh, have with you, if that's the case. I can handle a hammer as well as a dice-box.

SIR OLIVER [*aside*]: Oh, the profligates!

CHARLES: Come, Moses, you shall be appraiser if we want one. Gad's life, little Premium, you don't seem to like the business.

SIR OLIVER: Oh, yes, I do, vastly. Ha, ha, ha! Yes, yes, I think it a rare joke to sell one's family by auction. Ha, ha! [*Aside*] Oh, the prodigal!

CHARLES: To be sure! When a man wants money, where the plague should he get assistance if he can't make free with his own relations?
    [*Exeunt.*]

ACT IV

Scene i

Picture room at CHARLES SURFACE'*s house.*

[*Enter* CHARLES SURFACE, SIR OLIVER SURFACE, MOSES, *and* CARELESS.]

CHARLES: Walk in, gentlemen, pray walk in. Here they are, the family of the Surfaces, up to the Conquest.

SIR OLIVER: And, in my opinion, a goodly collection.

CHARLES: Aye, aye, these are done in the true spirit of portrait painting – no volunteer grace and expression, not like the works of your modern Raphael,[1] who gives you the strongest resemblance, yet contrives to make your own portrait independent of you, so that you may sink the original and not hurt the picture. No, no; the merit of these is the inveterate likeness – all stiff and awkward as the originals, and like nothing in human nature beside.

SIR OLIVER: Ah! we shall never see such figures of men again.

CHARLES: I hope not. Well, you see, Master Premium, what a domestic character I am. Here I sit of an evening surrounded by my family. But come, get to your pulpit, Mr Auctioneer. Here's an old gouty chair of my grandfather's will answer the purpose.

CARELESS: Aye, aye, this will do. But, Charles, I have ne'er a hammer – and what's an auctioneer without his hammer?

CHARLES: Egad, that's true. [*Takes down a roll*] What parchment have we here? *Richard, heir to Thomas*. Oh, our genealogy in full. Here, Careless, you shall have no common bit of mahogany –

1. *modern Raphael*: Sir Joshua Reynolds (1723–92).

here's the family tree for you, you rogue. This shall be your hammer, and now you may knock down my ancestors with their own pedigree.

SIR OLIVER [aside]: What an unnatural rogue – an ex post facto[2] parricide!

CARELESS: Yes, yes, here's a list of your generation indeed. Faith, Charles, this is the most convenient thing you could have found for the business, for 'twill serve not only as a hammer but a catalogue into the bargain. But come, begin. A-going, a-going, a-going!

CHARLES: Bravo, Careless. Well, here's my great-uncle Sir Richard Raveline, a marvellous good general in his day, I assure you. He served in all the Duke of Marlborough's wars, and got that cut over his eye at the Battle of Malplaquet.[3] What say you, Mr Premium? Look at him – there's a hero for you! Not cut out of his feathers,[4] as your modern clipped captains are, but enveloped in wig and regimentals, as a general should be. What do you bid?

MOSES: Mr Premium would have you speak.

CHARLES: Why, then, he shall have him for ten pounds, and I'm sure that's not dear for a staff-officer.

SIR OLIVER [aside]: Heaven deliver me! His famous uncle Richard for ten pounds! [Aloud] Very well, sir, I take him at that.

CHARLES: Careless, knock down my uncle Richard. Here now is a maiden sister of his, my great-aunt Deborah, done by Kneller,[5] thought to be in his best manner, and a very formidable likeness. There she is, you see, a shepherdess feeding her flock. You shall have her for five pounds ten – the sheep are worth the money.

SIR OLIVER [aside]: Ah, poor Deborah – a woman who set such value on herself! [Aloud] Five pounds ten – she's mine.

CHARLES: Knock down my aunt Deborah. Here now are two that were a sort of cousins of theirs. You see, Moses, these pictures were done some time ago, when beaux wore wigs, and the ladies their own hair.

---

2. *ex post facto*: after the event; retroactive.
3. *Battle of Malplaquet*: fought on 11 September 1709.
4. *feathers*: plumes.
5. *Kneller*: Sir Godfrey Kneller (1646–1723).

SIR OLIVER: Yes, truly, head-dresses appear to have been a little lower in those days.

CHARLES: Well, take that couple for the same.

MOSES: 'Tis good bargain.

CHARLES: Careless! This now is a grandfather of my mother's, a learned judge, well known on the western circuit. What do you rate him at, Moses?

MOSES: Four guineas.

CHARLES: Four guineas! Gad's life, you don't bid me the price of his wig. Mr Premium, you have more respect for the woolsack;[6] do let us knock his lordship down at fifteen.

SIR OLIVER: By all means.

CARELESS: Gone.

CHARLES: And these are two brothers of his, William and Walter Blunt, Esquires, both Members of Parliament and noted speakers; and what's very extraordinary, I believe this is the first time they were ever bought and sold.

SIR OLIVER: That is very extraordinary, indeed! I'll take them at your own price, for the honour of Parliament.

CARELESS: Well said, little Premium! I'll knock them down at forty.

CHARLES: Here's a jolly fellow. I don't know what relation, but he was Mayor of Manchester. Take him at eight pounds.

SIR OLIVER: No, no; six will do for the mayor.

CHARLES: Come, make it guineas, and I'll throw you the two aldermen there into the bargain.

SIR OLIVER: They're mine.

CHARLES: Careless, knock down the Lord Mayor and aldermen. But, plague on't, we shall be all day retailing in this manner. Do let us deal wholesale, what say you, little Premium? Give us three hundred pounds for the rest of the family in the lump.

CARELESS: Aye, aye, that will be the best way.

SIR OLIVER: Well, well, anything to accommodate you: they are mine. But there is one portrait which you have always passed over.

CARELESS: What, that ill-looking little fellow over the settee?

6. *woolsack*: Lord Chancellor's cushion in the House of Lords, or judges in general.

SIR OLIVER: Yes, sir, I mean that, though I don't think him so ill-looking a little fellow by any means.

CHARLES: What, that? Oh, that's my uncle Oliver; 'twas done before he went to India.

CARELESS: Your uncle Oliver! Gad, then you'll never be friends, Charles. That now to me is as stern a looking rogue as ever I saw – an unforgiving eye and a damned disinheriting countenance. An inveterate knave, depend on't. Don't you think so, little Premium?

SIR OLIVER: Upon my soul, sir, I do not; I think it is as honest a looking face as any in the room, dead or alive. But I suppose your Uncle Oliver goes with the rest of the lumber?

CHARLES: No, hang it! I'll not part with poor Noll. The old fellow has been very good to me, and egad I'll keep his picture while I've a room to put it in.

SIR OLIVER [aside]: The rogue's my nephew after all! [Aloud] But, sir, I have somehow taken a fancy to that picture.

CHARLES: I'm sorry for't, for you certainly will not have it. Oons, haven't you got enough of them?

SIR OLIVER [aside]: I forgive him for everything! [Aloud] But, sir, when I take a whim in my head, I don't value money. I'll give you as much for that as for all the rest.

CHARLES: Don't tease me, master broker. I tell you I'll not part with it, and there's an end of it.

SIR OLIVER [aside]: How like his father the dog is! [Aloud] Well, well, I have done. [Aside] I did not perceive it before, but I think I never saw such a striking resemblance. [Aloud] Well, sir, here's a draft for your sum.

CHARLES: Why, 'tis for eight hundred pounds!

SIR OLIVER: You will not let Sir Oliver go?

CHARLES: Zounds, no! I tell you once more.

SIR OLIVER: Then never mind the difference, we'll balance that another time; but give me your hand on the bargain. You are an honest fellow, Charles – I beg pardon, sir, for being so free. Come, Moses.

CHARLES [aside]: Egad, this is a whimsical old fellow! [Aloud] But hark'ee, Premium, you'll prepare lodgings for these gentlemen.

SIR OLIVER: Yes, yes, I'll send for them in a day or two.

CHARLES: But hold! Do, now, send a genteel conveyance for them, for, I assure you, they were most of them used to ride in their own carriages.

SIR OLIVER: I will, I will – for all but Oliver.

CHARLES: Aye, all but the little nabob.[7]

SIR OLIVER: You're fixed on that?

CHARLES: Peremptorily.

SIR OLIVER [aside]: A dear extravagant rogue! [Aloud] Good day! Come, Moses. [Aside] Let me hear now who dares call him profligate!

[Exeunt SIR OLIVER and MOSES.]

CARELESS: Why, this is the oddest genius of the sort I ever saw.

CHARLES: Egad, he's the prince of brokers, I think. I wonder how the devil Moses got acquainted with so honest a fellow. Ha! here's Rowley. Do, Careless, say I'll join the company in a few moments.

CARELESS: I will; but don't let that old blockhead persuade you to squander any of that money on old musty debts, or any such nonsense; for tradesmen, Charles, are the most exorbitant fellows!

CHARLES: Very true, and paying them is only encouraging them.

CARELESS: Nothing else.

CHARLES: Aye, aye, never fear.

[Exit CARELESS.]

So this was an odd old fellow, indeed! Let me see, two-thirds of this is mine by right – five hundred and thirty odd pounds. 'Fore heaven! I find one's ancestors are more valuable relations than I took 'em for! Ladies and gentlemen, your most obedient and very grateful humble servant.

[Enter ROWLEY.]

Ha, old Rowley! Egad, you are just come in time to take leave of your old acquaintance.

ROWLEY: Yes, I heard they were a-going. But I wonder you can have such spirits under so many distresses.

CHARLES: Why, there's the point – my distresses are so many, that I can't afford to part with my spirits. But I shall be rich and splenetic

---

7. *nabob*: someone who has returned to England from India with a large fortune acquired there.

all in good time. However, I suppose you are surprised that I am not more sorrowful at parting with so many near relations. To be sure, 'tis very affecting; but, rot 'em, you see they never move a muscle, so why should I?

ROWLEY: There's no making you serious a moment.

CHARLES: Yes, faith, I am so now. Here, my honest Rowley, here, get me this changed directly, and take a hundred pounds of it immediately to old Stanley.

ROWLEY: A hundred pounds! Consider only –

CHARLES: Gad's life, don't talk about it: poor Stanley's wants are pressing, and if you don't make haste, we shall have someone call that has a better right to the money.

ROWLEY: Ah, there's the point! I never will cease dunning you with the old proverb –

CHARLES: 'Be just before you're generous', hey? Why, so I would if I could; but Justice is an old lame hobbling beldame,[8] and I can't get her to keep pace with Generosity for the soul of me.

ROWLEY: Yet, Charles, believe me, one hour's reflection –

CHARLES: Aye, aye, it's all very true; but, hark'ee, Rowley, while I have, by heaven I'll give; so damn your economy, and now for hazard.

[*Exeunt.*]

Scene ii

The Parlour at CHARLES SURFACE's *house.*

[*Enter* SIR OLIVER SURFACE *and* MOSES.]

MOSES: Well, sir, I think, as Sir Peter said, you have seen Mr Charles in high glory; 'tis great pity he's so extravagant.

SIR OLIVER: True, but he wouldn't sell my picture.

MOSES: And loves wine and women so much.

SIR OLIVER: But he wouldn't sell my picture.

---

8. *beldame*: an aged woman or hag.

MOSES: And games so deep.

SIR OLIVER: But he wouldn't sell my picture. Oh, here's Rowley.

[*Enter* ROWLEY.]

ROWLEY: So, Sir Oliver, I find you have made a purchase.

SIR OLIVER: Yes, yes, our young rake has parted with his ancestors like old tapestry.

ROWLEY: And here has he commissioned me to re-deliver you part of the purchase-money – I mean, though, in your necessitous character of old Stanley.

MOSES: Ah, there is the pity of all; he is so damned charitable.

ROWLEY: And I left a hosier and two tailors in the hall, who, I'm sure, won't be paid, and this hundred would satisfy them.

SIR OLIVER: Well, well, I'll pay his debts, and his benevolence too. But now I am no more a broker and you shall introduce me to the elder brother as old Stanley.

ROWLEY: Not yet awhile. Sir Peter, I know, means to call there about this time.

[*Enter* TRIP.]

TRIP: Oh, gentlemen, I beg pardon for not showing you out; this way. Moses, a word.

[*Exeunt* TRIP *and* MOSES.]

SIR OLIVER: There's a fellow for you! Would you believe it, that puppy intercepted the Jew on our coming and wanted to raise money before he got to his master.

ROWLEY: Indeed.

SIR OLIVER: Yes, they are now planning an annuity business. Ah, Master Rowley, in my days servants were content with the follies of their masters, when they were worn a little threadbare; but now they have their vices, like their birthday clothes,[9] with the gloss on.

[*Exeunt.*]

9. *birthday clothes*: for the monarch's birthday celebrations.

Scene iii

[JOSEPH SURFACE *and* SERVANT *in the library in* JOSEPH's *house.*]

JOSEPH: No letter from Lady Teazle?

SERVANT: No, sir.

JOSEPH [*aside*]: I am surprised she has not sent, if she is prevented from coming. Sir Peter certainly does not suspect me. Yet, I wish I may not lose the heiress, through the scrape I have drawn myself in with the wife; however, Charles's imprudence and bad character are great points in my favour.

[*Knocking heard without.*]

SERVANT: Sir, I believe that must be Lady Teazle.

JOSEPH: Hold! See whether it is or not before you go to the door; I have a particular message for you, if it should be my brother.

SERVANT: 'Tis her ladyship, sir; she always leaves her chair at the milliner's in the next street.

JOSEPH: Stay, stay; draw that screen before the window – that will do. My opposite neighbour is a maiden lady of so curious a temper.

[SERVANT *draws the screen, and exit.*]

I have a difficult hand to play in this affair. Lady Teazle has lately suspected my views on Maria; but she must by no means be let into the secret – at least, not till I have her more in my power.

[*Enter* LADY TEAZLE.]

LADY TEAZLE: What! Sentiment in soliloquy now? Have you been very impatient? O lud, don't pretend to look grave. I vow I couldn't come before.

JOSEPH: Oh, madam, punctuality is a species of constancy, a very unfashionable quality in a lady.

LADY TEAZLE: Upon my word, you ought to pity me. Do you know Sir Peter is grown so ill-tempered to me of late – and so jealous of Charles too! That's the best of the story, isn't it?

JOSEPH [*aside*]: I am glad my scandalous friends keep that up.

LADY TEAZLE: I am sure I wish he would let Maria marry him and then perhaps he would be convinced; don't you, Mr Surface?

JOSEPH [*aside*]: Indeed I do not. [*Aloud*] Oh, certainly I do. For then my dear Lady Teazle would also be convinced how wrong her suspicions were of my having any design on the silly girl.

LADY TEAZLE: Well, well, I'm inclined to believe you. But isn't it provoking, to have the most ill-natured things said of one? And there's my friend Lady Sneerwell has circulated I don't know how many scandalous tales of me, and all without any foundation too – that's what vexes me.

JOSEPH: Aye, madam, to be sure, that is the provoking circumstance – without foundation. Yes, yes, there's the mortification, indeed; for, when a scandalous story is believed against one, there certainly is no comfort like the consciousness of having deserved it.

LADY TEAZLE: No, to be sure, then I'd forgive their malice. But to attack me, who am really so innocent and who never say an ill-natured thing of anybody – that is, of any friend; and then Sir Peter, too, to have him so peevish and so suspicious, when I know the integrity of my own heart – indeed, 'tis monstrous!

JOSEPH: But, my dear Lady Teazle, 'tis your own fault if you suffer it. When a husband entertains a groundless suspicion of his wife and withdraws his confidence from her, the original compact is broken, and she owes it to the honour of her sex to endeavour to outwit him.

LADY TEAZLE: Indeed! So that if he suspects me without cause, it follows that the best way of curing his jealousy is to give him reason for it?

JOSEPH: Undoubtedly – for your husband should never be deceived in you; and in that case it becomes you to be frail in compliment to his discernment.

LADY TEAZLE: To be sure, what you say is very reasonable, and when the consciousness of my own innocence –

JOSEPH: Ah, my dear madam, there is the great mistake! 'Tis this very conscious innocence that is of the greatest prejudice to you. What is it makes you negligent of forms, and careless of the world's opinion? Why, the consciousness of your own innocence. What makes you thoughtless in your conduct, and apt to run into a thousand little imprudences? Why, the consciousness of your own innocence. What makes you impatient of Sir Peter's temper, and outrageous at his suspicions? Why, the consciousness of your innocence.

LADY TEAZLE: 'Tis very true.

JOSEPH: Now, my dear Lady Teazle, if you would but once make a trifling *faux pas*, you can't conceive how cautious you would grow, and how ready to humour and agree with your husband.

LADY TEAZLE: Do you think so?

JOSEPH: Oh, I am sure on't; and then you would find all scandal would cease at once, for, in short, your character at present is like a person in a plethora,[10] absolutely dying from too much health.

LADY TEAZLE: So, so; then I perceive your prescription is that I must sin in my own defence, and part with my virtue to secure my reputation?

JOSEPH: Exactly so, upon my credit, ma'am.

LADY TEAZLE: Well, certainly this is the oddest doctrine, and the newest receipt for avoiding calumny.

JOSEPH: An infallible one, believe me. Prudence, like experience, must be paid for.

LADY TEAZLE: Why, if my understanding were once convinced –

JOSEPH: Oh, certainly, madam, your understanding should be convinced. Yes, yes – heaven forbid I should persuade you to do anything you thought wrong. No, no, I have too much honour to desire it.

LADY TEAZLE: Don't you think we may as well leave honour out of the argument?

JOSEPH: Ah, the ill effects of your country education, I see, still remain with you.

LADY TEAZLE: I doubt they do indeed; and I will fairly own to you that if I could be persuaded to do wrong, it would be by Sir Peter's ill usage sooner than your honourable logic after all.

JOSEPH: Then, by this hand, which he is unworthy of – [*Taking her hand*]

    [*Enter* SERVANT.]

'Sdeath, you blockhead – what do you want?

SERVANT: I beg your pardon, sir, but I thought you wouldn't choose Sir Peter to come up without announcing him.

---

10. *plethora*: excess, especially of red corpuscles in the blood.

JOSEPH: Sir Peter! Oons – the devil!

LADY TEAZLE: Sir Peter! O lud, I'm ruined! I'm ruined!

SERVANT: Sir, 'twasn't I let him in.

LADY TEAZLE: Oh, I'm undone! What will become of me now, Mr Logic? Oh, mercy, he's on the stairs. I'll get behind here – and if ever I'm so imprudent again –

[*Hides behind screen.*]

JOSEPH: Give me that book.

[*Sits down. Servant pretends to adjust his hair.*]

[*Enter* SIR PETER TEAZLE.]

SIR PETER: Aye, ever improving himself! Mr Surface, Mr Surface –

JOSEPH: Oh, my dear Sir Peter, I beg your pardon. [*Gaping, and throws away the book.*] I have been dozing over a stupid book. Well, I am much obliged to you for this call. You haven't been here, I believe, since I fitted up this room. Books, you know, are the only things I am a coxcomb in.

SIR PETER: 'Tis very neat indeed. Well, well, that's proper; and you make even your screen a source of knowledge – hung, I perceive, with maps.

JOSEPH: Oh, yes, I find great use in that screen.

SIR PETER: I dare say you must. Certainly when you want to find anything in a hurry.

JOSEPH [*aside*]: Aye, or to hide anything in a hurry either.

SIR PETER: Well, I have a little private business –

JOSEPH [*to* SERVANT]: You needn't stay.

SERVANT: No, sir.

[*Exit.*]

JOSEPH: Here's a chair, Sir Peter. I beg –

SIR PETER: Well, now we are alone, there is a subject, my dear friend, on which I wish to unburden my mind to you – a point of the greatest moment to my peace; in short, my dear friend, Lady Teazle's conduct of late has made me extremely unhappy.

JOSEPH: Indeed! I am very sorry to hear it.

SIR PETER: Aye, 'tis too plain she has not the least regard for me; but, what's worse, I have pretty good authority to suppose she must have formed an attachment to another.

JOSEPH: Indeed! You astonish me!

SIR PETER: Yes; and, between ourselves, I think I've discovered the person.

JOSEPH: How! You alarm me exceedingly.

SIR PETER: Aye, my dear friend, I knew you would sympathize with me.

JOSEPH: Yes – believe me, Sir Peter, such a discovery would hurt me just as much as it would you.

SIR PETER: I am convinced of it. Ah, it is a happiness to have a friend whom one can trust even with one's family secrets. But have you no guess who I mean?

JOSEPH: I haven't the most distant idea. It can't be Sir Benjamin Backbite?

SIR PETER: Oh, no! What say you to Charles?

JOSEPH: My brother! Impossible!

SIR PETER: Ah, my dear friend, the goodness of your own heart misleads you. You judge of others by yourself.

JOSEPH: Certainly, Sir Peter, the heart that is conscious of its own integrity is ever slow to credit another's treachery.

SIR PETER: True, but your brother has no sentiment; you never hear him talk so.

JOSEPH: Yet I can't but think Lady Teazle herself has too much principle.

SIR PETER: Aye, but what is principle against the flattery of a handsome, lively young fellow?

JOSEPH: That's very true.

SIR PETER: And then, you know, the difference of our ages makes it very improbable that she should have any very great affection for me; and, if she were to be frail, and I were to make it public, why, the town would only laugh at me – the foolish old bachelor who had married a girl.

JOSEPH: That's true, to be sure – they would laugh.

SIR PETER: Laugh -- aye, and make ballads and paragraphs and the devil knows what of me.

JOSEPH: No, you must never make it public.

SIR PETER: But then, again, that the nephew of my old friend, Sir Oliver, should be the person to attempt such a wrong, hurts me more nearly.

JOSEPH: Aye, there's the point. When ingratitude barbs the dart of injury, the wound has double danger in it.

SIR PETER: Aye. I that was, in a manner, left his guardian, in whose house he had been so often entertained – who never in my life denied him my advice!

JOSEPH: Oh, 'tis not to be credited! There may be a man capable of such baseness, to be sure; but, for my part, till you can give me positive proofs, I cannot but doubt it. However, if it should be proved on him, he is no longer a brother of mine; I disclaim kindred with him; for the man who can break the laws of hospitality and attempt the wife of his friend, deserves to be branded as the pest of society.

SIR PETER: What a difference there is between you! What noble sentiments!

JOSEPH: Yet I cannot suspect Lady Teazle's honour.

SIR PETER: I am sure I wish to think well of her, and to remove all ground of quarrel between us. She has lately reproached me more than once with having made no settlement on her, and in our last quarrel she almost hinted that she should not break her heart if I was dead. Now, as we seem to differ in our ideas of expense, I have resolved she shall have her own way and be her own mistress in that respect for the future; and if I were to die, she will find that I have not been inattentive to her interest while living. Here, my friend, are the drafts of two deeds, which I wish to have your opinion on. By one she will enjoy eight hundred a year independent while I live; and, by the other, the bulk of my fortune at my death.

JOSEPH: This conduct, Sir Peter, is indeed truly generous. [*Aside*] I wish it may not corrupt my pupil.

SIR PETER: Yes, I am determined she shall have no cause to complain, though I would not have her acquainted with the latter instance of my affection yet awhile.

JOSEPH [*aside*]: Nor I, if I could help it.

SIR PETER: And now, my dear friend, if you please, we will talk over the situation of your affairs with Maria.

JOSEPH [*softly*]: Oh, no, Sir Peter; another time, if you please.

SIR PETER: I am sensibly chagrined at the little progress you seem to make in her affection.

JOSEPH [*softly*]: I beg you will not mention it. What are my disappointments when your happiness is in debate! [*Aside*] 'Sdeath, I shall be ruined every way.

SIR PETER: And though you are so averse to my acquainting Lady Teazle with your passion for Maria, I'm sure she's not your enemy in the affair.

JOSEPH: Pray, Sir Peter, now, oblige me. I am really too much affected by the subject we have been speaking of, to bestow a thought on my own concerns. The man who is entrusted with his friend's distresses can never –

[*Enter* SERVANT.]

Well, sir?

SERVANT: Your brother, sir, is speaking to a gentleman in the street, and says he knows you are within.

JOSEPH: 'Sdeath, blockhead, I'm not within; I'm out for the day.

SIR PETER: Stay, hold, a thought has struck me. You shall be at home.

JOSEPH: Well, well, let him up.

[*Exit* SERVANT.]

[*Aside*] He'll interrupt Sir Peter, however.

SIR PETER: Now, my good friend, oblige me, I entreat you. Before Charles comes, let me conceal myself somewhere; then do you tax him on the point we have been talking on, and his answers may satisfy me at once.

JOSEPH: Oh, fie, Sir Peter! Would you have me join in so mean a trick – to trepan[11] my brother too?

SIR PETER: Nay, you tell me you are sure he is innocent; if so, you do him the greatest service by giving him an opportunity to clear himself, and you will set my heart at rest. Come, you shall not refuse me. Here, behind this screen will be – [*Goes to the screen.*] Hey! What the devil! There seems to be one listener there already. I'll swear I saw a petticoat.

JOSEPH: Ha, ha, ha! Well, this is ridiculous enough. I'll tell you, Sir Peter, though I hold a man of intrigue to be a most despicable character, yet, you know, it doesn't follow that one is to be an

11. *trepan*: entrap.

absolute Joseph[12] either. Hark'ee, 'tis a little French milliner, a silly rogue that plagues me – and having some character to lose, on your coming, sir, she ran behind the screen.

SIR PETER: Ah, you rogue! But, egad, she has overheard all I have been saying of my wife.

JOSEPH: Oh, 'twill never go any farther, you may depend upon't.

SIR PETER: No? Then i'faith let her hear it out. Here's a closet will do as well.

JOSEPH: Well, go in then.

SIR PETER: Sly rogue! sly rogue!

    [*Goes into the closet.*]

JOSEPH: A narrow escape, indeed, and a curious situation I'm in, to part man and wife in this manner.

LADY TEAZLE [*peeping from the screen*]: Couldn't I steal off?

JOSEPH: Keep close, my angel.

SIR PETER [*peeping*]: Joseph, tax him home.

JOSEPH: Back, my dear friend.

LADY TEAZLE [*peeping*]: Couldn't you lock Sir Peter in?

JOSEPH: Be still, my life.

SIR PETER [*peeping*]: You're sure the little milliner won't blab?

JOSEPH: In, in, my good Sir Peter, 'Fore gad, I wish I had a key to the door.

    [*Enter* CHARLES SURFACE.]

CHARLES: Hullo, brother, what has been the matter? Your fellow would not let me up at first. What, have you had a Jew or a wench with you?

JOSEPH: Neither, brother, I assure you.

CHARLES: But what has made Sir Peter steal off? I thought he had been with you.

JOSEPH: He *was* brother, but hearing you were coming, he did not choose to stay.

CHARLES: What! Was the old gentleman afraid I wanted to borrow money of him?

JOSEPH: No, sir. But I am sorry to find, Charles, you have lately given that worthy man grounds for great uneasiness.

12. *Joseph*: see Genesis, Ch. 39.

CHARLES: Yes, they tell me I do that to a great many worthy men. But how so, pray?

JOSEPH: To be plain with you, brother, he thinks you are endeavouring to gain Lady Teazle's affections from him.

CHARLES: Who, I? O lud, not I, upon my word. Ha, ha, ha! So the old fellow has found out that he has got a young wife, has he? Or, what is worse, her ladyship has found out she has an old husband?

JOSEPH: This is no subject to jest on, brother. He who can laugh –

CHARLES: True, true, as you were going to say. Then, seriously, I never had the least idea of what you charge me with, upon my honour.

JOSEPH [aloud]: Well, it will give Sir Peter great satisfaction to hear this.

CHARLES: To be sure, I once thought the lady seemed to have taken a fancy to me; but, upon my soul, I never gave her the least encouragement. Besides, you know my attachment to Maria.

JOSEPH: But sure, brother, even if Lady Teazle had betrayed the fondest partiality for you –

CHARLES: Why, look'ee, Joseph, I hope I shall never deliberately do a dishonourable action; but if a pretty woman was purposely to throw herself in my way – and that pretty woman married to a man old enough to be her father –

JOSEPH: Well?

CHARLES: Why, I believe I should be obliged to borrow a little of your morality, that's all. But brother, do you know now that you surprise me exceedingly by naming *me* with Lady Teazle; for, faith, I always understood you were her favourite.

JOSEPH: Oh, for shame, Charles! This retort is foolish.

CHARLES: Nay, I swear I have seen you exchange such significant glances –

JOSEPH: Nay, nay, sir, this is no jest –

CHARLES: Egad, I'm serious. Don't you remember, one day, when I called here –

JOSEPH: Nay, prithee, Charles –

CHARLES: And found you together –

JOSEPH: Zounds, sir, I insist –

CHARLES: And another time, when your servant –

JOSEPH: Brother, brother, a word with you. [*Aside*] Gad, I must stop him.

CHARLES: Informed me, I say, that –

JOSEPH: Hush! I beg your pardon, but Sir Peter has overheard all we have been saying. I knew you would clear yourself, or I should not have consented.

CHARLES: How, Sir Peter! Where is he?

JOSEPH: Softly. There!

[*Points to the closet.*]

CHARLES: Oh, 'fore heaven, I'll have him out. Sir Peter, come forth!

JOSEPH: No, no –

CHARLES: I say, Sir Peter, come into court. [*Pulls in* SIR PETER.] What! My old guardian! What, turn inquisitor and take evidence incog.?[13]

SIR PETER: Give me your hand, Charles. I believe I have suspected you wrongfully; but you mustn't be angry with Joseph. 'Twas my plan.

CHARLES: Indeed!

SIR PETER: But I acquit you. I promise you I don't think near so ill of you as I did. What I have heard has given me great satisfaction.

CHARLES: Egad, then, 'twas lucky you didn't hear any more. [*Apart to* JOSEPH] Wasn't it Joseph?

SIR PETER: Ah, you would have retorted on him.

CHARLES: Aye, aye, that was a joke.

SIR PETER: Yes, yes, I know his honour too well.

CHARLES: But you might as well have suspected him as me in this matter for all that. [*Apart to* JOSEPH] Mightn't he, Joseph?

SIR PETER: Well, well, I believe you.

JOSEPH [*aside*]: Would they were both well out of the room!

[*Enter* SERVANT *and whispers* JOSEPH.]

SIR PETER: And in future, perhaps, we may not be such strangers.

[*Exit* SERVANT.]

JOSEPH: Gentlemen, I beg your pardon, I must wait on you downstairs. Here is a person come on particular business.

CHARLES: Well, you can see him in another room. Sir Peter and I

13. *incog.*: incognito, with one's identity concealed.

have not met a long time, and I have something to say to him.

JOSEPH [*aside*]: They must not be left together. [*Aloud*] I'll send this man away and return directly. [*Apart to* SIR PETER *and goes out.*] Sir Peter, not a word of the French milliner.

SIR PETER [*apart to* JOSEPH]: I? Not for the world. [*Aloud*] Ah, Charles, if you associated more with your brother, one might indeed hope for your reformation. He is a man of sentiment. Well, there is nothing in the world so noble as a man of sentiment.

CHARLES: Pshaw, he is too moral by half – and so apprehensive of his good name, as he calls it, that I suppose he would as soon let a priest into his house as a girl.

SIR PETER: No, no! Come, come, you wrong him. No, no, Joseph is no rake, but he is no such saint either in that respect. [*Aside*] I have a great mind to tell him; we should have a laugh.

CHARLES: Oh, hang him, he's a very anchorite, a young hermit.

SIR PETER: Hark'ee, you must not abuse him: he may chance to hear of it again, I promise you.

CHARLES: Why, you won't tell him?

SIR PETER: No. But this way. [*Aside*] Egad, I'll tell him. [*Aloud*] Hark'ee, have you a mind to have a good laugh at Joseph?

CHARLES: I should like it of all things.

SIR PETER: Then, i'faith, we will! [*Aside*] I'll be quit with him for discovering me. [*Aloud*] He had a girl with him when I called.

CHARLES: What! Joseph? You jest.

SIR PETER: Hush! A little French milliner. And the best of the jest is – she's in the room now.

CHARLES: The devil she is!

SIR PETER: Hush! I tell you.

[*Points to the screen.*]

CHARLES: Behind the screen! 'Slife, let's unveil her.

SIR PETER: No, no, he's coming – you shan't indeed.

CHARLES: Oh, egad, we'll have a peep at the little milliner.

SIR PETER: Not for the world! Joseph will never forgive me.

CHARLES: I'll stand by you.

SIR PETER: Odds, here he is!

[JOSEPH *enters just as* CHARLES *throws down the screen.*]

CHARLES: Lady Teazle – by all that's wonderful!

255

SIR PETER: Lady Teazle, by all that's damnable!

CHARLES: Sir Peter, this is one of the smartest French milliners I ever saw. Egad, you seem all to have been diverting yourselves here at hide and seek – and I don't see who is out of the secret. Shall I beg your ladyship to inform me? Not a word! Brother, will you be pleased to explain this matter? What, is morality dumb too? Sir Peter, though I found you in the dark, perhaps you are not so now? All mute. Well, though I can make nothing of the affair, I suppose you perfectly understand one another, so I'll leave you to yourselves. [*Going*] Brother, I'm sorry to find you have given that worthy man cause for so much uneasiness. Sir Peter, there's nothing in the world so noble as a man of sentiment!

[*Exit* CHARLES. *They stand for some time looking at each other.*]

JOSEPH: Sir Peter, notwithstanding I confess that appearances are against me, if you will afford me your patience, I make no doubt – but I shall explain everything to your satisfaction.

SIR PETER: If you please, sir.

JOSEPH: The fact is, sir, that Lady Teazle, knowing my pretensions to your ward, Maria – I say, sir – Lady Teazle, being apprehensive of the jealousy of your temper – and knowing my friendship to the family – she, sir, I say – called here – in order that – I might explain these pretensions – but on your coming – being apprehensive – as I said – of your jealousy – she withdrew – and this, you may depend on it, is the whole truth of the matter.

SIR PETER: A very clear account, upon my word; and I dare swear the lady will vouch for every article of it.

LADY TEAZLE: For not one word of it, Sir Peter.

SIR PETER: How? Don't you even think it worth while to agree in the lie?

LADY TEAZLE: There is not one syllable of truth in what that gentleman has told you.

SIR PETER: I believe you, upon my soul, ma'am.

JOSEPH [*aside to* LADY TEAZLE]: 'Sdeath, madam, will you betray me?

LADY TEAZLE: Good Mr Hypocrite, by your leave, I'll speak for myself.

SIR PETER: Aye, let her alone, sir; you'll find she'll make out a better story than you, without prompting.

LADY TEAZLE: Hear me, Sir Peter! I came hither on no matter relating to your ward, and even ignorant of this gentleman's pretensions to her. But I came seduced by his insidious arguments, at least to listen to his pretended passion, if not to sacrifice your honour to his baseness.

SIR PETER: Now I believe the truth is coming indeed!

JOSEPH: The woman's mad!

LADY TEAZLE: No, sir, she has recovered her senses, and your own arts have furnished her with the means. Sir Peter, I do not expect you to credit me, but the tenderness you expressed for me, when I am sure you could not think I was a witness to it, has penetrated so to my heart, that had I left the place without the shame of this discovery, my future life should have spoken the sincerity of my gratitude. As for that smooth-tongued hypocrite, who would have seduced the wife of his too credulous friend, while he affected honourable addresses to his ward – I behold him now in a light so truly despicable that I shall never again respect myself for having listened to him.

[Exit.]

JOSEPH: Notwithstanding all this, Sir Peter, heaven knows –

SIR PETER: That you are a villain! And so I leave you to your conscience.

JOSEPH: You are too rash, Sir Peter; you shall hear me. The man who shuts out conviction by refusing to –

[Exeunt, JOSEPH SURFACE following and speaking.]

ACT V

Scene i

The library in JOSEPH SURFACE'*s house.*

[*Enter* JOSEPH SURFACE *and* SERVANT.]

JOSEPH: Mr Stanley! And why should you think I would see him? You must know he comes to ask something.

SERVANT: Sir, I should not have let him in, but that Mr Rowley came to the door with him.

JOSEPH: Pshaw, blockhead! to suppose that I should now be in a temper to receive visits from poor relations! Well, why don't you show the fellow up?

SERVANT: I will, sir. Why, sir, it was not my fault that Sir Peter discovered my lady –

JOSEPH: Go, fool!

[*Exit* SERVANT.]

Sure, Fortune never played a man of my policy such a trick before. My character with Sir Peter, my hopes with Maria, destroyed in a moment! I'm in a rare humour to listen to other people's distresses. I shan't be able to bestow even a benevolent sentiment on Stanley. – So, here he comes, and Rowley with him. I must try to recover myself and put a little charity into my face, however.

[*Exit.*]

[*Enter* SIR OLIVER SURFACE *and* ROWLEY.]

SIR OLIVER: What, does he avoid us? That was he, was it not?

ROWLEY: It was, sir. But I doubt you are come a little too abruptly. His nerves are so weak that the sight of a poor relation may be too much for him. I should have gone first to break it to him.

SIR OLIVER: Oh, plague of his nerves! Yet this is he whom Sir Peter extols as a man of the most benevolent way of thinking.

ROWLEY: As to his way of thinking, I cannot pretend to decide; for, to do him justice, he appears to have as much speculative benevolence as any private gentleman in the kingdom, though he is seldom so sensual as to indulge himself in the exercise of it.

SIR OLIVER: Yet he has a string of charitable sentiments, I suppose, at his fingers' ends.

ROWLEY: Or, rather, at his tongue's end, Sir Oliver, for I believe there is no sentiment he has such faith in as that 'Charity begins at home'.

SIR OLIVER: And his, I presume, is of that domestic sort which never stirs abroad at all.

ROWLEY: I doubt you'll find it so. But he's coming. I mustn't seem to interrupt you; and you know immediately as you leave him, I come in to announce your arrival in your real character.

SIR OLIVER: True; and afterwards you'll meet me at Sir Peter's.

ROWLEY: Without losing a moment.

  [*Exit.*]

  [*Enter* JOSEPH SURFACE.]

SIR OLIVER: I don't like the complaisance of his features.

JOSEPH: Sir, I beg you ten thousand pardons for keeping you a moment waiting. Mr Stanley, I presume.

SIR OLIVER: At your service.

JOSEPH: Sir, I beg you will do me the honour to sit down. – I entreat you, sir.

SIR OLIVER: Dear sir, there's no occasion. [*Aside*] Too civil by half.

JOSEPH: I have not the pleasure of knowing you, Mr Stanley, but I am extremely happy to see you look so well. You were nearly related to my mother, I think, Mr Stanley?

SIR OLIVER: I was, sir; so nearly that my present poverty, I fear, may do discredit to her wealthy children; else I should not have presumed to trouble you.

JOSEPH: Dear sir, there needs no apology: he that is in distress, though a stranger, has a right to claim kindred with the wealthy. I am sure I wish I was of that class and had it in my power to offer you even a small relief.

SIR OLIVER: If your uncle, Sir Oliver, were here, I should have a friend.

JOSEPH: I wish he was, sir, with all my heart. You should not want an advocate with him, believe me, sir.

SIR OLIVER: I should not need one – my distresses would recommend me. But I imagined his bounty had enabled you to become the agent of his charity.

JOSEPH: My dear sir, you were strangely misinformed. Sir Oliver is a worthy man, a very worthy man; but avarice, Mr Stanley, is the vice of age. I will tell you, my good sir, in confidence, what he has done for me has been a mere nothing; though people, I know, have thought otherwise, and for my part, I never chose to contradict the report.

SIR OLIVER: What! Has he never transmitted you bullion – rupees, pagodas?[1]

JOSEPH: Oh, dear sir, nothing of the kind! No, no. A few presents now and then – china, shawls, congou tea,[2] avadavats,[3] and India crackers – little more, believe me.

SIR OLIVER [aside]: Here's gratitude for twelve thousand pounds! Avadavats and India crackers!

JOSEPH: Then, my dear sir, you have heard, I doubt not, of the extravagance of my brother. There are very few would credit what I have done for that unfortunate young man.

SIR OLIVER [aside]: Not I, for one!

JOSEPH: The sums I have lent him! Indeed I have been exceedingly to blame. It was an amiable weakness; however, I don't pretend to defend it; and now I feel it doubly culpable, since it has deprived me of the pleasure of serving you, Mr Stanley, as my heart dictates.

SIR OLIVER [aside]: Dissembler! [Aloud] Then, sir, you can't assist me?

JOSEPH: At present, it grieves me to say, I cannot; but, whenever I have the ability, you may depend upon hearing from me.

SIR OLIVER: I am extremely sorry –

1. *rupees, pagodas*: Indian coinage.
2. *congou tea*: a black, Chinese tea.
3. *avadavats*: Indian song birds.

JOSEPH: Not more than I, believe me. To pity without the power to relieve is still more painful than to ask and be denied.

SIR OLIVER: Kind sir, your most obedient humble servant.

JOSEPH: You leave me deeply affected, Mr Stanley. William, be ready to open the door.

SIR OLIVER: Oh, dear sir, no ceremony.

JOSEPH: Your very obedient –

SIR OLIVER: Sir, your most obsequious –

JOSEPH: You may depend upon hearing from me, whenever I can be of service.

SIR OLIVER: Sweet sir, you are too good!

JOSEPH: In the meantime I wish you health and spirits.

SIR OLIVER: Your ever grateful and perpetual humble servant.

JOSEPH: Sir, yours as sincerely.

SIR OLIVER [*aside*]: Charles, you are my heir!
    [*Exit.*]

JOSEPH [*alone*]: This is one bad effect of a good character; it invites application from the unfortunate, and there needs no small degree of address to gain the reputation of benevolence without incurring the expense. The silver ore of pure charity is an expensive article in the catalogue of a man's good qualities; whereas the sentimental French plate I use instead of it makes just as good a show, and pays no tax.
    [*Enter* ROWLEY.]

ROWLEY: Mr Surface, your servant. I was apprehensive of interrupting you, though my business demands immediate attention – as this note will inform you.

JOSEPH: Always happy to see Mr Rowley. [*Reads.*] How? 'Sir Oliver Surface'! – my uncle arrived?

ROWLEY: He is, indeed: we have just parted. Quite well after a speedy voyage, and impatient to embrace his worthy nephew.

JOSEPH: I am astonished! William, stop Mr Stanley, if he's not gone.

ROWLEY: Oh, he's out of reach, I believe.

JOSEPH: Why didn't you let me know this when you came in together?

ROWLEY: I thought you had particular business. But I must be gone to inform your brother and appoint him here to meet his uncle. He will be with you in a quarter of an hour.

THE SCHOOL FOR SCANDAL

JOSEPH: So he says. Well, I am strangely overjoyed at his coming. [*Aside*] Never to be sure was anything so damned unlucky!

ROWLEY: You will be delighted to see how well he looks.

JOSEPH: Oh, I'm rejoiced to hear it. [*Aside*] Just at this time!

ROWLEY: I'll tell him how impatiently you expect him.

JOSEPH: Do, do; pray give my best duty and affection. Indeed, I cannot express the sensations I feel at the thought of seeing him!

[*Exit* ROWLEY.]

JOSEPH [*alone*]: Certainly his coming just at this time is the cruellest piece of ill fortune.

[*Exit.*]

Scene ii

SIR PETER TEAZLE'S

[*Enter* MRS CANDOUR *and* MAID.]

MAID: Indeed, ma'am, my lady will see nobody at present.

MRS CANDOUR: Did you tell her it was her friend Mrs Candour?

MAID: Yes, ma'am; but she begs you will excuse her.

MRS CANDOUR: Do go again – I shall be glad to see her if it be only for a moment, for I am sure she must be in great distress.

[*Exit* MAID.]

Dear heart, how provoking! I'm not mistress of half the circumstances. We shall have the whole affair in the newspapers, with the names of the parties at length, before I have dropped the story at a dozen houses.

[*Enter* SIR BENJAMIN BACKBITE.]

Oh, Sir Benjamin, you have heard, I suppose –

SIR BENJAMIN: Of Lady Teazle and Mr Surface –

MRS CANDOUR: And Sir Peter's discovery –

SIR BENJAMIN: Oh, the strangest piece of business, to be sure!

MRS CANDOUR: Well, I never was so surprised in my life. I am so sorry for all parties, indeed.

SIR BENJAMIN: Now, I don't pity Sir Peter at all; he was so extravagantly partial to Mr Surface.

MRS CANDOUR: Mr Surface! Why, 'twas with Charles Lady Teazle was detected.

SIR BENJAMIN: No, no, I tell you; Mr Surface is the gallant.

MRS CANDOUR: No such thing! Charles is the man. 'Twas Mr Surface brought Sir Peter on purpose to discover them.

SIR BENJAMIN: I tell you I had it from one –

MRS CANDOUR: And I have it from one –

SIR BENJAMIN: Who had it from one, who had it –

MRS CANDOUR: From one immediately. But here comes Lady Sneerwell; perhaps she knows the whole affair.

[*Enter* LADY SNEERWELL.]

LADY SNEERWELL: So, my dear Mrs Candour, here's a sad affair of our friend Lady Teazle.

MRS CANDOUR: Aye, my dear friend, who would have thought –

LADY SNEERWELL: Well, there is no trusting appearances, though indeed she was always too lively for me.

MRS CANDOUR: To be sure, her manners were a little too free; but then she was so young!

LADY SNEERWELL: And had, indeed, some good qualities.

MRS CANDOUR: So she had, indeed. But have you heard the particulars?

LADY SNEERWELL: No; but everybody says that Mr Surface –

SIR BENJAMIN: Aye, there; I told you Mr Surface was the man.

MRS CANDOUR: No, no; indeed, the assignation was with Charles.

LADY SNEERWELL: With Charles? You alarm me, Mrs Candour!

MRS CANDOUR: Yes, yes; he was the lover. Mr Surface, to do him justice, was only the informer.

SIR BENJAMIN: Well, I'll not dispute with you, Mrs Candour; but, be it which it may, I hope that Sir Peter's wound will not –

MRS CANDOUR: Sir Peter's wound! Oh, mercy! I didn't hear a word of their fighting.

LADY SNEERWELL: Nor I, not a syllable.

SIR BENJAMIN: No? What, no mention of the duel?

MRS CANDOUR: Not a word.

SIR BENJAMIN: Oh, Lord, yes: they fought before they left the room.

LADY SNEERWELL: Pray let us hear.

MRS CANDOUR: Aye, do oblige us with the duel.

SIR BENJAMIN: 'Sir', says Sir Peter, immediately after the discovery, 'you are a most ungrateful fellow'.

MRS CANDOUR: Aye, to Charles –

SIR BENJAMIN: No, no, to Mr Surface. 'A most ungrateful fellow; and old as I am, sir', says he, 'I insist on immediate satisfaction'.

MRS CANDOUR: Aye, that must have been to Charles; for 'tis very unlikely Mr Surface should fight in his own house.

SIR BENJAMIN: Gad's life, ma'am, not at all – 'Giving me immediate satisfaction'. On this, ma'am, Lady Teazle, seeing Sir Peter in such danger, ran out of the room in strong hysterics, and Charles after her, calling out for hartshorn[4] and water; then, madam, they began to fight with swords –

[*Enter* CRABTREE.]

CRABTREE: With pistols, nephew – pistols: I have it from undoubted authority.

MRS CANDOUR: Oh, Mr Crabtree, then it is all true?

CRABTREE: Too true, indeed, madam, and Sir Peter is dangerously wounded –

SIR BENJAMIN: By a thrust in seconde[5] quite through his left side –

CRABTREE: By a bullet lodged in the thorax.

MRS CANDOUR: Mercy on me! Poor Sir Peter!

CRABTREE: Yes, madam; though Charles would have avoided the matter, if he could.

MRS CANDOUR: I knew Charles was the person.

SIR BENJAMIN: My uncle, I see, knows nothing of the matter.

CRABTREE: But Sir Peter taxed him with the basest ingratitude.

SIR BENJAMIN: That I told you, you know –

CRABTREE: Do, nephew, let me speak! – and insisted on immediate –

SIR BENJAMIN: Just as I said –

CRABTREE: Odds life, nephew, allow others to know something too. A pair of pistols lay on the bureau (for Mr Surface, it seems, had come home the night before late from Salthill, where he had been

4. *hartshorn*: aqueous solution of ammonia; smelling salts.
5. *seconde*: 'the second of the eight parries recognized in sword-play' (*O.E.D.*).

to see the Montem[6] with a friend, who has a son at Eton), so, unluckily, the pistols were left charged.

SIR BENJAMIN: I heard nothing of this.

CRABTREE: Sir Peter forced Charles to take one, and they fired, it seems, pretty nearly together. Charles's shot took place, as I told you, and Sir Peter's missed; but, what is very extraordinary, the ball struck against a little bronze Pliny that stood over the fireplace, grazed out of the window at a right angle, and wounded the postman, who was just coming to the door with a double letter from Northamptonshire.

SIR BENJAMIN: My uncle's account is more circumstantial, I confess; but I believe mine is the true one, for all that.

LADY SNEERWELL [aside]: I am more interested in this affair than they imagine, and must have better information.

[Exit LADY SNEERWELL.]

SIR BENJAMIN [after a pause looking at each other]: Ah, Lady Sneerwell's alarm is very easily accounted for.

CRABTREE: Yes, yes, they certainly do say – but that's neither here nor there.

MRS CANDOUR: But, pray, where is Sir Peter at present?

CRABTREE: Oh, they brought him home, and he is now in the house, though the servants are ordered to deny it.

MRS CANDOUR: I believe so, and Lady Teazle, I suppose, attending him.

CRABTREE: Yes, yes; I saw one of the faculty[7] enter just before me.

SIR BENJAMIN: Hey! Who comes here?

CRABTREE: Oh, this is he – the physician, depend on't.

MRS CANDOUR: Oh, certainly. It must be the physician; and now we shall know.

[Enter SIR OLIVER SURFACE.]

CRABTREE: Well, doctor, what hopes?

MRS CANDOUR: Aye, doctor, how's your patient?

SIR BENJAMIN: Now, doctor, isn't it a wound with a small sword?

CRABTREE: A bullet lodged in the thorax, for a hundred!

---

6. *Montem*: annual money-collecting festival at Eton College.
7. *faculty*: of medicine.

SIR OLIVER: Doctor! A wound with a small sword! And a bullet in the thorax? Oons, are you mad, good people?

SIR BENJAMIN: Perhaps, sir, you are not a doctor?

SIR OLIVER: Truly, I am to thank you for my degree, if I am.

CRABTREE: Only a friend of Sir Peter's, then, I presume. But, sir, you must have heard of his accident?

SIR OLIVER: Not a word!

CRABTREE: Not of his being dangerously wounded?

SIR OLIVER: The devil he is!

SIR BENJAMIN: Run through the body —

CRABTREE: Shot in the breast —

SIR BENJAMIN: By one Mr Surface —

CRABTREE: Aye, the younger.

SIR OLIVER: Hey! What the plague! You seem to differ strangely in your accounts. However you agree that Sir Peter is dangerously wounded.

SIR BENJAMIN: Oh, yes, we agree there.

CRABTREE: Yes, yes, I believe there can be no doubt of that.

SIR OLIVER: Then, upon my word, for a person in that situation, he is the most imprudent man alive; for here he comes, walking as if nothing at all was the matter.

[*Enter* SIR PETER TEAZLE.]

Odds heart, Sir Peter, you are come in good time, I promise you; for we had just given you over.

SIR BENJAMIN: Egad, uncle, this is the most sudden recovery!

SIR OLIVER: Why, man, what do you out of bed with a small sword through your body, and a bullet lodged in your thorax?

SIR PETER: A small sword, and a bullet!

SIR OLIVER: Aye, these gentlemen would have killed you without law or physic, and wanted to dub me a doctor to make me an accomplice.

SIR PETER: Why, what is all this?

SIR BENJAMIN: We rejoice, Sir Peter, that the story of the duel is not true and are sincerely sorry for your other misfortune.

SIR PETER [*aside*]: So, so; all over the town already.

CRABTREE: Though, Sir Peter, you were certainly vastly to blame to marry at all at your years.

SIR PETER: Sir, what business is that of yours?

MRS CANDOUR: Though, indeed, as Sir Peter made so good a husband, he's very much to be pitied.

SIR PETER: Plague on your pity, ma'am! I desire none of it.

SIR BENJAMIN: However, Sir Peter, you must not mind the laughing and jests you will meet on this occasion.

SIR PETER: Sir, I desire to be master in my own house.

CRABTREE: 'Tis no uncommon case, that's one comfort.

SIR PETER: I insist on being left to myself. Without ceremony I insist on your leaving my house directly!

MRS CANDOUR: Well, well, we are going – and depend on't, we'll make the best report of you we can.

SIR PETER: Leave my house!

CRABTREE: And tell how hardly you have been treated.

SIR PETER: Leave my house!

SIR BENJAMIN: And how patiently you bear it.

SIR PETER: Fiends! Vipers! Furies! Oh, that their own venom would choke them!

[*Exeunt* MRS CANDOUR, SIR BENJAMIN BACKBITE, CRABTREE.]

SIR OLIVER: They are very provoking indeed, Sir Peter.

[*Enter* ROWLEY.]

ROWLEY: I heard high words – what has ruffled you, Sir Peter?

SIR PETER: Pshaw! what signifies asking? Do I ever pass a day without my vexations?

ROWLEY: Well, I'm not inquisitive.

SIR OLIVER: Well, Sir Peter, I have seen both my nephews in the manner we proposed.

SIR PETER: A precious couple they are!

ROWLEY: Yes, and Sir Oliver is convinced that your judgment was right, Sir Peter.

SIR OLIVER: Yes, I find Joseph is indeed the man, after all.

ROWLEY: Aye, as Sir Peter says, he is a man of sentiment.

SIR OLIVER: And acts up to the sentiments he professes.

ROWLEY: It certainly is edification to hear him talk.

SIR OLIVER: Oh, he's a model for the young men of the age! But how's this, Sir Peter, you don't join us in your friend Joseph's praise, as I expected.

SIR PETER: Sir Oliver, we live in a damned wicked world, and the fewer we praise the better.

ROWLEY: What? Do you say so, Sir Peter, who were never mistaken in your life?

SIR PETER: Pshaw! Plague on you both! I see by your sneering you have heard the whole affair. I shall go mad among you.

ROWLEY: Then, to fret you no longer, Sir Peter, we are indeed acquainted with it all. I met Lady Teazle coming from Mr Surface's so humbled that she deigned to request me to be her advocate with you.

SIR PETER: And does Sir Oliver know all this?

SIR OLIVER: Every circumstance.

SIR PETER: What? Of the closet and the screen, hey?

SIR OLIVER: Yes, yes, and the little French milliner. Oh, I have been vastly diverted with the story! Ha, ha, ha!

SIR PETER: 'Twas very pleasant.

SIR OLIVER: I never laughed more in my life, I assure you. Ha, ha, ha!

SIR PETER: Oh, vastly diverting. Ha, ha, ha!

ROWLEY: To be sure, Joseph with his sentiments! Ha, ha, ha!

SIR PETER: Yes, yes, his sentiments! Ha, ha, ha! Hypocritical villain!

SIR OLIVER: Aye, and that rogue Charles to pull Sir Peter out of the closet! Ha, ha, ha!

SIR PETER: Ha, ha! 'Twas devilish entertaining, to be sure.

SIR OLIVER: Ha, ha, ha! Egad, Sir Peter, I should like to have seen your face when the screen was thrown down. Ha, ha!

SIR PETER: Yes, yes, my face when the screen was thrown down. Ha, ha, ha! Oh, I must never show my head again.

SIR OLIVER: But, come, come, it isn't fair to laugh at you neither, my old friend, though, upon my soul, I can't help it.

SIR PETER: Oh, pray don't restrain your mirth on my account: it does not hurt me at all. I laugh at the whole affair myself. Yes, yes, I think being a standing jest for all one's acquaintance a very happy situation. Oh, yes, and then of a morning to read the paragraphs about Mr S—, Lady T—, and Sir P— will be so entertaining.

ROWLEY: Without affectation, Sir Peter, you may despise the ridicule of fools. But I see Lady Teazle going towards the next room; I am sure you must desire a reconciliation as earnestly as she does.

SIR OLIVER: Perhaps my being here prevents her coming to you. Well, I'll leave honest Rowley to mediate between you; but he must bring you all presently to Mr Surface's, where I am now returning, if not to reclaim a libertine, at least to expose hypocrisy.

SIR PETER: Ah, I'll be present at your discovering yourself there with all my heart, though 'tis a vile unlucky place for discoveries.

ROWLEY: We'll follow.

[*Exit* SIR OLIVER.]

SIR PETER: She is not coming here, you see, Rowley.

ROWLEY: No, but she has left the door of that room open, you perceive. See, she is in tears.

SIR PETER: Certainly a little mortification appears very becoming in a wife. Don't you think it will do her good to let her pine a little?

ROWLEY: Oh, this is ungenerous in you.

SIR PETER: Well, I know not what to think. You remember, Rowley, the letter I found of hers evidently intended for Charles?

ROWLEY: A mere forgery, Sir Peter, laid in your way on purpose. This is one of the points which I intend Snake shall give you conviction on.

SIR PETER: I wish I were once satisfied of that. She looks this way. What a remarkably elegant turn of the head she has! Rowley, I'll go to her.

ROWLEY: Certainly.

SIR PETER: Though, when it is known that we are reconciled, people will laugh at me ten times more.

ROWLEY: Let them laugh, and retort their malice only by showing them you are happy in spite of it.

SIR PETER: I'faith, so I will! And, if I'm not mistaken, we may yet be the happiest couple in the country.

ROWLEY: Nay, Sir Peter, he who once lays aside suspicion –

SIR PETER: Hold, Master Rowley! If you have any regard for me, never let me hear you utter anything like a sentiment: I have had enough of them to serve me the rest of my life.

[*Exeunt.*]

Scene iii

The library in JOSEPH SURFACE'*s house.*

[*Enter* JOSEPH SURFACE *and* LADY SNEERWELL.]

LADY SNEERWELL: Impossible! Will not Sir Peter immediately be reconciled to Charles, and, of course, no longer oppose his union with Maria? The thought is distraction to me.

JOSEPH: Can passion furnish a remedy?

LADY SNEERWELL: No, nor cunning neither. Oh, I was a fool, an idiot, to league with such a blunderer!

JOSEPH: Sure, Lady Sneerwell, I am the greatest sufferer; yet you see I bear the accident with calmness.

LADY SNEERWELL: Because the disappointment doesn't reach your heart; your interest only attached you to Maria. Had you felt for her what I have for that ungrateful libertine, neither your temper nor hypocrisy could prevent your showing the sharpness of your vexation.

JOSEPH: But why should your reproaches fall on me for this disappointment?

LADY SNEERWELL: Are you not the cause of it? What had you to do to bate in your pursuit of Maria to pervert Lady Teazle by the way? Had you not a sufficient field for your roguery in blinding Sir Peter, and supplanting your brother, but you must endeavour to seduce his wife? I hate such an avarice of crimes; 'tis an unfair monopoly, and never prospers.

JOSEPH: Well, I admit I have been to blame. I confess I deviated from the direct road of wrong, but I don't think we're so totally defeated neither.

LADY SNEERWELL: No!

JOSEPH: You tell me you have made a trial of Snake since we met, and that you still believe him faithful to us?

LADY SNEERWELL: I do believe so.

JOSEPH: And that he has undertaken, should it be necessary, to swear and prove that Charles is at this time contracted by vows and honour to your ladyship – which some of his former letters to you will serve to support.

LADY SNEERWELL: This, indeed, might have assisted.

JOSEPH: Come, come; it is not too late yet. [*Knocking at the door.*] But hark! This is probably my uncle, Sir Oliver: retire to that room; we'll consult farther when he's gone.

LADY SNEERWELL: Well, but if he should find you out too?

JOSEPH: Oh, I have no fear of that. Sir Peter will hold his tongue for his own credit's sake – and you may depend on't I shall soon discover Sir Oliver's weak side!

LADY SNEERWELL: I have no diffidence of your abilities; only be constant to one roguery at a time.

[*Exit.*]

JOSEPH: I will, I will! So, 'tis confounded hard, after such bad fortune, to be baited by one's confederate in evil. Well, at all events my character is so much better than Charles's that I certainly – hey! what? This is not Sir Oliver but old Stanley again. Plague on't that he should return to tease me just now. We shall have Sir Oliver come and find him here and –

[*Enter* SIR OLIVER SURFACE.]

Gad's life, Mr Stanley, why have you come back to plague me just at this time? You must not stay now, upon my word.

SIR OLIVER: Sir, I hear your uncle Oliver is expected here, and though he has been so penurious to you, I'll try what he'll do for me.

JOSEPH: Sir, 'tis impossible for you to stay now, so I must beg – come any other time, and I promise you, you shall be assisted.

SIR OLIVER: No: Sir Oliver and I must be acquainted.

JOSEPH: Zounds, sir! Then I insist on your quitting the room directly.

SIR OLIVER: Nay, sir –

JOSEPH: Sir, I insist on't: here, William! show this gentleman out. Since you compel me, sir, not one moment – this is such insolence.

[*Going to push him out.*]

[*Enter* CHARLES SURFACE.]

CHARLES: Hey day! what's the matter now? What the devil, have you got hold of my little broker here? Zounds, brother, don't hurt little Premium. What's the matter, my little fellow?

JOSEPH: So! he has been with you too, has he?

CHARLES: To be sure he has. Why, he's as honest a little – but sure, Joseph, you have not been borrowing money too, have you?

JOSEPH: Borrowing? No. But, brother, you know we expect Sir Oliver here every –

CHARLES: O Gad, that's true! Noll mustn't find the little broker here, to be sure.

JOSEPH: Yet, Mr Stanley insists –

CHARLES: Stanley! Why his name is Premium.

JOSEPH: No, no, Stanley.

CHARLES: No, no, Premium.

JOSEPH: Well, no matter which, but –

CHARLES: Aye, aye, Stanley or Premium, 'tis the same thing, as you say; for I suppose he goes by half a hundred names, besides A.B. at the coffee-houses.

[Knocking.]

JOSEPH: 'Sdeath! here's Sir Oliver at the door. Now I beg, Mr Stanley –

CHARLES: Aye, aye, and I beg, Mr Premium –

SIR OLIVER: Gentlemen –

JOSEPH: Sir, by heaven you shall go.

CHARLES: Aye, out with him, certainly.

SIR OLIVER: This violence –

JOSEPH: Sir, 'tis your own fault.

CHARLES: Out with him, to be sure. [Both forcing SIR OLIVER out.]

[Enter SIR PETER and LADY TEAZLE, MARIA, and ROWLEY.]

SIR PETER: My old friend, Sir Oliver – hey! What in the name of wonder? Here are dutiful nephews – assault their uncle at a first visit.

LADY TEAZLE: Indeed, Sir Oliver, 'twas well we came in to rescue you.

ROWLEY: Truly it was; for I perceive, Sir Oliver, the character of old Stanley was no protection to you.

SIR OLIVER: Nor of Premium either. The necessities of the former could not extort a shilling from that benevolent gentleman; and now, egad, I stood a chance of faring worse than my ancestors and being knocked down without being bid for.

[*After a pause,* JOSEPH *and* CHARLES *turning to each other.*]

JOSEPH: Charles!

CHARLES: Joseph!

JOSEPH: 'Tis now complete.

CHARLES: Very!

SIR OLIVER: Sir Peter, my friend, and Rowley, too, look on that elder nephew of mine. You know what he has already received from my bounty; and you know also how gladly I would have regarded half my fortune as held in trust for him. Judge then my disappointment in discovering him to be destitute of truth, charity, and gratitude.

SIR PETER: Sir Oliver, I should be more surprised at this declaration if I had not myself found him to be mean, treacherous, and hypocritical.

LADY TEAZLE: And if the gentleman pleads not guilty to these, pray let him call *me* to his character.

SIR PETER: Then, I believe, we need add no more. If he knows himself, he will consider it as the most perfect punishment that he is known to the world.

CHARLES [*aside*]: If they talk this way to honesty, what will they say to me by and by?

SIR OLIVER: As for that prodigal, his brother there –

CHARLES [*aside*]: Aye, now comes my turn: the damned family pictures will ruin me.

JOSEPH: Sir Oliver, uncle, will you honour me with a hearing?

CHARLES [*aside*]: Now, if Joseph would make one of his long speeches, I might recollect myself a little.

SIR OLIVER [*to* JOSEPH]: I suppose you would undertake to justify yourself entirely?

JOSEPH: I trust I could.

SIR OLIVER [*to* CHARLES]: Well, sir, and you could justify yourself too, I suppose?

CHARLES: Not that I know of, Sir Oliver.

SIR OLIVER: What? Little Premium has been let too much into the secret, I suppose?

CHARLES: True, sir; but they were family secrets and should not be mentioned again, you know.

ROWLEY: Come, Sir Oliver, I know you cannot speak of Charles's follies with anger.

SIR OLIVER: Odd's heart, no more I can – nor with gravity either. Sir Peter, do you know the rogue bargained with me for all his ancestors, sold me judges and generals by the foot, and maiden aunts as cheap as broken china?

CHARLES: To be sure, Sir Oliver, I did make a little free with the family canvas, that's the truth on't. My ancestors may certainly rise in judgment against me, there's no denying it. But believe me sincere when I tell you, and upon my soul I would not say it if I was not, that if I do not appear mortified at the exposure of my follies, it is because I feel at this moment the warmest satisfaction in seeing you, my liberal benefactor.

SIR OLIVER: Charles, I believe you. Give me your hand again: the ill-looking little fellow over the settee has made your peace.

CHARLES: Then, sir, my gratitude to the original is still increased.

LADY TEAZLE: Yet I believe, Sir Oliver, here is one whom Charles is still more anxious to be reconciled to.

SIR OLIVER: Oh, I have heard of his attachment there; and, with the young lady's pardon, if I construe right that blush –

SIR PETER: Well, child, speak your sentiments!

MARIA: Sir, I have little to say, but that I shall rejoice to hear that he is happy. For me, whatever claim I had to his affection, I willingly resign to one who has a better title.

CHARLES: How, Maria!

SIR PETER: Hey day! what's the mystery now? While he appeared an incorrigible rake, you would give your hand to no one else; and now that he is likely to reform, I warrant you won't have him.

MARIA: His own heart and Lady Sneerwell know the cause.

CHARLES: Lady Sneerwell!

JOSEPH: Brother, it is with great concern I am obliged to speak on this point, but my regard to justice compels me, and Lady Sneerwell's injuries can no longer be concealed.

[*Opens the door.*]

[*Enter* LADY SNEERWELL.]

SIR PETER: So, another French milliner! Egad, he has one in every room in the house, I suppose.

LADY SNEERWELL: Ungrateful Charles! Well may you be surprised, and feel for the indelicate situation which your perfidy has forced me into.

CHARLES: Pray, Uncle, is this another plot of yours? For, as I have life, I don't understand it.

JOSEPH: I believe, sir, there is but the evidence of one person more necessary to make it extremely clear.

SIR PETER: And that person, I imagine, is Mr Snake. Rowley, you were perfectly right to bring him with us, and pray let him appear.

ROWLEY: Walk in, Mr Snake.

[*Enter* SNAKE.]

I thought his testimony might be wanted; however, it happens unluckily, that he comes to confront Lady Sneerwell, not to support her.

LADY SNEERWELL: Villain! Treacherous to me at last! [*Aside*] Speak, fellow, have you too conspired against me?

SNAKE: I beg your ladyship ten thousand pardons. You paid me extremely liberally for the lie in question; but I unfortunately have been offered double to speak the truth.

SIR PETER: Plot and counterplot, egad!

LADY SNEERWELL: The torments of shame and disappointment on you all!

LADY TEAZLE: Hold, Lady Sneerwell. Before you go, let me thank you for the trouble you and that gentleman have taken in writing letters from me to Charles, and answering them yourself. And let me also request you to make my respects to the scandalous college of which you are president, and inform them, that Lady Teazle, licentiate, begs leave to return the diploma they gave her, as she leaves off practice, and kills characters no longer.

LADY SNEERWELL: You too, madam! Provoking insolent! May your husband live these fifty years.

[*Exit.*]

SIR PETER: Oons! what a fury!

LADY TEAZLE: A malicious creature, indeed!

SIR PETER: Hey! Not for her last wish?

LADY TEAZLE: Oh, no!

SIR OLIVER: Well, sir, and what have you to say now?

JOSEPH: Sir, I am so confounded to find that Lady Sneerwell could be guilty of suborning Mr Snake in this manner, to impose on us all, that I know not what to say. However, lest her revengeful spirit should prompt her to injure my brother, I had certainly better follow her directly.

[*Exit.*]

SIR PETER: Moral to the last drop!

SIR OLIVER: Aye, and marry her, Joseph, if you can. Oil and vinegar, egad! You'll do very well together.

ROWLEY: I believe we have no more occasion for Mr Snake at present.

SNAKE: Before I go, I beg your pardon once for all, for whatever uneasiness I have been the humble instrument of causing to the parties present.

SIR PETER: Well, well, you have made atonement by a good deed at last.

SNAKE: But I must request of the company that it shall never be known.

SIR PETER: Hey! What the plague! Are you ashamed of having done a right thing once in your life?

SNAKE: Ah, sir, consider. I live by the badness of my character. I have nothing but my infamy to depend on, and, if it were once known that I had been betrayed into an honest action, I should lose every friend I have in the world.

SIR OLIVER: Well, well, we'll not traduce you by saying anything in your praise, never fear.

[*Exit* SNAKE.]

SIR PETER: There's a precious rogue!

LADY TEAZLE: See, Sir Oliver, there needs no persuasion now to reconcile your nephew and Maria.

[CHARLES *and* MARIA *apart.*]

SIR OLIVER: Aye, aye, that's as it should be, and, egad, we'll have the wedding tomorrow morning.

CHARLES: Thank you, dear Uncle.

SIR PETER: What, you rogue, don't you ask the girl's consent first?

CHARLES: Oh, I have done that a long time – above a minute ago – and she has looked *yes*.

MARIA: For shame, Charles! I protest, Sir Peter, there has not been a word.

SIR OLIVER: Well then, the fewer the better. May your love for each other never know abatement!

SIR PETER: And may you live as happily together as Lady Teazle and I intend to do!

CHARLES: Rowley, my old friend, I am sure you congratulate me; and I suspect that I owe you much.

SIR OLIVER: You do, indeed, Charles.

ROWLEY: If my efforts to serve you had not succeeded, you would have been in my debt for the attempt; but deserve to be happy and you overpay me.

SIR PETER: Aye, honest Rowley always said you would reform.

CHARLES: Why, as to reforming, Sir Peter, I'll make no promises, and that I take to be a proof that I intend to set about it. But here shall be my monitor, my gentle guide. Ah, can I leave the virtuous path those eyes illumine?

> Though thou, dear maid, shouldst waive thy beauty's sway,
> Thou still must rule, because I will obey.
> An humbled fugitive from folly view,
> No sanctuary near but love and you.

> [*To the audience.*]
> You can, indeed, each anxious fear remove,
> For even Scandal dies, if you approve!

EPILOGUE

BY MR COLMAN[1]
Spoken by LADY TEAZLE

I, who was late so volatile and gay,
Like a trade-wind must now blow all one way,
Bend all my cares, my studies, and my vows,
To one dull rusty weathercock – my spouse!
So wills our virtuous bard – the motley Bayes[2]
Of crying epilogues and laughing plays.
Old bachelors, who marry smart young wives,
Learn from our play to regulate your lives:
Each bring his dear to town, all faults upon her –
London will prove the very source of honour.
Plunged fairly in, like a cold bath it serves,
When principles relax, to brace the nerves.
Such is my case; and yet I must deplore
That the gay dream of dissipation's o'er.
And say, ye fair, was ever lively wife,
Born with a genius for the highest life,
Like me untimely blasted in her bloom,
Like me condemned to such a dismal doom?
Save money, when I just knew how to waste it!
Leave London, just as I began to taste it!
Must I then watch the early-crowing cock,
The melancholy ticking of a clock
In a lone rustic hall forever pounded,
With dogs, cats, rats, and squalling brats surrounded?
With humble curate can I now retire
(While good Sir Peter boozes with the squire)
And at backgammon mortify my soul,

---

1. *Colman*: George Colman the elder (1732–94).
2. *Bayes*: the name under which Dryden was attacked in Buckingham's *The Rehearsal* (1671).

That pants for loo,[3] or flutters at a vole?[4]
'Seven's the main!'[5] – dear sound that must expire,
Lost at hot cockles[6] round a Christmas fire.
The transient hour of fashion too soon spent,
Farewell[7] the tranquil mind, farewell content!
Farewell the plumèd head, the cushioned *tête*,
That takes the cushion from its proper seat!
That spirit-stirring drum! (card drums,[8] I mean –
Spadille,[9] odd trick, pam,[10] basto,[11] king and queen!)
And you, ye knockers that with brazen throat
The welcome visitors' approach denote.
Farewell all quality of high renown,
Pride, pomp, and circumstance of glorious town!
Farewell! your revels I partake no more,
And Lady Teazle's occupation's o'er!
All this I told our bard; he smiled and said 'twas clear,
I ought to play deep tragedy next year.
Meanwhile he drew wise morals from his play
And in these solemn periods stalked away:
'Blessed were the fair like you, her faults who stopped,
And closed her follies when the curtain dropped –
No more in vice or error to engage
Or play the fool at large on life's great stage'.

3. *loo*: a card game.
4. *vole*: winning all the tricks.
5. *'Seven's the main'*: 'the main' was the number called out (here 'seven') by the caster in the dice-game of hazard.
6. *hot cockles*: country game where a blindfolded player had to guess who had struck him.
7. *Farewell . . . o'er*: cf. *Othello*, III, iii, 348–57.
8. *drums*: assemblies at private houses; parties.
9. *spadille*: ace of spades in the card games quadrille and ombre.
10. *pam*: knave of clubs.
11. *basto*: ace of clubs in quadrille and ombre.

APPENDIX

Lydia's Books (*The Rivals*, Act I, Scene ii)

1   *The Reward of Constancy*: probably *The Happy Pair, or Virtue and Constancy Rewarded* (1771).

2   *The Fatal Connection* by Mrs Fogerty (1773).

3   *The Mistakes of the Heart* by Pierre Henri Treyssac de Vergy (1769).

4   *The Delicate Distress* by Elizabeth Griffith (1769).

5   *The Memoirs of Lady Woodford* (1771).

6   *The Gordian Knot* by Richard Griffith (1769).

7   *The Adventures of Peregrine Pickle* includes *The Memoirs of a Lady of Quality*. It is by Tobias Smollett (1751; 5th edn, 1773).

8   *The Tears of Sensibility*. 'Translated from the French of M. D'Arnaud by J. Murdoch' (2 vols., 1773).

9   *The Expedition of Humphry Clinker* by Tobias Smollett (1771).

10 *A Sentimental Journey through France and Italy* by Laurence Sterne (1768).

11 *The Whole Duty of Man* (1659).

12 *The Adventures of Roderick Random* by Tobias Smollett (1748).

13 *The Innocent Adultery*: either the 1722 translation of Paul Scarron's *L'Adultère innocente* or *Harriet, or The Innocent Adultress* (1771).

14 *The History of Lord Aimsworth* (1773).

15 Ovid: Publius Ovidius Naso (43 BC–AD 17); presumably a translation of one of his works.

16 *The Man of Feeling* by Henry Mackenzie (1771).

17 Mrs Chapone: *Letters on the Improvement of the Mind* by Mrs Chapone (1773).

18 Fordyce's *Sermons*: *Sermons to Young Women* by James Fordyce (1765).

19 Lord Chesterfield's *Letters*: *Letters written by the . . . Earl of Chesterfield, to his Son, Philip Stanhope, Esq.* (2 vols., 1774).

TEXTUAL NOTES TO
The School for Scandal

These notes give textual variants for *The School for Scandal* and show how the 1821 edition (see M below) has here been emended from earlier manuscripts. For a full discussion of the complex textual problems of *The School for Scandal*, see both Cecil Price, *The Dramatic Works of Richard Brinsley Sheridan* (Oxford, 1973), and F. W. Bateson, *The School for Scandal* (London, 1979).

The following abbreviations have been used to indicate the manuscripts and other works consulted:

L: Lord Chamberlain's copy, Yale University.
C: Crewe M S, Georgetown University.
B: Buckinghamshire M S, Yale University.
T: Tickell M S, Oxford University.
M: The 1821 edition of *The Works of the Late Right Honourable Richard Brinsley Sheridan*, published by Murray, Ridgway & Wilkie.

Act I, Scene i

p. 192, l. 7 hint: *C, B, L*; tint, *M, T*.
p. 193, ll. 33–4 He . . . lover: *C, B, L*; *omitted, M, T*.
p. 194, l. 3 arraigning: *C, B, L*; rallying, *M, T*.
p. 195, l. 3 further: *C, B, L, T*; farther, *M*.
p. 198, l. 7 one's: *C, B, L, T*; our, *M*.
p. 198, l. 28 I'll: *C, B, L*; I, *M, T*.
p. 200, l. 19 difficulty of breeding: *C, B, L*; breeding, *M, T*.
p. 201, l. 11 Synagogue: *C, B, L, T*; all the synagogues, *M*.

Act I, Scene ii

p. 202, l. 30 miserablest: *C, B, L, T*; most miserable, *M*.

p. 204, l. 7 eastern: *C, B, L, T*; *omitted, M.*
p. 204, l. 29 however: *C, B, L, T*; *omitted, M.*

Act II, Scene i

p. 207, l. 1 Lord, Sir Peter: *C, B, L, T*; And, *M.*

Act II, Scene ii

p. 215, l. 34 intemperance: *C, B*; interference, *L, M, T.*
p. 215, l. 35 ungovernable: *C, B, L*; uncontrollable, *M, T.*

Act II, Scene iii

p. 218, l. 31 as: *C, B, L, T*; *omitted, M.*

Act III, Scene i

p. 220, l. 9 once: *C, B, L, T*; *omitted, M.*
p. 220, l. 11 since . . . confinement: *C, B, L*; *omitted, M, T.*
p. 223, l. 16 Yes: *C, B, L, T*; *omitted, M.*
p. 224, l. 1 further: *C, B* [*L, line destroyed by fire*], *T*; farther, *M.*
p. 226, l. 18 certainly: *C, B, L, T*; *omitted, M.*
p. 226, l. 22 narrowly: *C, B, L*; seriously, *M, T.*
p. 228, l. 2 miserablest: *C, B, L, T*; most miserable, *M.*

Act III, Scene ii

p. 230, l. 2 insure: *C, B, L, T*; I'll ensure, *M.*

Act III, Scene iii

p. 234, l. 23 beau-pots: *C, B*; beaux pots, *L*; Bow Pots, *T*; bough pots, *M.*
p. 235, l. 28 That's droll: *C, B, L*; *omitted, M, T.*
p. 236, l. 14 complete: *C, B, L, T*; compact, *M.*

Act IV, Scene i

p. 238, l. 20 grandfather's: *C, B, L, T*; father's, *M.*
p. 238, l. 21 have ne'er: *C, B, L, T*; hav'n't a, *M.*
p. 238, l. 24 Richard . . . Thomas: *C, B, L*; *omitted, M, T.*
p. 239, l. 6 list: *C, B, L*; bit, *M, T.*
p. 239, l. 14 for you: *C*; *omitted, B, L, M, T.*

p. 239, l. 21 Very well: *C*, *B*, *L*, *T*; well, *M*.
p. 241, l. 10 your: *C*, *B*, *L*, *T*; *omitted, M*.
p. 241, l. 26 Well, sir: *C*, *B*, *L*, *T*; *omitted, M*.
p. 242, l. 9 dares call: *C*, *B*; calls, *L*, *M*, *T*.
p. 242, ll. 13–14 the devil: *C*, *B*, *L*, *T*; *omitted, M*.
p. 242, l. 27 humble: *C*, *B*, *L*; *omitted, M, T*.
p. 243, l. 3 rot 'em: *C*, *B*, *L*, *T*; *omitted, M*.
p. 243, l. 15 hey?: *C*, *B* [*L*, *line destroyed by fire*], *T*; *omitted, M*.

Act IV, Scene iii

p. 245, l. 18 curious: *C*, *B*, *L*; anxious, *M*, *T*.
p. 246, l. 20 endeavour to: *C*, *B*, *L*; *omitted, M, T*.
p. 247, l. 24 argument: *C*, *B*, *L*, *T*; question, *M*.
p. 248, l. 5 mercy: *C*, *B*, *L*; *omitted, M, T*.
p. 249, l. 26 then: *C*, *B*, *L*, *T*; there's, *M*.
p. 250, l. 11 attempt: *C*, *B*, *L*, *T*; tempt, *M*.
p. 254, l. 3 me: *C*, *B*, *L*, *T*; *omitted, M*.
p. 255, l. 20 laugh: *C*, *B*, *L*, *T*; *M adds* at Joseph *after* laugh.
p. 256, l. 28 even: *C*, *B*, *T*; *omitted, M, L*.

Act V, Scene i

p. 259, l. 7 I suppose: *C*, *B*, *L*; *omitted, M, T*.
p. 260, l. 6 had enabled: *C*, *B*, *L*, *T*; would enable, *M*.
p. 261, l. 28 How?: *C*, *B* [*L*, *line destroyed by fire*]; *omitted, M, T*.

Act V, Scene ii

p. 265, l. 5 place: *C*, *B*, *L*, *T*; effect, *M*.
p. 265, l. 7 Pliny: *C*, *B*, *L*; Shakespeare, *M*, *T*.
p. 265, l. 22 it: *C*, *B*, [*L*, *line destroyed by fire*], *T*; him, *M*.
p. 266, l. 37 at all: *C*, *B*, *L*, *T*; *omitted, M*.
p. 267, l. 20 Sir Peter: *C*, *B*, *L*; sir, *M*, *T*.
p. 269, l. 15 Rowley: *C*, *B*, *L*; *omitted, M, T*.
p. 269, l. 19 on: *C*, *B*, *L*; of, *M*, *T*.

Act V, Scene iii

p. 270, ll. 19–20 What . . . way: *C*, *B*, *L*, *T*; *omitted, M*.
p. 270, l. 21 blinding: *C*, *B*, *L*, *T*; imposing upon, *M*.

p. 271, l. 18 We: *C, B*, [*L, line destroyed by fire*], *T*; I, *M*.
p. 272, l. 10 no, no: *C, B, L, T*; no, sir, *M*.
p. 273, l. 10 truth: *C, B, L*; faith, *M, T*.
p. 274, l. 8 certainly: *C, B, L, T*; *omitted, M*.
p. 275, l. 2 which: *C, B*, [*L, line destroyed by fire*], *T*; *omitted, M*.
p. 276, l. 36 above, *C*; *omitted, B, L, T, M*.